Recreation and Leisure in New Communities

Raymond J. Burby, III

Ballinger Publishing Company • Cambridge, Massachusetts
A Subsidiary of J.B. Lippincott Company

This book is printed on recycled paper.

NSF–RA–E '75–026

All of the material incorporated in this work was developed with the support of National Science Foundation grant number APR 72–03425. However, any opinions, findings, conclusions or recommendations expressed
herein are those of the author and do not necessarily reflect the views of
the National Science Foundation.

International Standard Book Number: 0–88410–448–6

Library of Congress Catalog Card Number: 76–17871

Printed in the United States of America

Library of Congress Cataloging in Publication Data

Burby, Raymond J 1942–
  Recreation and leisure in new communities.

(New communities research series)
  1. Outdoor recreation—United States. 2. Leisure—United
States. 3. New towns—United States. I. Title.
GV191.4.B85   301.5'7   76–17871
ISBN 0–88410–448–6

Recreation
and Leisure
in New
Communities

New Communities Research Series

Shirley F. Weiss and *Raymond J. Burby, III,* series editors
Center for Urban and Regional Studies,
The University of North Carolina at Chapel Hill

- Access, Travel, and Transportation in New Communities by Robert B. Zehner

- Economic Integration in New Communities: An Evaluation of Factors Affecting Policies and Implementation by Helene V. Smookler

- Health Care in New Communities by Norman H. Loewenthal and Raymond J. Burby, III

- Indicators of the Quality of Life in New Communities by Robert B. Zehner

- Recreation and Leisure in New Communities by Raymond J. Burby, III

- Residential Mobility in New Communities: An Analysis of Recent In-movers and Prospective Out-movers by Edward J. Kaiser

- Schools in New Communities by Raymond J. Burby, III and Thomas G. Donnelly

Contents

List of Figures and Tables

Preface

This volume is one of a series of books that summarizes the results of a nationwide study and evaluation of new community development in the United States. The study was initiated in May 1972 under the direction of Dr. Shirley F. Weiss, principal investigator, and co-principal investigators Dr. Raymond J. Burby, III, Dr. Thomas G. Donnelly, Dr. Edward J. Kaiser and Dr. Robert B. Zehner, at the Center for Urban and Regional Studies of The University of North Carolina at Chapel Hill. Financial support for the project was provided by the Research Applied to National Needs Directorate of the National Science Foundation.

The New Communities Study grew out of our concern for the lack of information about the outcomes of new community development in this country. When the original prospectus for the study was prepared, new community development was attracting an increasing amount of attention from both the private and the public sectors. Beginning with a few pioneering new community projects started in the 1940s and 1950s, such as Park Forest and the Levittowns, the 1960s saw a significant expansion in community building. By the end of the decade, over 60 private new community ventures were reported to be under development in eighteen states. The prospect for further expansion in new community development was greatly enhanced by the passage of Title IV of the 1968 Housing and Urban Development Act and the Urban Growth and New Community Development Act of 1970, which provided federal loan guarantees and other forms of assistance for approved new community projects. In the early 1970s, officials of the Department of Housing and Urban

Development were confidently projecting that ten new communities per year would be started under the federal new communities program.

Increasing public involvement in community building was accompanied by heightened expectations about the public benefits that would result from new community development. The Urban Growth and New Community Development Act of 1970 indicated that the Congress expected new communities to improve the quality of life in the nation by: (1) increasing for all persons, particularly members of minority groups, the available choices of locations for living and working; (2) helping to create neighborhoods designed for easier access between the places where people live and the places where they work and find recreation; and (3) providing adequate public, community, and commercial facilities (including facilities needed for education, health and social services, recreation and transportation). Congressional expectations about the benefits from new community development, however, were not shared by all observers of the new communities movement.

On the basis of an in-depth study of new communities in California conducted in the mid-1960s, Edward P. Eichler and Marshall Kaplan (1967, p. 160) concluded that, ". . . community building, even with public aid or under public sponsorship, can do little to solve the serious problems confronting American society." Three years later William Alonso reviewed many of the potential benefits of new community development, but ended up by concluding that, "On the whole, a national policy of settling millions of people in new towns is not likely to succeed and would not significantly advance the national welfare if it could be done" (1970, p. 16). The Twentieth Century Fund Task Force on the Governance of New Towns, which reported its findings in 1971, felt that few large-scale developments in the United States were living up to the promise of the new community concept, and Clapp (1971, p. 287) concluded that existing public programs ". . . to date appear inadequate to further the satisfaction of the major objectives of the new town concept."

Obviously, whether the benefits from new community development are real or imagined is a matter of crucial importance in the formulation of national urban growth policies. Since passage of the 1968 and 1970 federal new communities legislation, seventeen new communities have been approved for assistance. Loan guarantee commitments by the federal government now total $361 million. When completed in about 20 years, these new communities are expected to house almost one million persons, with private investments running into the billions of dollars. Given the conflicting opinions about the benefits of new communities and the major public and private investments involved in their development, it seemed appropriate to propose, and for the National Science Foundation to support, a full-scale evaluation of new communities now under development in the United States.

The need for objective information about the performance of new communities has been further underscored by the devastating impacts of the national economic recession, which has produced severe financial problems for the projects participating in the federal new communities program. During 1974 no new loan guarantee commitments were made by the New Communities Administration in the Department of Housing and Urban Development, and on January 14, 1975 the Department suspended further processing of applications for assistance. Faced with mounting financial difficulties with assisted projects, attention within the federal government and the new communities industry has shifted away from the outputs of the program to more pressing concerns for the economic viability of assisted new community ventures. However, the outputs of the program cannot be ignored. If new communities are to receive continued and expanded federal support, they not only must survive as financially viable undertakings, they must also produce benefits that could not be as readily achieved through conventional urban growth.

THE NEW COMMUNITIES STUDY

The University of North Carolina New Communities Study was undertaken to provide federal, state and local officials, as well as public and private developers, with an improved information base to use in judging the merits of new community development as an urban growth alternative. To assure that new communities do, in fact, realize the "quality of life" objectives set forth by the Congress, the study also sought to determine the critical factors affecting the success or failure of new communities in attracting socially balanced populations and meeting the needs of all of their residents.

In pursuing these two goals, the new communities study was designed to provide answers to five major policy questions: (1) Are federally guaranteed new communities contributing more to residents' quality of life than non-guaranteed new communities and less planned environments? (2) Which characteristics of housing, neighborhood design, community facilities and governmental mechanisms contribute most to the quality of life of new community residents, including minorities, low-income families, the elderly and teenagers?

(3) Which factors in the developer decision process lead to new community characteristics that contribute most to the quality of life of new community residents? (4) How has the federal new community development program influenced developer decisions regarding housing, neighborhood design, community facilities and governmental mechanisms? (5) How can the federal new community development program be applied most effectively to produce communities which promise to improve the quality of life of their residents?

The research design that was formulated to answer these questions is based on the belief that an evaluation of new community development must involve more than a study of new communities. To provide a sound basis for conclusions about new community performance, comparisons using the same measurement techniques must be made between new communities and alternative conventional forms of urban development. This research strategy led to the selection of a sample of seventeen communities to represent different types of new communities that are under development in the United States and nineteen conventional communities. The new community sample includes two communities that are participating in the federal new communities program, thirteen nonfederally assisted new communities that were initiated prior to the federal program and two retirement new communities designed specifically for older households. Fifteen of the conventional communities were selected by pairing each of the two federally assisted and thirteen nonfederally assisted new communities with a nearby community containing housing similar to that available in the new community in terms of age, type and price range. Because the paired conventional communities did not have sufficient black and low- and moderate-income populations for comparison with the new communities, four additional conventional communities were selected. These included two suburban communities with subsidized housing and two suburban communities with predominantly black residential areas.

Data collection in the sample new and conventional communities was begun during the spring of 1973 and continued through the summer of 1974. Four types of information were assembled to answer the research questions. First, data on people's attitudes and behavior were collected through 90-minute interviews with 5511 new and conventional community adult residents and self-administered questionnaires returned by 974 young adults (age 14 to 20) living in the sample communities. Second, data about community characteristics, including the number, accessibility and quality of facilities and services available and selected housing and neighborhood characteristics, were obtained from community inventories completed for all 36 sample communities and 'from interviews with professional personnel serving the communities. Third, professionals' observations about the communities, as well as factual information about community service systems, were collected through interviews with 577 professional personnel, including school district superintendents, school principals, health officials and practitioners, recreation administrators and community association leaders. Finally, the plans and activities of developers, governments, and other institutions involved in the development of the new and conventional communities were secured during preliminary reconnaissance interviews in each community, two waves of interviews with developer personnel, accounts published in newspapers and other secondary sources, discussions with local governmental officials and also from the professional personnel survey.

NEW COMMUNITIES U.S.A.

The major findings and conclusions emerging from the new communities study are summarized in *New Communities U.S.A.* (D.C. Heath and Co., 1976). Capsuling three years of research, the summary report focuses on the strengths and weaknesses of new community development in the United States, key factors which account for variation in new community performance and public policy options.

In comparison with conventional modes of suburban growth and development, new communities were found to be superior in five major respects. *First*, better land use planning and community design resulted in the provision of a wider choice of housing types for purchase or rent, more neighborhood amenities and services and safer access to them. *Second*, new community households tended to accumulate less annual automobile mileage, in part because of consistently better access to community facilities and services. *Third*, new communities were characterized by better recreational facilities and services, which resulted in somewhat higher participation in outdoor recreational activities and much higher levels of resident satisfaction with community recreational service systems. *Fourth*, new community residents tended to give higher ratings to the overall livability of their communities and were more likely than conventional community residents to recommend their communities as particularly good places to which to move. *Fifth*, new communities were found to provide satisfying living environments for target populations— black households, low- and moderate-income residents of subsidized housing, and older persons—than the comparison conventional communities.

Given these benefits and assuming that the costs of new community development are no greater than those incurred in conventional urban growth, the study findings provide ample justification for federal efforts to encourage the increased production of new communities in this country. In fact, federal participation in the new communities field appears to be necessary if new communities are to serve as one means of achieving the goals set forth by the Congress in the Urban Growth and New Community Development Act of 1970.

While producing substantial benefits, new community development in the United States has fallen short of achieving the full potential of the new community concept for solving urban problems and creating a better urban environment. Aspects of community development and life where few overall differences were found between the new and conventional communities studied included: evaluations of housing and neighborhood livability; residents' social perspectives, rates of participation in neighboring, community organizations, and community politics, and satisfaction with various life domains and with life as a whole; the provision of some community services; and the organization and operation of community governance. Clearly, in some cases planners have been overly optimistic about the influence of improvements in the physical environment on people's attitudes and behavior. However, in many cases, including the attainment of population balance and the provision of superior public services, the gap between concept and reality can be traced to a variety of factors subject to change through public policy.

In order to optimize the potential that new communities offer for a quantum improvement in the character of urban growth and development, some means must be found to overcome the private developer's limited ability to assume public sector responsibilities and local government's inability to cope with fragmented urban service responsibilities and the debilitating effects of insufficient financial resources. The need to assist developers and local governments in the provision of public and community services was recognized in the Urban Growth and New Community Development Act of 1970, but many of the provisions of the Act designed to achieve this purpose were never implemented.

With the federal new communities program at a standstill, two basic, though not mutually exclusive, policy options are available. First, given waning developer interest in larger scale new communities, the program could be reoriented toward smaller scale planned unit developments, villages and experimental new communities. At the same time that assistance is directed toward smaller scale development, the existing new communities legislation could be amended to recharge those new communities already participating in the federal program. This would require expanded support for low- and moderate-income housing in new communities and the design of new incentives for the provision of high quality and innovative community service systems. Additionally, eligibility for such assistance could be extended to new communities not now federally assisted, if they subscribe to the goals of the program.

Another option, not excluded by the first, would be to return to the basic purposes embraced in the 1970 Urban Growth and New Community Development Act and link the production of new communities to the implementation of a national urban growth policy. If new communities are to be an integral part of a national urban growth policy, stronger measures than exist in current legislation for private developer and state and local government participation in new community development must be provided. This would require full funding and implementation of the 1970 new communities legislation as a first step. Beyond this, federal incentives are needed to encourage state government participation in new community projects, including state oversight of land use and development regulations, state initiatives to establish new governmental structures for new communities and state financial assistance in meeting the public overhead and front-end costs of new community development projects.

NEW COMMUNITIES RESEARCH SERIES

The seven volumes in the *New Communities Research Series*, published by Ballinger Publishing Company, explore in depth key facets of new community development in the United States. The books in this series are designed to give community development professionals and researchers in architecture, design, education, health care, housing, planning, recreation, social services, transportation and allied professions a fuller and more detailed description and analysis of the new community experience than could be provided in a summary report. In addition to their utility to persons concerned with new community development, these books summarize the results of a pioneering social science research effort. They report the findings of one of the first, and probably the most comprehensive, attempts to trace through sequences of actions and consequences in the community development process—from the decisions which led to the provision of housing and the production of facilities and services through their effects on individual and household attitudes and behavior.

A central premise of the new community concept has been that through comprehensive planning better relationships can be attained among many of the key variables that influence travel behavior. In *Access, Travel, and Transportation in New Communities* Robert B. Zehner examines the availability of transportation and other community facilities and services in new communities and how they influence travel behavior. Particular attention is given to alternatives to the automobile, including walking and community transit, the journey to work, automobile ownership rates and annual household automobile mileage. By analyzing relationships between demographic and community characteristics on the one hand, and residents' travel behavior on the other, Dr. Zehner shows how community design can result in reduced travel and potential energy savings.

Economic Integration in New Communities: An Evaluation of Factors Affecting Policies and Implementation by Helene V. Smookler describes the processes of income and racial integration (and nonintegration) in fifteen new communities. The communities are analyzed to determine what factors made integration possible and how they contributed to the effectiveness of the integration programs and strategies that were utilized. The early effects of federal involvement in new community development are described. Dr. Smookler also examines the correlates of residents' integration attitudes, showing that significant differences in attitudes characterize communities with varying amounts of income and racial integration. Finally, the benefits of integration are analyzed in terms of the actual attitudes and perceptions of low-income and black residents living in integrated new communities.

Planned new communities have been viewed as ideal settings in which to develop better ways of organizing and delivering health care services. As described in *Health Care in New Communities* by Norman H. Loewenthal and Raymond J. Burby, III, however, a number of factors have prevented many new communities from achieving this potential. In addition to describing the approaches to health care that have characterized community building in the United States, the authors examine the impacts of available health care resources on residents' satisfaction with and utilization of health care facilities and services. Health care resources that are analyzed in the study include the provision of physicians' services, hospital care and ambulance service, social service programs, nursing and convalescent care facilities, public health facilities and health maintenance programs. Objective characteristics of health care systems, residents' attitudes and behavior, and health professionals' evaluations are interrelated and used as a basis for the formulation of health care policies for the next generation of new communities to be built in this country.

During the past five years increasing interest has been expressed in the quality of life in the United States and how it can and should be measured. The strategy used to assess the quality of life of new and conventional community residents, reported in *Indicators of the Quality of Life in New Communities* by Robert B. Zehner, is eclectic, ranging from measures focused on specific functional community service areas to more global concepts, such as residents' overall life satisfaction. A unique aspect of the data presented in this book is the discussion of residents' individual perceptions of the factors that influence the quality of life as they have defined it for themselves. Dr. Zehner also explores residents' satisfactions with a number of life domains—standard of living, use of leisure time, health, family life, marriage and work, among others. He also shows how satisfaction with each domain relates to satisfaction with life as a whole. Differences in the quality of life among nineteen classifications of residents, including blacks, low- and moderate-income persons and the elderly, are highlighted, as well as observed differences in the quality of life between new and conventional communities.

Recreation and Leisure in New Communities by Raymond J. Burby, III provides a comprehensive description and analysis of this key community service system. A comparative evaluation of the experiences of fifteen new communities in developing recreational service systems is presented. Key agents and their roles in developing community recreational resources are identified. Dr. Burby also discusses the administration of recreational service systems, including their governance, approaches to recreational planning and methods of financing facilities and services. The effectiveness of alternative approaches to organizing the provision of recreational services is evaluated in terms of recreational resources produced and residents' use of and satisfaction with facilities and services. Particular attention is given to how the recreational needs of young adults, elderly persons, women, blacks and subsidized housing residents have been met. Recreational service system characteristics that influenced residents' participation in outdoor recreational activities, satisfaction with the facilities and services used most often, and overall evaluations of community recreational resources are identified and used as a basis for suggestions about the best approaches to the design and development of community recreational facilities and services.

Who moves to new communities and why? Why are families considering moving from new communities? What factors attract black families and low- and moderate-income households to new and conventional suburban communities? How do residential mobility processes shape the population profiles of new communities? These and related questions are addressed in *Residential Mobility in New Communities: An Analysis of Recent In-movers and Prospective Out-movers* by Edward J. Kaiser. In this book, Dr. Kaiser examines the inflow of residents to new communities, paying particular attention to the characteristics of recent in-movers, their reasons for selecting a home in a new community and the improvements that were realized as a result of the move. Because the number and profile of out-movers influence the profile of residents left behind, Dr. Kaiser also examines the rate and type of household being lost to new communities through out-mobility. The characteristics of those households most likely to move are identified, together with the key reasons for their moving intentions. Separate chapters are devoted to the retrospective residential choices and prospective mobility of black households, subsidized housing residents, and the residents of federally assisted new communities.

The last book in the series, *Schools in New Communities* by Raymond J. Burby, III and Thomas G. Donnelly, examines school development processes and outcomes in the sample of new and conventional communities. Five topics are covered in this study. First, the capacity of school districts to cope with large-scale community development projects is examined through an analysis of the experiences of twenty-seven school districts in developing educational programs for and building new schools in nonfederally and federally assisted new communities. School districts' experiences in serving new communities are traced from each district's initial contacts with developers, through various phases of the school development process, to current issues in the operation of new community schools. Second, school development outcomes are evaluated in terms of both the objective characteristics of school plants and educational programs and the subjective attitudes of educators and parents. Third, links between characteristics of the schools and parents' evaluations of the schools attended by their children are identified. Fourth, the impact of school availability on the attractiveness of new communities to various population groups is reported, including the contribution of public schools to households' decisions to move to new communities and their satisfaction with the community as a place to live after they have occupied their homes. Finally, suggestions for increasing the effectiveness of school development processes are offered.

THE RESEARCH TEAM

The New Communities Study, summary report, and monographs in the *New Communities Research Series* were made possible by the combined efforts of a large team of researchers and supporting staff assembled at the Center for Urban and Regional Studies of The University of North Carolina at Chapel Hill. The team members and their roles in the study were the following:

Dr. Shirley F. Weiss, principal investigator and project director, who had primary responsibility for management of the study and coordination of the research efforts of the team of co-principal investigators and research associates. Dr. Weiss's research focused on the overall new community development process, implementation, fiscal concerns and federal assistance, as well as shopping center and other commercial facilities.

Dr. Raymond J. Burby, III, co-principal investigator and deputy project director, who assumed primary responsibility for implementation of the research design and preparation of the project summary report. Dr. Burby's research focused on new community planning and governance, the recreation and leisure service system, schools and health care planning and delivery.

Dr. Thomas G. Donnelly, co-principal investigator, who assumed primary responsibility for the extensive data processing for the study. Dr. Donnelly's research focused on the development and utilization of efficient computation routines for the data analyses and on educational development processes in new communities.

Dr. Edward J. Kaiser, co-principal investigator, who helped formulate the original research design and research management strategy, and offered invaluable advice throughout the study. Dr. Kaiser's research focused on residential mobility processes in new communities.

Dr. Robert B. Zehner, co-principal investigator, who assumed primary responsibility for the design and conduct of the household survey. Dr. Zehner's research focused on transportation and travel in new communities, neighborhood and community satisfaction and the quality of life of new community residents.

David F. Lewis, research associate, who prepared a comparative analysis of the population characteristics of new communities, their host counties, and host SMSAs, and contributed to the analysis of housing and neighborhood satisfaction in new communities.

Norman H. Loewenthal, research associate, who undertook a major portion of the professional personnel survey design and field work and assumed primary responsibility for the analysis of health care service systems in new communities.

Mary Ellen McCalla, research associate, who assumed responsibility for immediate supervision of the household survey sampling, field work, and coding operations, supervision of the community inventory map measurement and professional personnel survey coding, and contributed to the analysis of the social life of new communities.

Dr. Helene V. Smookler, research associate, who assumed primary responsibility for the design and conduct of developer decision studies and the analysis of economic integration in new communities.

Invaluable assistance throughout the study was provided by Barbara G. Rodgers, who served as administrative aide, research assistant and publications manager.

The research work was supported by a staff of technical specialists, research assistants, interviewers, coders and office personnel too extensive for a complete listing. In particular, the efforts of the following persons should be recognized: research assistants Jerry L. Doctrow, Mary C. Edeburn, Leo E. Hendricks, Christopher G. Olney and Raymond E. Stanland, Jr.; and secretaries Cathy A. Albert, Lisa D. McDaniel, Linda B. Johnson, Lucinda D. Peterson and Diana Pettaway.

THE NATIONAL SCIENCE FOUNDATION

The new communities study was made possible by research grant APR 72−03425 from the Research Applied to National Needs Directorate of the National Science Foundation. Throughout the course of the study, the research team benefited greatly from the continuing interest and constant encouragement of Dr. George W. Baker, the project's program manager. Dr. Baker worked with the research team to achieve scientific excellence in each phase of the study.

Of course, the findings, opinions, conclusions or recommendations arising out of this research grant are those of the authors, and it should not be implied that they represent the views of the National Science Foundation.

SITE AND ADVISORY COMMITTEES

The process of refining the initial research design was aided by the expert advice of the Site Visit Committee and the panel of anonymous peer reviewers whose ideas were synthesized by Dr. George W. Baker.

An important source of guidance and consultation was made possible by the project's Advisory Committee, drawn from experts in new community development, city planning, economics, political science and sociology. Jonathan B. Howes, Director, Center for Urban and Regional Studies, The University of North Carolina at Chapel Hill, ably served as chairman of the Advisory Committee which included: Dr. George W. Baker, National Science Foundation; Professor F. Stuart Chapin, Jr., The University of North Carolina at Chapel Hill; Dr. Amos H. Hawley, The University of North Caolina at Chapel Hill; Morton Hoppenfeld, The Rouse Company (resigned March 5, 1975); Dr. Richard M. Langendorf, University of Miami; Floyd B. McKissick, McKissick Enterprises, Inc.; Dr. Frederick A. McLaughlin, Jr., New Communities Administration, Department of Housing and Urban Development (appointed in 1973); Dr. Peter H. Rossi, University of Massachusetts; Dr. Joseph J. Spengler, Duke University; Dr. Lawrence Susskind, Massachusetts Institute of Technology; Dr. Dorothy S. Williams, Department of Housing and Urban Development (1972–73); and Dr. Deil S. Wright, The University of North Carolina at Chapel Hill.

While their collective and individual contributions to the conduct of the study are gratefully acknowledged, it goes without saying that neither the Site Committee, the Advisory Committee, nor any individual members bear responsibility for the findings and interpretations in the *New Communities Research Series* and other publications of the project.

NEW COMMUNITIES POLICY APPLICATIONS WORKSHOP

A New Communities Policy Applications Workshop was held in Chapel Hill at The University of North Carolina from November 17 to 19, 1974. The workshop brought together invited representatives of federal, state, local, private and academic user communities to review the methodology and preliminary findings of the study. The workshop was structured to insure that critical feedback to the research team would be secured from formal and informal discussion sessions and to provide a forum for the consideration of broad issues in new community development.

The Policy Applications Workshop was an invaluable part of the research process. The following participants offered many astute observations and critical comments which were helpful to the research team.

Representing the federal government: Dr. Harvey A. Averch, National Science Foundation; Dr. George W. Baker, National Science

Foundation; Bernard P. Bernsten, U.S. Postal Service; Larry W. Colaw, Tennessee Valley Authority; Dr. James D. Cowhig, National Science Foundation; Dr. Frederick J. Eggers, U.S. Department of Housing and Urban Development; Richard L. Fore, U.S. Department of Housing and Urban Development; James L. Gober, Tennessee Valley Authority; George Gross, House Budget Committee, U.S. House of Representatives; Charles A. Gueli, U.S. Department of Housing and Urban Development; Benjamin McKeever, Subcommittee on Housing of the Committee on Banking and Currency, U.S. House of Representatives; Dr. Frederick A. McLaughlin, Jr., U.S. Department of Housing and Urban Development; Paul W. Rasmussen, U.S. Department of Transportation; Dr. Salvatore Rinaldi, U.S. Office of Education; Ali F. Sevin, Federal Highway Administration; Dr. Frederick T. Sparrow, National Science Foundation; Otto G. Stolz, U.S. Department of Housing and Urban Development; Jack Underhill, U.S. Department of Housing and Urban Development; Margaret L. Wireman, U.S. Department of Housing and Urban Development; and Theodore W. Wirths, National Science Foundation.

Representing state, local and community government: D. David Brandon, New York State Urban Development Corporation; W.C. Dutton, Jr., The Maryland-National Capital Park and Planning Commission; Brendan K. Geraghty, Newfields New Community Authority; James L. Hindes, Office of Planning and Budget, State of Georgia; Mayor Gabrielle G. Pryor, City of Irvine, Calif.; Roger S. Ralph, Columbia Park and Recreation Association; Anne D. Stubbs, The Council of State Governments; and Gerald W. von Mayer, Office of Planning and Zoning, Howard County, Md.

Representing new community developers: James E. Bock, Gerald D. Hines Interests; Dwight Bunce, Harbison Development Corporation; David J. Burton, Harbison Development Corporation; Gordon R. Carey, Warren Regional Planning Corporation; David Scott Carlson, Riverton Properties, Inc.; Eva Clayton, Soul City Foundation; Mark H. Freeman, League of New Community Developers; Morton Hoppenfeld, DEVCO—The Greater Hartford Community Development Corporation; Joseph T. Howell, Seton Belt Village; Floyd B. McKissick, The Soul City Company; Richard A. Reese, The Irvine Company; Jeffrey B. Samet, Harbison Development Corporation; Elinor Schwartz, League of New Community Developers; Michael D. Spear, The Rouse Company; and Francis C. Steinbauer, Gulf-Reston, Inc.

Representing public interest groups and new community/urban affairs consultants: Mahlon Apgar, IV, McKinsey and Company; Evans Clinchy, Educational Planning Associates; Ben H. Cunningham,

The Hodne-Stageberg Partners; Harvey B. Gantt, Gantt/Huberman Associates; John E. Gaynus, National Urban League, Inc.; James J. Gildea, Barton-Aschman Associates; Nathaniel M. Griffin, Urban Land Institute; Guy W. Hager, Planning and Management Consultant; William H. Hoffman, National Corporation for Housing Partnerships; Jack Linville, Jr., American Institute of Planners; Hugh Mields, Jr., Academy for Contemporary Problems; William Nicoson, Urban Affairs Consultant; Dr. Carl Norcross, Advisor on New Communities; Robert M. O'Donnell, Harman, O'Donnell and Henninger Associates; Donald E. Priest, Urban Land Institute; Edward M. Risse, Richard P. Browne Associates; George M. Stephens, Jr., Stephens Associates; Eugene R. Streich, System Development Corporation; and Doris Wright, REP Associates.

Representing the academic community: Dr. Allen H. Barton, Columbia University; Professor David L. Bell, North Carolina State University; Professor Richard D. Berry, University of Southern California; Donald W. Bradley, Michigan State University; William A. Brandt, Jr., University of Chicago; David J. Brower, The University of North Carolina at Chapel Hill; Lynne C. Burkhart, University of Massachusetts; Professor F. Stuart Chapin, Jr., The University of North Carolina at Chapel Hill; Dr. Lewis Clopton, The University of North Carolina at Chapel Hill; Dr. Robert H. Erskine, The University of North Carolina at Chapel Hill; Dr. Sylvia F. Fava, Brooklyn College of The City University of New York; Dr. Nelson N. Foote, Hunter College of The City University of New York; Russell C. Ford, The University of North Carolina at Chapel Hill; Dr. Gorman Gilbert, The University of North Carolina at Chapel Hill; Dr. David R. Godschalk, The University of North Carolina at Chapel Hill; Dr. Gideon Golany, The Pennsylvania State University; Professor Philip P. Green, Jr., The University of North Carolina at Chapel Hill; Dr. George C. Hemmens, The University of North Carolina at Chapel Hill; Dean George R. Holcomb, The University of North Carolina at Chapel Hill; Jonathan B. Howes, The University of North Carolina at Chapel Hill; Frederick K. Ickes, The University of North Carolina at Chapel Hill; Dr. Suzanne Keller, Princeton University; Joseph E. Kilpatrick, The University of North Carolina at Chapel Hill; Professor Alan S. Kravitz, Ramapo College of New Jersey; Dr. Richard M. Langendorf, University of Miami; Dean Claude E. McKinney, North Carolina State University; Dr. Robert W. Marans, The University of Michigan; Susan L. Marker, Bryn Mawr College; Dr. Michael J. Minor, University of Chicago; Professor Roger Montgomery, University of California, Berkeley; Daniel W. O'Connell, Harvard University; Dean Kermit C. Parsons, Cornell University; David R. Paulson, The University of

North Carolina at Chapel Hill; Dr. Francine F. Rabinovitz, University of California, Los Angeles; Dr. Peter H. Rossi, University of Massachusetts; Dr. Arthur B. Shostak, Drexel University; Dr. Michael A. Stegman, The University of North Carolina at Chapel Hill; Dr. Robert Sullivan, Jr., Duke University; Dr. Lawrence Susskind, Massachusetts Institute of Technology; Professor Maxine T. Wallace, Howard University; Dr. William A. Wallace, Carnegie-Mellon University; Kenneth Weeden, The University of North Carolina at Chapel Hill; Professor Warren J. Wicker, The University of North Carolina at Chapel Hill; Dr. Deil S. Wright, The University of North Carolina at Chapel Hill; and Dr. Mary Wylie, The University of Wisconsin—Madison.

Representing the press: Barry Casselman, *Appleseeds* and *Many Corners* newspapers; Thomas Lippman, *The Washington Post*; William B. Richards, *The Washington Post*; and Barry Zigas, *Housing and Development Reporter.*

Foreign observers: Asel Floderus, The National Swedish Institute for Building Research; and Hans Floderus, Building and Town Planning Department, Avesta, Sweden.

To list all the people who contributed to this study is impossible. Among others, these would include 6485 residents who spent time responding to the household survey interview, the 577 professionals who shared their knowledge and opinions about the study communities and the 173 informed individuals who were interviewed in connection with the developer decision studies.

A final note of thanks is due the new community developers and their staffs who were generous in making available their time and expert knowledge to the research team. In reciprocation, this series is offered as an aid in their continuing efforts to realize better communities and a more livable environment.

Shirley F. Weiss and **Raymond J. Burby, III**

The University of North Carolina
at Chapel Hill
December 10, 1975

Author's Note

The assembly of data and other material for this book was made possible by the cooperation and assistance of a number of persons and agencies. I would like to thank the new community developers and recreation professionals in all parts of the nation who generously contributed their time and knowledge of recreation in new communities. I am also indebted to Dr. Robert W. Marans, Survey Research Center, The University of Michigan; Dr. Francine F. Rabinovitz, University of California, Los Angeles; Roger S. Ralph, Columbia Park and Recreation Association; and Elinor Schwartz, League of New Community Developers, who offered many useful comments on an earlier version of the manuscript.

My colleagues, Drs. Thomas G. Donnelly, Edward J. Kaiser, Shirley F. Weiss and Robert B. Zehner, are due a special note of thanks for their substantive research contributions throughout this study.

Finally, I would like to acknowledge the contributions of present and former staff members of the Center for Urban and Regional Studies. Norman H. Loewenthal conducted portions of the field work and assembled the data on recreational resources and professionals' opinions about recreational services in new communities. Jerry L. Doctrow, Leo E. Hendricks and David F. Lewis conducted portions of the recreation professional survey and community inventory fieldwork. Mary Ellen McCalla assisted in the preparation of the household survey instruments, conduct of the household survey fieldwork and supervised data coding operations. Mary C. Edeburn provided assistance in all phases of data processing. Barbara G. Rodgers supervised the central office staff and the typing and production of the final manuscript.

Raymond J. Burby, III

The University of North Carolina
at Chapel Hill
January 7, 1976

Chapter 1

Summary of Findings

Recreation is a key element in the design and development of new communities. Together with related open space, recreational areas and facilities involve major commitments of developer and public personnel and financial resources, consume large portions of community land devoted to public uses, and are essential in marketing new communities as desirable places to live. However, although much has been written about new communities, recreation and leisure have received very little attention.

This book focuses on this neglected component of new community development. The experiences of fifteen new communities in developing recreational service systems are explored and evaluated. Key decision agents and the roles they played in securing recreational resources for each community are identified. The administration of recreational service systems is described, including alternative approaches that have been used in governing recreational organizations, planning recreational areas and financing recreational facilities and services.

The effectiveness of recreational service systems is evaluated in terms of the recreational resources provided for community residents, residents' participation in recreational activities and their satisfaction with recreational facilities and services. Particular attention is given to how well recreational service systems have satisfied the needs of young adults, older persons, women, blacks and subsidized housing residents. To provide guidance in planning future recreational service systems, service system characteristics that are associated with higher than average facility utilization rates and consumer satisfaction are identified. Additional analyses highlight the influence of open space and recreational facilities on households' decisions to move to new communities, residents' evaluations of community livability and residents' satisfaction with the overall quality of their lives.

METHODS OF THE STUDY

The new communities studied included thirteen communities developed by the private sector without federal assistance, two communities that are participating in the federal new communities program and, to provide a basis for analyses of recreation and the elderly, two retirement new communities designed specifically for older households.

Nineteen conventional communities were included in the study to provide a basis for evaluations of new communities in comparison with less planned traditional modes of urban development and to control for contextual factors, such as climate. Each of the nonfederally assisted and federally assisted new communities was paired with a significantly less planned conventional community that was similar to the new community in terms of the age, price range and type of housing available and location. Because the sample of paired conventional communities did not have sufficient black and low- and moderate-income populations for comparison with the new communities, information was gathered in four additional conventional communities. These included two suburban communities with subsidized housing and two suburban communities with predominantly black residential areas.

Locations of the new and conventional communities are illustrated in Figure 1-1. The nonfederally assisted new communities are: Columbia, Md., Reston, Va., and North Palm Beach, Fla., on the East Coast; Forest Park, Oh., Elk Grove Village, Ill., and Park Forest, Ill., in the Midwest; Sharpstown, Tex., and Lake Havasu City, Ariz., in the Southwest; and in California, Foster City, outside San Francisco, and Valencia, Westlake Village, Irvine, and Laguna Niguel in the Los Angeles area.

The federally assisted new communities are Jonathan, Minn., and Park Forest South, Ill., two of the first three new communities to be approved for assistance. The retirement new communities are Rossmoor Leisure World, Laguna Hills, Calif., and Sun City Center, Fla.

Within each community, three types of data were collected. First, interviews with professional recreation personnel, officials of automatic homes (community) associations, school principals and new community developers were conducted during 1973 and 1974 to

Figure 1–1. New and Conventional Communities

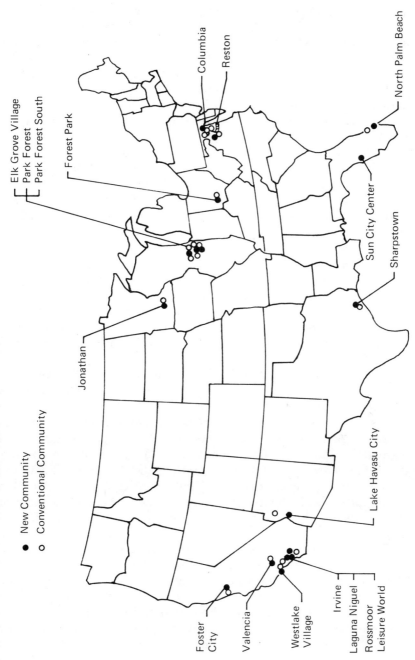

• New Community
o Conventional Community

Elk Grove Village
Park Forest
Park Forest South
Forest Park
Columbia
Reston
North Palm Beach
Sun City Center
Sharpstown
Jonathan
Lake Havasu City
Foster City
Valencia
Westlake Village
Irvine
Laguna Niguel
Rossmoor
Leisure World

obtain information about the organization and management of community recreational service systems and objective data on recreational resources. Second, additional data on the characteristics of recreational resources were collected during the spring of 1973 through a field inventory and evaluation of facilities and services available in each community and through a series of map measurements and calculations. Third, data on residents' participation in recreational activities, utilization of recreational facilities, and satisfaction with recreational service systems were collected through interviews conducted in the spring of 1973 with 5511 new and conventional community adult residents and self-administered questionnaires returned by 974 young adults in the fourteen to twenty year age bracket. A complete description of sampling and data collection procedures is provided in Appendix A. A series of brief vignettes that summarize selected characteristics of the new and conventional communities is provided in Appendix B.

Before reviewing the findings of the study, several limitations of the research methods should be noted. The results of the study presented here have been derived from cross-sectional data collected in new and conventional communities during 1973 and 1974. Although the results of earlier studies and subsequent changes were taken into account where data were available, longitudinal analysis and monitoring of new communities over time will be required for a dynamic view of recreation and leisure in new communities.

It should also be stressed that the new and conventional communities studied were by no means completed communities. Some new communities had gone farther in the development process than others—Park Forest, for example, had achieved about 90 percent of its target population—but, on average, the study new communities were only about one-fifth completed. Thus, this is a book about developing new communities rather than about completed communities. Particular circumstances in individual new and conventional communities will change over time as their populations grow and the provision of more recreational facilities and services becomes possible.

The two federally assisted new communities and their paired conventional communities were in the very initial stages of development. The findings for them provide an early empirical picture of the results of the federal new communities program and benchmarks for comparison with later studies of these two and other federally assisted communities. They should not, however, be used to judge the entire federal new communities program.

ORGANIZATION OF RECREATIONAL SERVICE SYSTEMS

In the usual pattern of urban growth and development, urban facilities and services have traditionally been provided in stages, beginning with basic facilities, such as streets, water and sewer systems and police and fire protection, and only over time encompassing social amenities such as parks, open space and recreational facilities. New communities have been expected to depart from traditional patterns of service delivery in two ways. First, the distinction between basic public services and social amenities in ordering priorities is viewed as relatively meaningless in the new community context. Instead, each is seen as an integral and essential part of the new community environment and as necessary for the economic and social success of a community. Second, a key component of the new community concept has been preservicing, with facilities and services provided before, rather than after, each neighborhood and village is occupied. Actually achieving these goals, however, has challenged the ingenuity of new community developers, planners and citizens.

The early need for a full array of recreational facilities and services, combined with the limited capacity of development organizations, local governments and other institutions to fill the need, caused serious organizational and management problems in a number of new communities. Developers were faced with two basic choices. On the one hand, they could seek to assure that high quality recreational facilities and services were provided by establishing developer-controlled institutions to manage the recreational service system. On the other hand, the economics of new community development required that developers share the costs of recreational facilities and services with the residents and local governments. Unfortunately, these goals conflicted, since the more costs were shared, the less control developers had over the characteristics of the recreational system.

Depending on the importance they attached to each goal, developers chose to follow one of three approaches to the organization of recreational service systems. One approach, characterized by the community-wide homes associations used in Columbia, Jonathan and Reston, gave developers the greatest amount of control over the characteristics of the recreational service system but entailed the greatest developer financial responsibility and, initially, the least cost sharing. A second approach combined developer control of the provision of neighborhood amenities (through developer design and construction of neighborhood recreational facilities and transfer of responsibility for their maintenance and operation to a series of small homes associations) with provision of community recreational facilities by public agencies and commercial establishments. This approach characterized new communities in California. It maximized developers' control of the recreational service system at the point of sale—the neighborhoods surrounding the developers' housing products—and minimized their financial contributions and responsibility for community-wide recreational facilities. A third approach, which characterized most of the older new communities studied, involved resident and public assumption of responsibility for the entire community recreational system. In this approach developer control was minimized, but so were the heavy front-end costs and other financial burdens involved in preservicing recreational facilites.

In general, the more developers chose to exchange control of new community recreational service systems for cost sharing, the more fragmented became the organization of recreational service delivery systems. This result occurred because there was no effective way for developers or new community residents to provide recreational services through public agencies during the initial stages of the development process. Instead, developers and residents were forced to patch together organizational structures for the provision of recreational services using whatever public and private institutions were most available and most amenable to servicing residents' needs. The array of institutions that were used to provide recreational services in new communities included voluntary associations, county park and recreation districts and departments, municipal park and recreation departments, independent park and recreation districts, county maintenance districts, county service districts, school districts and state agencies. An average of 4.5 different types of organizations provided major recreational services in each of the new communities studied.

RECREATIONAL RESOURCES

In spite of the many obstacles developers and residents faced in organizing recreational service systems, new communities as a whole were quite successful in providing recreational resources. New community performance, in comparison with the less planned conventional communities, was evaluated on the basis of eight measures of resource availability. These were: (1) recreational and open space acreage per capita; (2) recreational sites available; (3) variety of recreational facilities; (4) adequacy of facilities in comparison with national standards; (5) accessibility of facilities; (6) recreational leadership personnel; (7) variety of recreational programming; and

(8) per capita annual operating expenditures for recreational services.

New community recreational service systems provided an average of 406 acres of recreational and open space land per 10,000 residents, almost double the 216 acres per 10,000 population found in the paired conventional communities. The large amount of open space and recreational land provided in new communities was matched by a greater number of recreational sites. Six new communities, but only two of the conventional communities, had 30 or more recreational sites. On a per capita basis new communities provided over twice as many recreational sites as their paired conventional communities. This advantage carried over to recreational facilities. Of 21 different types of facilities inventoried, new communities provided from two to seven times the number per capita as were provided in the paired conventional communities. Facilities that were provided in much greater abundance in new communities included tot lots, walking paths, bicycle trails, fishing lakes, boating facilities, swimming facilities, recreational centers, arts and crafts rooms, teen centers and playing fields. The conventional communities were superior for two of the twenty-one facility types—basketball courts and baseball diamonds. New communities met or exceeded national standards for ten of the eleven facilities for which minimal standards have been established. Swimming facilities, community recreational centers, golf courses and gymnasiums were each provided at over twice the minimal standard. In contrast, the conventional communities failed to meet national standards for four of the facilities compared.

To gauge the accessibility of recreational facilities in new communities, two types of measures were used. The road distance from each sample cluster of households (groups of from five to seven dwelling units) was measured to the nearest of each of five types of recreational facilities, including parks and playgrounds for children under twelve years old, golf courses, swimming facilities, tennis courts and walking paths. In each case the median road distance to the nearest facility was less in the new communities than in the paired conventional communities. In addition to road-distance measures, the availability of thirteen types of indoor and outdoor recreational and entertainment facilities in each respondent's neighborhood was recorded. New community residents were significantly more likely than conventional community residents to have a park or playground, swimming facility, walking path, picnic area and neighborhood or community center in their neighborhoods. On the other hand, differences in the neighborhood availability of tennis courts, teen centers, bars and taverns, billiard parlors, bowling alleys, movie theaters, ice skating rinks and roller skating rinks were not statistically significant.

Recreational facilities provide places for people to go and equipment to use for their recreational pursuits. In addition, many people want opportunities to engage in a variety of activities that by their very nature must be organized. To offer such opportunities, the recreational system must provide leadership personnel who can organize programs and activities for a community's residents. In ten of the thirteen nonfederally assisted new communities and one of the two federally assisted communities, the new community had a larger number of recreational employees than its paired conventional community. Overall, new communities provided 55 full- and part-time recreational employees per 10,000 population, more than double the recreational personnel per 10,000 population employed in the conventional communities. The greater number of recreational employees in new communities was matched by a greater variety of recreational programming. Of twenty-one types of supervised recreational programs that were checked in each community, baseball was the only activity offered in more conventional than new communities. Finally, annual per capita operating expenditures for recreational services were over twice as large in the new communities as in the paired conventional communities.

Community-wide homes associations proved to be the most effective vehicles for providing recreational resources. They were more effective than recreational systems centered on neighborhood homes associations, municipalities and special districts, and county and state agencies on six of the eight types of measures—recreational sites per capita, variety of recreational facilities, adequacy of facilities, accessibility of facilities, recreational personnel per capita and community recreational expenditures per capita. Recreational systems based on neighborhood homes associations and those based on municipalities/ park districts tended to be about equal in their ability to marshal recreational resources. Recreational systems in which county or state agencies played the major roles tended to be the least effective in providing resources.

Although new community recreational systems as a whole were more effective than those in the conventional communities, all new communities were not equally effective in providing recreational resources. Based on an index of recreational resources provided, the most effective nonfederally assisted new communities were, in order: Columbia, Reston, Lake Havasu City, Valencia, Elk Grove Village, Park Forest, Foster City, Irvine, Laguna Niguel, Westlake Village, North Palm Beach, Forest Park and Sharpstown. Among the federally assisted new communities, Jonathan had had somewhat greater success in providing recreational resources than Park Forest South.

RESIDENTS' RESPONSES TO
RECREATIONAL SERVICE SYSTEMS

In addition to considering recreational resources, a full evaluation of the effectiveness of new community recreational service systems must also consider the outputs of these systems—their effects on the individuals and households living in new communities. The analysis of residents' responses to recreational service systems included examinations of children's outdoor play, young adults' recreational behavior and attitudes and the recreation participation rates and satisfactions of adult residents.

The inventory of recreational resources indicated that new communities had more tot lots per 10,000 population than any other recreational facility except basketball courts and baseball diamonds. Were they used? Overwhelmingly, both new and conventional community children tended to play in their own or their neighbors' yards. Streets and parking lots ranked second in terms of the places parents said their children usually played, with undeveloped open space following close behind. Only 9 percent of the new community parents and 4 percent of the conventional community parents said that their children usually played at a park or playground.

One reason why children did not usually play at parks and playgrounds may have been their inaccessibility. In both the new and the conventional communities fewer than 30 percent of the parks and playgrounds that parents were aware of were within one-eighth mile (easy walking distance for a child) of their homes. Sixty-one percent of the parents whose children lived that close to a park or playground said that their children used the facility at least once a week. Among all new community parents, only 38 percent said that their children used a park or playground once a week or more often. Parents were also asked how they felt about places near their homes for children under twelve years old to play outdoors. Three-fourths of the new community parents and two-thirds of the conventional community parents rated such places as either excellent or good.

Almost a quarter of the households living in new communities had one or more young adult member in the fourteen to twenty year age bracket. Although new communities tended to pay more attention to young adults' recreational needs than did the conventional communities, neither type of community was very successful in this regard. For example, of those young adults who knew of available teen recreational centers, only 20 percent of those living in the new communities and 15 percent living in the conventional communities claimed to use them at least once a week. Low usage was probably caused by young adults' low regard for these facilities. Two-thirds of the new community young adults rated available teen centers as average, below average or poor. Ratings in the conventional communities were only slightly better. Fewer than half of the young adults living in both settings said they were happy with organized recreational activities and programs. Even more disturbing, about 40 percent of the young adults could not rate organized teen activities because they had never participated in them. However, when asked about the specific recreational facilities they used most often, young adults reported much higher levels of satisfaction. Over 80 percent of the young adults were satisfied with the facilities they most often used for their favorite out-of-home activities and for bicycling, swimming and walking and hiking.

In spite of their high levels of satisfaction with some facilities, young adults' dissatisfaction with teen-oriented facilities carried over to their overall evaluations of recreational facilities in their communities. In contrast to generally high overall ratings given by their parents, over two-thirds of the young adults living in the new and conventional communities rated community recreational facilities and services as average or below. In addition, over a third were neutral or dissatisfied with the ways in which they spent their leisure time. To find out how their ratings could be improved, young adults were asked what kinds of additional facilities were needed. Over a quarter of the new community young adults expressed a need for teen centers and an equal proportion wanted more cultural, entertainment and shopping facilities in their communities, including theaters, places for dances and parties, shopping malls, fast food places and libraries. In contrast with new community young adults, those living in the conventional communities were more likely to indicate a need for more indoor and outdoor recreational facilities.

Adult residents were asked about their participation in five outdoor recreational activities (golf, swimming, tennis, bicycling and walking and hiking) during the previous year. Surprisingly, although new communities provided more facilities for these activities, participation rates were only slightly higher than in the conventional communities. The margin of difference (in favor of new communities) in the proportions of respondents who participated in the activities ranged from a high of only 7 percent for golf to a low of 2 percent for participation in tennis. In addition, new community residents were not consistently more likely to use facilities within their own communities or to report that they were satisfied with the facilities they most often used. For example, although new community residents were significantly more likely than conventional community residents to golf, swim and walk or hike within their own communities, no differences were evident for bicycling, and a significantly higher proportion of conventional community residents played tennis within their own communities. New community residents were somewhat more likely to be satisfied with the swimming, bicycling and walking facilities they most often used, but were somewhat less likely to be satisfied with the golf and tennis facilities they used. As was also true of recreational resources, participation and facility satisfaction rates varied among new communities. The top ranking new communities in this case were Westlake Village, Reston, Lake Havasu City, Irvine, Valencia and Columbia.

Analyses of the relationships between facility characteristics and recreational participation indicated that planners can influence participation rates through the location and design of recreational facilities. Higher quality and more accessible recreational facilities were associated with much higher rates of participation than lower quality facilities that were less accessible to users.

Golf course characteristics that were associated with frequent (over 50 times during the preceding year) participation in golf included private ownership of the course used most often, availability of a clubhouse and bar, location of the course in the user's own community, availability of a driving range at the course, night lighting and generous landscaping.

Swimming facility characteristics that were most associated with higher participation rates included location (frequent participation was almost 20 percent higher than average for swimming facilities located within one-quarter mile of users), ownership by a homes association, outdoor pool or lake beach, heated water, adjacent clubhouse and longer operating season.

Like golf and swimming, frequent participation in tennis was also associated with the characteristics of the tennis courts players most often used. Frequent participation was higher among tennis players who used a court within one-eighth mile of their homes and dropped steadily with increasing distance. Participation was also higher among tennis players who used courts that were open twelve or more hours per day, required payment of a use fee and that had correspondingly more elaborate facilities, including lighted courts, pro shop and locker room, clubhouse and a bar. Participation was also higher at tennis facilities that were generously landscaped and well maintained.

Higher participation rates tended to be induced by the sociability aspect of outdoor recreation. Frequent participation in golf, swimming and tennis was greater at facilities that offered organized social activities for users, while organized sports activities, such as tournaments, had no effect on rates of frequent participation. Although new community development has not yet resulted in much greater than usual participation in outdoor activities, these results show that careful attention to the location, design and operation of recreational facilities can produce more active new communities.

In addition to the five outdoor activities that were examined for all respondents (bicycling, golf, swimming, tennis and walking and hiking), residents were asked to specify their favorite out-of-home activities. New community residents' favorite activities, in order of the frequency with which they were mentioned, were: golf, swimming, gardening, walking and hiking, bowling, tennis, boating, fishing, bicycling, arts and crafts and playing cards. The ability of new community recreational service systems to accommodate people's favorite activities provides another measure of service system effectiveness.

For each of the top ten favorite activities except gardening, which most people did in their own yards, new community residents who mentioned an activity as their favorite were more likely to participate in their own communities than were residents of the conventional communities. The difference was statistically significant for boating, swimming and tennis. Over three-fourths of the new community residents who mentioned gardening, walking, arts and crafts, swimming, boating, bicycling, tennis or golf as their favorite activity were satisfied with the facility they most often used for the activity. However, new community residents were no more satisfied with the facilities they used for their favorite activities than were residents of the conventional communities. The only favorite activities for which there was a 10 percent or greater difference in satisfaction levels were walking and fishing. Twelve percent more new community residents who said that walking was their favorite out-of-home activity were satisfied with the place used for walking, while 10 percent more conventional community residents who said that fishing was their favorite out-of-home activity were satisfied with the place they used for fishing. Neither difference is statistically significant. Thus, it appears that regardless of whether a community provides facilities for their favorite activities, residents will find a place to participate that suits their needs. Bowling and fishing were the only favorite activities where less than three-fourths of the respondents were satisfied with the facilities they most often used.

To summarize their overall responses to community recreational service systems, residents were asked to rate recreational facilities and services in comparison with their previous places of residence, to rate facilities and services in terms of their overall quality and to indicate whether community expenditures for outdoor recreational facilities were adequate. The superiority of new communities in providing recreational resources was clearly reflected in residents' responses to the questions. New community residents were significantly more likely than residents of the conventional communities, 63 percent versus 49 percent, to believe that community recreational facilities were better than those availabe in the communities from which they had moved. Seventy-seven percent of the new community respondents rated recreational facilities in their communities as excellent or good. Only 62 percent of the conventional community respondents rated facilities that highly. Finally, 66 percent of the new community respondents versus 60 percent living in the conventional communities thought that community recreational expenditures were adequate.

Recreational service systems in new communities also succeeded in satisfying most segments of the population. Men and women were equally likely to rate facilities as excellent or good. Older residents, age 65 or more, gave somewhat higher ratings (82 percent excellent or good) than younger residents (76 percent). In five new communities with subsidized housing, 83 percent of both the subsidized housing and nonsubsidized housing residents rated recreational facilities and services as above average. Black residents were only slightly (although significantly) less likely than white residents (67 percent versus 75 percent) to rate facilities as excellent or good in the five new communities where special subsamples of black residents were interviewed. Residents of single-family houses, townhouses and apartments, and owners and renters did not rate facilities differently, nor did residents who had lived for varying lengths of time in new communities. In fact, the only clearly disaffected group living in new communities was young adults. Compared with excellent or good ratings from 77 percent of the adult respondents, only 32 percent of the young adults rated recreational facilities and services that highly.

Comparisons of various characteristics of recreational facilities and services in new communities with residents' ratings provide some clues as to how ratings might be improved. For example, residents who participated more in recreational activities tended to rate facilities higher than non-participants. Inducing greater participation, as discussed above, should improve residents' evaluations of the recreational service system. Second, residents who had to travel shorter distances to participate in various activities also rated the recreational system as a whole higher. Critical distances from facilities used included: park or playground, under one-eighth mile; swimming facilities and tennis courts, under one-fourth mile; and golf courses, under two miles. People who lived within these distances of the recreational facilities they used most often tended to rate facilities as a whole highest.

Regardless of whether they used them or not, people who had various recreational facilities available in their neighborhood tended to rate the recreational service system as a whole highly. Also, a community's overall effort in providing recreational resources was related to ratings of the recreational system. Higher overall ratings tended to be given to recreational service systems with higher per capita annual operating expenditures, more community recreational and open space land per 10,000 population, and a greater variety of outdoor recreational facilities. The association of a number of objective characteristics of the recreational service system with service system ratings shows that residents' evaluations were not an arbitrary or random phenomenon. More and better recreational facilities resulted in more satisfied residents.

RECREATIONAL FACILITIES AND COMMUNITY MARKETING

In addition to their intrinsic value in conjunction with residents' recreational pursuits, community recreational facilities may serve a number of other functions. For example, because open space and recreational facilities attract residents, they may be key elements in the marketing and economic success of a new community venture.

An examination of the reasons residents gave for moving to new communities indicated that open space and recreational facilities were not equally important at all stages of development or to all types of prospective residents. Perceived nearness to the outdoors and natural environment, for example, contributed much more to households' decisions to move to new communities that were in earlier rather than later stages of the development process. In seven of the thirteen nonfederally assisted new communities and both federally assisted new communities, nearness to the outdoors and natural environment was mentioned by over a quarter of the respondents as one of the three most important reasons for having moved to them. Each of these communities began development after 1960, and each was surrounded by large expanses of vacant land. In contrast, the six new communities in which nearness to the outdoors was an insignificant aspect of their market appeal each began development prior to 1960 and/or was located in a highly developed area.

Because of the transitory character of proximity to the natural environment and the threat of later resident discontent as the natural environment disappears with increased urbanization, developers must be cautious in their use of this feature in community marketing. When new community residents were asked to name the most important issues or problems facing their communities, over a fifth of the respondents mentioned increasing density and crowding as an important problem. The concern many residents expressed for increasing population density was also revealed in suggestions for making their communities better places in which to live. Almost a fifth of the respondents (19 percent) thought that continued growth of their communities should be controlled and that higher density development should be limited. This strong sentiment for limited growth, if translated into more stringent zoning requirements, could have disastrous consequences for the financial viability of many new community ventures. Thus, while extolling the virtues of a "City in the Country," developers would be wise to fully inform prospective residents about future development plans in order to diminish adverse reactions to continued community growth and development.

The availability of recreational facilities was less likely than nearness to the outdoors and natural environments to be mentioned as a reason for having moved to a new community. Overall, 12 percent of the respondents living in the nonfederally assisted new communities, 22 percent of those living in Jonathan, and 9 percent of the Park Forest South respondents cited recreational facilities as one of the three most important reasons for their selection of a new community home. However, recreational facilities were more important aspects of the appeal of some new communities and some types of housing than others. For example, in addition to Jonathan, over 20 percent of the respondents living in Lake Havasu City (30 percent), Irvine (21 percent) and the two retirement new communities (Rossmoor Leisure World, 30 percent; Sun City Center, 32 percent) mentioned the recreational facilities available as one of the three most important reasons for having moved to these communities. Recreational facilities also played a larger part in households' decisions to move to higher density housing. Twenty-two percent of the households who had moved to condominium apartments, 22 percent who had moved to rental townhouses and 18 percent who had moved to rental apartments did so, in part, because of the availability of recreational facilities.

Two additional pieces of evidence suggest that recreational facilities can be of more than marginal importance in marketing new communities to prospective residents. First, recreational facilities ranked fifth among nineteen features in the proportion of respondents who reported improvements as a result of their move to a new community (mentioned more often were overall planning of the community, layout and space of the dwelling and lot, appearance of the immediate neighborhood and the community as a place to raise children). Second, recreation was one of only two features (the other being community planning) that was mentioned significantly more often by new community respondents than by conventional community respondents as a reason for having moved to their community. In short, community recreational facilities can play an important part in the marketing and financial success of a new community venture.

RECREATION AND THE QUALITY
OF COMMUNITY LIFE

In addition to contributing to the economic success of new communities, open space and recreational facilities are key elements in residents' perceptions of the quality of community life. Ninety percent of the new community respondents and 86 percent of the conventional community respondents rated their communities as excellent or good places to live. To explore reasons underlying evaluations of community livability, respondents were asked to elaborate on their ratings. Lack of crowding and nearness to nature and the outdoors were mentioned most often as reasons for rating new communities highly (cited by 16 percent and 15 percent of the respondents, respectively). The convenience of recreational facilities was mentioned by 6 percent of the respondents, while 5 percent mentioned the quality of recreational facilities as reasons for their positive evaluations of community livability.

Among individual communities, open space and other natural features of the environment were mentioned most frequently as reasons for positive evaluations of five new communities: Irvine (31 percent); Laguna Niguel (29 percent); Reston (24 percent); Valencia (23 percent); and Westlake Village (23 percent). These results generally parallel those for nearness to the outdoors as a reason for having moved to a new community. That is, open space and other natural features were more important factors in moving decisions and evaluations of community livability in communities that had been under development a shorter period of time and where the area surrounding the community was mostly undeveloped.

Jonathan respondents (26 percent) were most likely to mention recreational facilities as a key aspect of community livability, followed by respondents living in Valencia (17 percent) and those living in five new communities—Irvine, Laguna Niguel, North Palm Beach, Elk Grove Village and Foster City—where from 13 to 15 percent mentioned recreational facilities as a reason for rating livability highly.

New community residents' evaluations of the quality of community recreational facilities were strongly associated (statistically) with their overall ratings of community livability. On the basis of simple correlation coefficients, residents' evaluations of community recreational facilities ranked third among nine community attributes in explaining the variance in overall evaluations of community livability. When respondents' personal and household characteristics were controlled in a multivariate analysis, evaluations of recreational facilities ranked second among the factors influencing livability ratings. Residents' evaluations of their neighborhoods had more influence on livability ratings, while satisfaction with dwelling unit livability had an equivalent effect. However, residents' evaluations of recreational facilities explained more of the variance in community livability ratings than their evaluations of schools, health care facilities and services, their community association, transportation, shopping or religious facilities. In comparison with their effect in new communities, evaluations of recreational facilities had much less influence on conventional community residents' overall evaluations of community livability.

The contribution of recreational facilities to residents' evaluations of new communities as places to live was greater for some residents than for others. Because of this, new community planners and developers need to be sensitive to the interests they are serving through recreational facilities and programs. For example, recreational facilities appear to be more important to the community livability evaluations of women rather than men, of younger and older persons rather than middle-aged persons and of persons with family incomes that are under $10,000. Efforts to increase residents' satisfaction with community livability through improvements in the quality of recreational facilities will produce greater changes in satisfaction among these types of residents than among other new community residents. Conversely, satisfaction with community livability among these residents will suffer most from inadequacies in the community recreational service system.

Although recreational facilities had a strong influence on residents' perceptions of community livability, they had much less effect on residents' satisfaction with their lives as a whole. Instead, life satisfaction was highly dependent on satisfaction with the use of leisure time, which, surprisingly, was not associated with evaluations of community recreational facilities. That is, whether residents rated community recreational facilities highly or poorly had no effect on whether or not they were satisfied with the ways in which they spent their spare time, or, in turn, on whether or not they were satisfied with their lives as a whole. In large part this may stem from a narrow conception of leisure in new community planning. Planners have emphasized outdoor recreation, but have neglected facilities and programs for nonathletic pursuits.

If new community development is to have a positive influence on residents' satisfaction with their lives, a broader definition of leisure is needed. Attention should be given to a larger portion of residents' discretionary time than just that spent in outdoor recreational pursuits, and much greater attention should be given to leisure time programming and personalized advice to residents on the use of their spare time. In computer terminology, new communities have done well in providing the hardware (facilities), but must now begin to concentrate on the software (personnel and programs) that can enable people to grow and achieve satisfying lives.

 *Chapter 2*

Recreational Service Systems
in Fifteen New Communities

The characteristics of the recreational service system that evolves in a new community are a function of both the orientation of the developer and the social and institutional setting in which a community is developed. Although the new community goal of preservicing recretational facilities—providing facilities prior to each increment of residential development—required extensive planning before the first residents moved to the new communities, planning for institutions to develop, operate and extend recreational areas and facilities was rare. In a few cases recreational service systems emerged from the drawing boards as full-fledged operating entities. In most cases, however, the recreational service systems gradually took shape over a period of years in response to changes in environmental conditions and to changes in the needs and desires of each community's residents. This process is clearly illustrated by the experiences of the fifteen new communities that are described in this chapter.

FIVE OLDER NEW COMMUNITIES

Five new communities—Park Forest, Sharpstown, North Palm Beach, Forest Park and Elk Grove Village—began development during the late 1940s through the mid–1950s. New communities initiated during this period were characterized by two major departures from traditional approaches to converting rural land to urban use. First, in contrast to the small scale of most suburban subdivisions, community builders assembled land for projects that encompassed thousands of acres. Second, in contrast to the notable lack of land use planning in many suburban areas and resultant suburban sprawl, community builders began development of their projects with carefully drawn master plans that reserved land for a variety of urban functions and included provisions for a variety of housing types. On the other hand, the early community builders paid relatively little attention to site planning, architectural excellence and community amenities that have since become a hallmark of new community development in the United States.

The new communities of the 1940s and 1950s were built and merchandised by developers who had their roots in the home building and real estate industries. Their major concerns were building housing for the broad middle and lower middle income segments of the housing market who were moving to suburban areas in increasing numbers and capturing returns from commercial development attracted by the market they had created. The innovative planning principles, such as superblocks, cluster development and neighborhood greenways, that were pioneered in the 1930s by Radburn, the Greenbelt communities of the federal Resettlement Administration and the British garden cities were not continued. In some cases developers relied on traditional land use planning concepts because of financial considerations; in others developers used planning engineers who did not embrace the advanced planning concepts; and in others local governmental land use regulations inhibited innovative community design. In addition, with the exception of Sharpstown, the residents played major roles in the development of each of the older new communities that were studied. Each community incorporated at an early stage in the development process (Sharpstown was annexed to the city of Houston) and municipal governments assumed responsibility for land use control and most community facilities and services.

Park Forest, Illinois

The development of Park Forest was begun in 1947 by American Community Builders, Inc., a partnership consisting of Nathan Manilow, Phillip M. Klutznick and Jerrold Loebl. The original master plan designated a number of areas for neighborhood and community parks, but their development and the initiation of recreational programming was left to the residents. Four months after the first residents moved to Park Forest a provisional town government was formed. The community incorporated as a village the following year in February 1949. Because severe financial difficulties were encountered by the new village government (see Jack Meltzer 1952), American Community Builders donated a number of park sites to the community, many of which were to be jointly developed as park-schools. Aside from this early help, however, the developer did not play a major role in community recreation. Instead, American Community Builders preferred to let the residents of Park Forest decide what types of facilities they wanted and could afford to finance and operate.

The weak financial condition of the village led to the establishment of a nonprofit community swimming pool corporation, which built and operated the Park Forest Aquacenter until the spring of 1975 when the facility was taken over by the YMCA of Metropolitan Chicago. Although the Aquacenter is privately owned and operated, the Park Forest Recreation and Parks Department has been the major provider of recreational facilities and programs. In 1973 the department maintained 275 acres of parks, operated a nine-hole golf course and supervised and staffed some 80 recreational programs ranging from preschool through adult activities. A recreation center building, owned by the village, was jointly used by the recreation and parks department and a local school district. In addition, Park Forest's 30,600 residents had access to wooded lands, owned by the Cook County Forest Preserve District, which bordered the community on the east. In recent years the village government has also taken an active role in open space preservation by acquiring some open space land and by encouraging the preservation of the Thorn Creek Woods on Park Forest's southern border. Future development of Park Forest's recreational service system is guided by the village comprehensive plan, which was adopted by the board of trustees in 1967.

Sharpstown, Texas

When Frank W. Sharp began building Sharpstown in 1953, the development site was located well outside the built-up areas of the city of Houston. To attract residents to his new community, Sharp constructed and operated the Sharpstown Country Club. Membership in the club, which included a swimming facility and an 18-hole golf course, was offered to all who purchased homes in Sharpstown.

Sharp also reserved three neighborhood park sites, totaling 20.6 acres, for public acquisition. These sites were developed by the Houston Department of Parks and Recreation after Sharpstown was annexed to the city. Another park site in Sharpstown was donated to Harris County by a private citizen and is operated as a county park. By 1973 a number of other organizations were also contributing to the provision of recreational opportunities in the community. A variety of voluntary associations offered recreational programs for youth, and the Sharpstown Civic Association took an active part in preserving recreational amenities. Formed in 1961 to enforce architectural and land use covenants in Sharpstown (Houston does not have a zoning ordinance), the association sued the developer to block conversion of the Sharpstown Country Club to a multifamily residential development. In addition to the public recreational facilities operated by the city of Houston and Harris County, a number of swimming pools and tennis courts were provided at apartment projects located in Sharpstown.

North Palm Beach, Florida

North Palm Beach Properties, like the developers of most of the older new communities described here, contributed very little to the development of North Palm Beach's recreational service system. However, municipal incorporation served as a means to organize the provision of recreational services. In 1956, well before the first residents had occupied homes in North Palm Beach, the developer incorporated the community as a village, elected a mayor and a village council and hired the first village manager.

During the early years of development, North Palm Beach Properties dredged the North Palm Beach Waterway (to provide waterfront lots) and, in cooperation with the village government, built a recreational area for children and a village marina. Additional recreational opportunities were provided by the North Palm Beach Country Club, a developer-owned golf course that offered memberships to village residents. For the most part, however, the recreational service system in North Palm Beach was developed by the citizens working through their elected village government.

In 1961 the village paid $1,025,000 to acquire the North Palm Beach Country Club and added a swimming pool to the club's facilities.[a] In 1964 a recreation advisory board was created by the village council, and in 1969 a village recreation department was formed with a full-time director. By 1973 the recreation department operated a variety of recreational programs at four park sites and on occasion at the country club. In addition, the recreation department worked very closely with the North Palm Beach Youth Activities Association which operated a variety of sports programs. Additional recreational facilities (for the most part swimming pools) were provided at the numerous condominium apartment projects that were located in North Palm Beach.

[a]Although the North Palm Beach Country Club is owned by the village, it is operated as a private club with membership discounts given to North Palm Beach residents. In 1973 the swimming pool was available for general public use by village residents on only four days.

Forest Park, Ohio

Forest Park is being developed on land that was originally part of the federal greenbelt community of Greenhills, Ohio. In 1952, a 3400–acre tract of land lying just north of Greenhills was declared surplus and was sold to the Cincinnati Community Development Corporation for the construction of a planned new community.[b] In 1954 the Community Development Corporation sold the 3400–acre tract to the Warner-Kanter Corporation which began comprehensive development of Forest Park.

The original master plan for Forest Park was prepared by Victor Gruen and Associates. In 1956 the first residents moved into the community. However, by 1964 a new comprehensive plan noted:

> It is quite obvious that what has been planned and what has been realized have no parallel. One could argue that vacant lots serve as children's playgrounds on a temporary basis, but the question is: how long will these sites remain vacant? . . . only eight years after initial development began, the village has an inadequate recreational system. (R. Paul Christiansen 1964)

In 1964 the only public recreational facilities within Forest Park were an elementary school playground and a baseball diamond that was leased by the Forest Park Recreation Association for use by the community's Little League baseball teams.

In the absence of a developer commitment to open space and community recreational facilities, Forest Park had to rely on voluntary efforts and its incorporated city government to provide community recreational resources. Voluntary organizations operated youth recreational programs in Forest Park and a swimming facility was built and is operated by a nonprofit community corporation. In 1961 Forest Park was incorporated, largely to avoid annexation by neighboring Greenhills. With the backing of the Forest Park Recreation Association, the city formed the Forest Park Recreation Commission in 1966 to operate a community-wide recreational program. In order to acquire land for and improve the community's recreational resources, a $130,000 recreation bond issue was approved by the voters in 1972. It was used to purchase 22 acres of park-land from the developer. Because of the shortage of developed recreational facilities, local school gymnasiums and playing fields have been used extensively by Forest Park residents for outdoor recreation.

[b]The federal government also dedicated land lying between Greenhills and Forest Park to the Hamilton County Park District which developed the site as Winton Woods Regional Park.

Elk Grove Village, Illinois

In 1956 the Centex Construction Company began developing Elk Grove Village on a 1300–acre parcel it had acquired near O'Hare Airport. The original plans for Elk Grove Village called for a large tract of single family detached homes with a neighborhood shopping center and a small light-industrial park. However, between 1956 and 1960 Centex quadrupled its land holdings and replanned Elk Grove Village as a full-scale new community with a target population of 58,500 residents. Centex's role in the recreational system was defined as follows in the corporation's 1960 master plan for Elk Grove Village:

> Certain of the recreational needs, such as swimming facilities, golf courses, tennis courts and bowling alleys can logically be provided by private capital or cooperative efforts of the developer and civic groups. It is illogical, however, to assume that agencies other than public bodies should assume responsibility for the construction and equipping of such facilities as playgrounds, playfields, picnic areas, etc. (Phillips, Proctor, Bowers & Associates 1960)

The corporation had insured that a public body was available by incorporating Elk Grove Village in 1956, fully thirteen months before the first homes in the community were occupied.

The initial plans for Elk Grove Village designated nine sites, containing 68 acres, for neighborhood parks. By 1960 five sites with paved access and utilities had been preserved. However, none had been developed by the village, which was served by a recreation advisory group with limited funds and authority. Instead, early recreational development in Elk Grove Village resulted from the efforts of private voluntary associations. The Lions Club, in cooperation with the developer, built a swimming club, and the Jaycees helped to develop a community park.

In 1966 the Elk Grove Village Park District was established by a referendum of the residents and a slate of park commissioners was elected. The sole purpose of the district was to provide park and recreational services. By 1973 the district operated recreational programs at nineteen park sites and at eight schools, a number of which had been developed according to the park-school concept. The acquisition and development of park sites was guided by a recreation and park master plan that had been adopted by the district in 1968.

In addition to the park district, a number of voluntary associations provided recreational services in Elk Grove Village, including the Athletic Association, which sponsored recreational programs for youth. Elk Grove Village residents also had access to the adjacent

3800-acre Ned Brown Forest Preserve which is owned and maintained by the Cook County Forest Preserve District.

A FREESTANDING NEW COMMUNITY:
LAKE HAVASU CITY, ARIZONA

Lake Havasu City is one of the few freestanding new communities in the United States. It is being developed by McCulloch Properties, Inc. in the Arizona desert on a 16,630-acre site adjacent to Lake Havasu (a large reservoir formed by Parker Dam on the Colorado River) in an unincorporated section of Mohave County. With 8500 residents in 1972, an eventual population of 60,000 is expected.

The master plan for Lake Havasu City reserved the lake shoreline for use as a state park and designated sites for 36 neighborhood parks. However, because public agencies did not have the funds to develop fully the reserved recreational areas, McCulloch Properties was forced to invest heavily in recreational facilities and services. The developer financed the construction of beach and day-use areas at Lake Havasu State Park and constructed two eighteen-hole golf courses, a nine-hole par-three golf course, a marina, a campground and recreational trailer park and a bowling alley and movie theater (which were later sold to private operators). In addition, McCulloch Properties frequently responded to citizen's requests for help by donating funds for recreational activities organized by voluntary associations and by sponsoring youth athletic teams.

Three public organizations and several voluntary associations also played instrumental roles in providing recreational opportunities in Lake Havasu City. The state of Arizona operated Lake Havasu State Park. The Lake Havasu Irrigation and Drainage District (a special district formed by McCulloch Properties to aid in the development of the community) started the Lake Havasu City Recreation Commission to operate a summer recreational program financed by user charges and donations. The Mohave County Union High School District operated a community school program at Lake Havasu City High School. In addition, the community's high school, junior high and two elementary schools were extensively used for recreational activities sponsored by voluntary associations.

In order to coordinate the recreational activities of voluntary associations, including those of the Jaycees, Lions and a variety of special interest groups, the Lake Havasu City Recreation Association was formed. Among its other activities, the association worked for the development of a proposed 1082-acre Special Activities Recreation Area, to be developed cooperatively by its member organizations on land leased by Mohave County from the United States Bureau of Land Management. The recreation area is to include a Little League baseball diamond, equestrian and rodeo area, athletic field, motorcycle training area and trails, rifle, pistol, skeet and trap shooting ranges, model airplane facilities, lighted tennis courts, picnic areas and hiking trails.

THE CALIFORNIA NEW COMMUNITIES

A number of factors combined to make California an especially fertile area for new community development. Rapid population growth in the Los Angeles and San Francisco areas provided the necessary markets for large-scale development projects. The existence of many large tracts of vacant land under single ownership eased land assembly problems that have thwarted new community development in regions with fragmented ownership patterns. The state's expanding freeway and interstate highway system improved the accessibility of previously isolated land holdings. Every new community in California is bisected by or adjacent to a freeway. Finally, the ready availability (and easy formation) of special districts to provide water, sewerage and other improvements made new community development feasible in areas far removed from existing urban service systems. As a result, by 1974 California was the location of 38 of the 175 existing and proposed new communities in the nation ("New Community Check List Update" 1974).

The California new communities represent a sharp departure in community building technique from the older and freestanding new communities described above. California community builders were among the first to recognize the market for communities that featured a variety of recreational amenities. Early new community developers were steeped in the lore of homebuilding. They marketed the home first and the community second. Land was reserved for recreational facilities, but its actual development was often left to the vagaries of municipal government and the market. In contrast, the California community builders took an alternative approach. They sought reputable builders who were able to market their own housing products and concentrated on producing and marketing their community's image.

California new communities paid much closer attention to landscaping and architectural style than was common in the older new communities or Lake Havasu City. Community facilities—particularly recreational facilities that contributed to community image—were provided earlier in the development process. Neighborhood site planning was emphasized, with homes often clustered and related to adjacent open space networks and path systems. The major tradeoff the California community builders made was in housing prices. While the older new communities and Lake Havasu City provided homes within the means of a broad segment of the population, the California community builders stuck largely to middle- and upper-middle-income markets that could afford elaborate community amenity packages.

Foster City, California

Foster City is being developed on 2600 acres of low-lying land along the shore of San Francisco Bay, 25 miles south of San Francisco. The property was acquired in 1959 by T. Jack Foster for a new community that was expected to grow to 36,000 residents when development was completed. The Foster City General Plan, prepared by the firm of Wilsey, Ham and Blair, was approved by the San Mateo County Board of Supervisors on June 18, 1961. In 1964 the first homes in Foster City were occupied.

The general plan for Foster City reserved land for all of the community facilities that would be needed in a complete city. Recreational areas and facilities included a system of lagoons for sailing (and storm drainage), a series of small neighborhood parks and a central park on a lake formed by one of the lagoons. Before these and other facilities could be developed, however, the land had to be reclaimed from San Francisco Bay. In order to finance the reclamation effort and various municipal services, the developer retained a bond council to draft state legislation that would create the first municipal improvement district in California. The enabling act gave the district most of the powers of a municipality (police powers were not included) and allowed it to issue tax-exempt bonds.

The Estero Municipal Improvement District was organized on September 8, 1960. The first board of directors was appointed by the San Mateo County Board of Supervisors, but the three men selected were chosen by Foster and his sons. Continued developer control of the district was to be maintained by distributing voting rights on the basis of one vote for every one dollar of assessed valuation in the community and by assessing undeveloped land owned by the Fosters on a benefits-to-be-received basis (that is, as if it had been fully developed and was ready for sale to builders).

Developer control of the Estero District and the Fosters' practice of capitalizing interest (using bond proceeds to make interest payments in order to reduce property taxes when the developer was the major landowner) subsequently caused extensive citizen unrest in

Foster City. In 1966 a Foster City resident initiated a law suit (that was ultimately denied in a four to three decision by the California Supreme Court) charging that the formation of the Estero District was unconstitutional and amounted to a wrongful use of a public agency for private purposes. The following year the Foster City Community Association arranged a compromise with the Fosters. The Estero board of directors was expanded from three to five members and the election of board members was staggered to assure that by November 1971 all five directors would be directly elected by the residents.

Although Estero District bonds provided a means to develop and operate recreational facilities in Foster City, the cost of reclamation and other services left little money for recreational programming and park development. By 1970 the district property tax was substantially higher than that of all other cities in San Mateo County. Its bonded debt, $63.86 million, was almost two times the county's assessed valuation of Foster City. In an effort to increase revenues, provide greater citizen control, and a basis for improved community services, in April 1971 Foster City residents voted to incorporate the community.

The new city government established a parks and recreation department and a twelve-member park and recreation advisory committee to the Estero Board (the district became a subsidiary of the city after incorporation). These two bodies then moved swiftly to improve community recreational facilities. Foster City secured federal and county grants for a regional marina-park, established a park dedication ordinance, acquired additional park lands and initiated a community recreational program. The voters of Foster City also approved a $13 million bond issue in 1971, of which $2 million was designated for parks and the construction of a community recreational center.

In addition to the Foster City Park and Recreation Department, several other organizations contributed to the community's recreational system. The two elementary schools and junior high school in Foster City were used for recreational purposes. The San Mateo County Department of Parks and Recreation owned and operated a fishing pier in Foster City, and several voluntary associations, including Little League and the Lions Club, provided recreational services. Centex West, Inc., which purchased the undeveloped land in the community from the Fosters in 1971, donated recreational sites through the city's park dedication ordinance. Also, Centex and other builders developed a number of swimming and tennis facilities in connection with townhouse and apartment projects.

Laguna Niguel, California

Laguna Niguel was begun in 1960 by the Laguna Niguel Company, a subsidiary of Cabot, Cabot & Forbes. The initial development plan for the 7936-acre community located in an unincorporated section of southern Orange County was prepared by Victor Gruen and Associates. Although the development plan reserved sites for a variety of recreational areas and facilities, the pace of residential development was far below expectations and few recreational facilities were actually completed during the 1960s. Recreational facilities developed by the Laguna Niguel Company were private in character. They included the El Niguel Country Club and Laguna Niguel Tennis Club, both of which were owned and operated by the company. In addition, neighborhood parks and recreational facilities were developed and deeded to three automatic homes associations, and land for two neighborhood parks was set aside, but not developed for park use.

In 1971, after nearly 2300 homes had been sold, the undeveloped land in Laguna Niguel was sold to the Avco Corporation. After forming Avco Community Developers, Inc., to continue development, the corporation established a recreation division with an annual budget of over $100,000, appointed a recreation and parks administrator and took a number of steps to improve Laguna Niguel's recreational system. Since 1971, two Orange County parks have opened in Laguna Niguel, including the 167-acre Niguel Regional Park, located on a tract donated to Orange County by the Laguna Niguel Company, and the Niguel Beach Park, located on eleven acres sold to the county for less than its market value by Avco. Avco built the parking area for the beach park under a turnkey agreement with the county. In 1972 Avco provided a community center for group meetings in Laguna Niguel. The community center was also used by the YMCA, which offered various recreational programs.

Although Avco invested heavily in Laguna Niguel to speed development and agreed to donate park sites as new residential development occurred, it also recognized that full-scale park and recreational development would require public financing and operation. Since Laguna Niguel was in an unincorporated portion of Orange County, the approach followed was to use a county special taxing area, Laguna Niguel County Service Area #3, to provide recreational services. In 1974 the Laguna Niguel Homeowners Association (a voluntary group) asked the Orange County Harbors, Beaches and Parks District and the county board of supervisors to prepare a master plan for local parks and a five-year implementation plan. Funds for the plan were provided from the County Service Area #3 budget, which was also used to improve an undeveloped park on land originally dedicated by the Laguna Niguel Company. In addition, Avco Community Developers continued the development of private recreational facilities. These included a proposed athletic club to provide a variety of recreational facilities for all residents of the community and neighborhood park and recreational facilities which were dedicated to and operated by small homes associations created for each new increment of development.

Valencia, California

Valencia is being developed by the Newhall Land and Farming Company on a 4000–acre tract of unincorporated land in the Santa Clara River Valley northeast of Los Angeles. The master plan, prepared by Thomas L. Sutton and Victor Gruen and Associates, was adopted by the Los Angeles County Regional Planning Commission in October 1965. The plan provided for a variety of recreational areas and facilities, including golf courses, paseos (pathways connecting homes with schools and parks), neighborhood and village parks and an open space system separating a series of planned villages. A variety of institutional mechanisms were used to implement the recreational and open space provisions of the plan.

Commercial recreational facilities were constructed and operated by the developer. These included two eighteen-hole golf courses and a par-three course. A $30 million family ride park (called Magic Mountain) was constructed on a 200–acre site adjacent to Valencia in 1971. Other commercial recreational facilities that were developed in Valencia included a public riding stable, a family recreation park for dune buggies and motorcyclists and a trailer park and campground.

Maintenance of the paseo system was provided by the Los Angeles County Park and Recreation Department and paid for with revenues from a special taxing district of the county. Three neighborhood parks were operated by the Los Angeles County Park and Recreation Department (at an annual expense of approximately $45,000). The Newhall Land and Farming Company donated the land and developed the facilities for the first park (Old Orchard Park School) before dedicating the site to the county. The other two parks were developed by the county on land donated by the company. Operating expenses for all three parks were paid from general county budget allocations to the park and recreation department. Finally, several small automatic homes associations were established by the developer to maintain and operate clubhouse, swimming and tennis facilities in neighborhoods without county-operated park facilities. The two apartment complexes in the community had their own swimming and tennis facilities. In addition to the community and neighborhood recreational facilities provided in Valencia, recreational and cultural opportunities were offered by two educational institutions, College of the Canyons, a two-year community college, and the California Institute of the Arts.

Westlake Village, California

Westlake Village was started in 1964 by the American-Hawaiian Steamship Company on the 11,605–acre Albertson Ranch, located 40 miles northwest of the Los Angeles Civic Center. According to a company brochure, its goal in developing Westlake Village was to create "a place for a home with all the essentials of a community where homeowners will enjoy the advantages and necessities of the mid-week home and the enjoyment and recreation of a weekend resort . . ." The original community master plan was prepared by the Bechtel Corporation during 1964 and 1965. Although the plan included a variety of recreational facilities and open spaces that were to be developed in conjunction with a series of neighborhood clusters, American-Hawaiian noted that, "The idea of the community plan is to make provision for all of these facilities but not all of these facilities will be provided by the developer" (American-Hawaiian Steamship Company 1972, p. 2).

Nevertheless, the American-Hawaiian Steamship Company invested in a number of major community recreational facilities. A central focus of Westlake Village is the $2–million, 150–acre Lake Westlake. The lake was built by the American-Hawaiian Steamship Company, which also assumed responsibility for lake maintenance during the initial years of development. Lake Westlake was not planned as a public recreational facility. Instead, a private lake management association, made up of representatives from adjacent residential neighborhoods, was formed. American-Hawaiian Steamship Company deeded the lake to the association in 1974. In addition to Lake Westlake, the developer built a night-lighted executive golf course, a tennis club and a motel complex, which were leased to a private operator, and made land available for a school of equitation and two riding stables. Ownership of the undeveloped property in Westlake Village passed from the American-Hawaiian Steamship Company to the Prudential Insurance Company in 1973. Prudential has since completed a second golf course.

Neighborhood recreational facilities and open space were developed through both private and public institutions. In 1973, thirteen of the sixteen neighborhoods in Westlake Village had small automatic homes associations. These associations were responsible for maintaining open space and neighborhood recreational facilities deeded to them by the developer and individual tract builders. The thirteen neighborhood home associations formed the Westlake Joint Board to represent their members before public agencies and to advise public recreation agencies of citizens' views about needed facilities.

Neighborhood parks were also operated by two public agencies. In the Los Angeles County portion of the community (Westlake Village straddles Los Angeles and Ventura counties and in Ventura County has been annexed by the city of Thousand Oaks) the Los Angeles County Park and Recreation Department operated a five-acre park located adjacent to an elementary school and a homes association recreational complex. Land for the park was donated by the developer. In the Ventura County/Thousand Oaks portion of the community, the Conejo Park and Recreation District owned three neighborhood park sites acquired with funds from a $3.3–million bond issue passed in 1970. The developer contributed funds for the partial development of two of these parks. Finally, the Ventura County Parks Department maintained the landscaping along a parkway and a flood plain walking path. The landscaping was installed by the developer and was maintained with funds provided by a county maintenance district.

Although Westlake Village had acquired parks and recreational facilities through the efforts of the developer and public agencies, the decentralization of authority for the recreational system made it difficult to provide recreational programs. Programs were not offered by either county or the Conejo Park and Recreation District, and most of the homes associations were too small to provide more than a few basic summer activities. To overcome this deficiency, the voluntary Westlake Athletic Association was formed by the citizens to provide a variety of sports activities for youth. The association used park and school facilities in Westlake Village for its programs and received financial support from the developer.

Irvine, California

The 88,000–acre Irvine Ranch encompasses three Mexican land grants located 40 miles south of Los Angeles in Orange County. In order to keep the ranch intact, it was deeded to the James Irvine Foundation in 1937. The foundation formed The Irvine Company to manage the ranch properties. By the late 1950s urbanization of Orange County was approaching the Irvine Ranch from the north and the company began to receive offers from developers interested in acquiring land for residential subdivisions. Two major freeways were planned through the ranch and taxes on the property began to reflect its potential for urban development. Rather than sell its land holdings, the Foundation decided to restructure The Irvine Company and to develop the property itself. The major stimulus to plan a new community on the Irvine Ranch occurred in 1959 when 1000 acres were donated by The Irvine Company to the University of California for a new campus. Initial residential building in the central portion of the ranch adjacent to the University of California at Irvine got underway in 1967.

From the first The Irvine Company relied heavily on the use of private homes associations to maintain and operate neighborhood recreational facilities that were built by the company and individual tract builders. Reliance on the homes association concept was based on several considerations. First, the company's residential developments were built around neighborhood recreational facilities, including tot lots, small parks, swimming pools and tennis courts. The use of automatic homes associations provided a way to insure that these facilities were maintained. At the same time, company officials thought that homes associations provided a source of exclusiveness, privacy, and community identity. Second, the company had had successful experiences with neighborhood homes associations in earlier developments on other parts of the ranch. Third, because development began in an unincorporated section of Orange County, there were few other options. (See Michael M. Hertel 1971.) By the end of 1973, 37 homes associations were operating in Irvine developments, eleven of them in the central sector community of Irvine.

In addition to homes associations, two other means were used to provide open space and recreational opportunities during the first years of development. Maintenance of two small parks, arterial highway landscaping and other public open space dedicated by The Irvine Company was financed by special service district taxes collected by Orange County. Golf facilities were provided at a public course constructed on a landfill by The Irvine Company.

The neighborhood homes association concept worked well, but it was not amenable to the development or operation of the full-scale recreational system planned for Irvine. In 1970, three years after residential occupancy of the first Irvine neighborhood, The Irvine Company published plans for the development of the central sector of the ranch. The plan called for an extensive array of open space and park facilities as an integral part of the land use scheme.[c] How-

[c]Included were proposals for 84 miles of bicycle trails; 56 miles of equestrian trails; 872 acres of arterial highway parkways; 409 acres of neighborhood parks; 597 acres of local community parks; 1007 acres of school playgrounds; 1227 acres of golf courses; 4554 acres of regional park land; and 5212 acres of scenic and wildlife habitat area.

ever, the means of achieving the plan were not detailed beyond a
proposal that a new city of Irvine be incorporated with an area
of influence of some 53,000 acres and an ultimate population of
430,000. In supporting incorporation of a new city, an Irvine Company official noted, "The largest problem faced by The Irvine Company in planning for open spaces has been finding some agency to
maintain the open space areas . . . with formation of a city, standards
for open spaces can be set and there will be some agency to assure
their care" (*Irvine World News*, December 16, 1971).

With the backing of The Irvine Company and the Council of the
Communities of Irvine, an organization formed by homes association
leaders, Irvine incorporated as a city in December 1971. After incorporation, a dual organization of the community recreational system
evolved. The Irvine Company and individual tract builders continued
to develop neighborhood recreational facilities, recoup their cost
through residential lot sales and deed them to neighborhood homes
associations. The city of Irvine focused its attention on the need for
larger community parks. The city's interim open space and parks plan
(see Haworth and Anderson 1973) noted that the lack of such parks
made it difficult to conduct community recreational programs. In
June 1974 the voters of Irvine passed a $16–million bond issue for
the acquisition and/or development of nine community parks located
throughout the city. Preliminary plans for the parks called for three
major community centers and three smaller multi-use centers, eighteen athletic fields, a swim center, twenty tennis courts, a performing
arts center and a senior citizen's center.

The city of Irvine also operated a community recreational program
that made use of school facilities owned by the Irvine Unified School
District. Finally, regional recreational areas were to be developed
in Irvine by the Orange County Harbors, Beaches and Parks District.
Its initial effort, a $750,000 45–acre first phase of the 345–acre
William R. Mason Regional Park opened in 1974. Land for the park
was donated by The Irvine Company.

NEW COMMUNITIES IN THE EAST

Two new communities in the Washington-Baltimore region—Reston
and Columbia—have been at the forefront of the new communities
movement in the United States. Reston and Columbia matched the
California new communities' concern for environmental design and
recreational amenities but added a concern for population balance
and diversity that was missing in the western communities. The California new communities represented suburban development at its

zenith. Columbia and Reston, on the other hand, were first attempts to create new cities in the suburbs.

Reston, Virginia

Reston began in March 1961 when its initial developer, Robert E. Simon, Jr., purchased 6750 acres of Virginia countryside for a large-scale new community. The first of seven goals Simon formulated as guides for building Reston was:

> that the widest choice of opportunities be made available for the full use of leisure time. This means that the New Town should provide a wide range of recreational and cultural facilities as well as an environment for privacy (The Reston Home Owners Association 1973, p. 2).

To achieve this goal, the Reston master plan designated 40 percent of the acreage in the community for various common uses.

As planning commenced for Reston's first two villages, Lake Anne and Hunters Woods, Simon established two automatic membership homes associations, First and Second, to maintain land and facilities—open space, swimming pools, lakes and tennis courts—that would be designed and constructed by the developer and dedicated to the associations.[d] This institutional structure was simplified in 1970 through the efforts of Gulf-Reston, Inc., which took over development from Simon in 1967. After a citywide vote, the First and Second homeowners associations were consolidated into one organization, the Reston Home Owners Association (RHOA).

When the First and Second homeowners associations were consolidated, village councils were created to provide a forum for citizen participation in the developer-controlled Reston Home Owners Association. Originally, the village councils were to represent village residents by advising the association about village affairs and by participating in an advisory Town Council composed of three resident-elected members of the RHOA board of directors and the village council chairmen. However, because of the stigma of developer control of the Reston Home Owners Association, since 1972 the village councils have been looked upon as totally autonomous bodies with no official connection with RHOA. The Town Council was also dropped in 1972 and was replaced by an Advisory Council composed

[d]As of February 1975, Gulf-Reston, Inc., Simon's successor, had deeded Lake Anne, tennis courts, stables, swimming pools, walkways and a pony barn—carrying a construction value of $2.622 million—to the Reston Home Owners Association. In addition, Gulf-Reston had deeded approximately 370 acres of common lands—valued at $1.5 million—to the Home Owners Association (*The Reston Times*, February 27, 1975).

of the three resident representatives on the RHOA board, representatives of the village councils and the executive director of the Home Owners Association. An additional change occurred in 1973 when the Advisory Council was replaced by the Reston Home Owners Association Council. The council together with the RHOA staff jointly recommend to the RHOA board of directors the proposed annual budget of the association. In 1972—73 annual expenditures of the Reston Home Owners Association were almost three quarters of a million dollars.

In addition to organizing Reston's initial homes associations, Simon established the Reston Foundation for Community Programs as a vehicle for securing grant money from outside sources and instituting innovative programs. In 1967 Simon and the foundation established the Nature Center as a means of providing environmental education and management. Since then the Nature Center has operated various environmental programs within Reston and, under an agreement with the Reston Home Owners Association, has assumed responsibility for contracting and supervising landscape maintenance (in return for RHOA and Gulf-Reson, Inc. budgetary support). Now known as the Environmental Office (of RHOA)—the Nature Center, the center has worked closely with environmental management committees which operate under village councils in the Reston Home Owners Association structure.

In 1973 the basic means of support for the Reston Home Owners Association came from a $50 annual assessment (which could be raised under certain conditions) on each residential lot in the community (the assessment of rental units was paid by their owners). Revenues from the annual assessment were adequate to support maintenance of common areas and facilities, but not full-scale recreational programming. In 1973 the association had one full-time staff person for recreational services and a budget of only $13,500 for programs. To overcome this problem a number of facilities (particularly swimming pools, tennis courts and equestrian facilities) were operated on a user-fee basis, and a number of voluntary associations were established to help maintain facilities and to participate in recreational programming. These included the Reston Tennis Association, Reston Riding Association, and Pools committees, as well as cultural organizations such as the Reston Players, Inc., Reston Ballet Company and Reston Chorale. The Reston Home Owners Association coordinated volunteer acitivites. Youth sports in Reston were coordinated by RHOA and by the Reston Youth Athletic Association, which was formed in 1971 from separate voluntary groups that were operating youth baseball, football and swimming programs (indoor soccer and basketball groups joined later).

In addition to the organizations which operated under the Reston Home Owners Association umbrella, several other agencies were active in providing recreational services in Reston. Gulf-Reston, Inc. owned and operated two golf courses in the community, one private and one public (which it subsidized), donated the use of athletic field sites to RHOA for recreational use pending their development for other purposes and made financial contributions to various recreational and cultural activities in Reston, including sponsorship of Reston Youth Athletic Association teams. Although the Fairfax County Park Authority had not acquired park sites in Reston, the Fairfax County Recreation Department (which operated programs, but did not own land) ran summer recreational programs (financed by RHOA) in two Reston elementary schools and supplied the staff and equipment for six-week teen centers during the summer. Finally, the Fairfax County school system allowed the Reston Home Owners Association to use the playgrounds and multipurpose rooms of the elementary schools in Reston.

Columbia, Maryland

Columbia was conceived by Baltimore mortgage banker and shopping center developer James Rouse in mid–1962. At that time he began secretly acquiring approximately 15,000 acres (13,690 were to be included in the new community) in rural Howard County midway between the beltways surrounding Baltimore and Washington. After several years of planning for a new community that would ultimately house 110,000 residents, the Columbia concept was approved by Howard County and in mid–1965 the development site was rezoned in accordance with a recently completed new-town section of the county zoning ordinance. To secure approval of the new community plan, Rouse agreed to devote a minimum of 20 percent of Columbia's acreage to permanent open space land uses. Fifty percent of this open space was to be available for public use.

In order to achieve the goal of providing the best possible environment for the growth of people, an extensive array of recreational facilities was planned for Columbia. In addition to some 3000 acres of open space, which would weave throughout Columbia's seven villages, each village was to have a community center and a recreational facility of some sort. Individual neighborhoods in the villages were each to have a neighborhood center, swimming pool and a park. To offer these amenities, together with a broad range of social services and recreational programs, and to assure that facilities were in place before each increment of population was added, it was apparent that a new means of providing facilities and services was needed.

The institution established for this purpose was the Columbia Park and Recreation Association. Incorporated on October 10, 1965, the Columbia Association, as it is commonly called, is a nonprofit organization which operates under recorded deed covenants for the maintenance of common property, the provision of all needed facilities and services not offered by Howard County and the operation of community programs. The Columbia Association differs from the Reston Home Owners Association and the small homes associations used in Irvine, Laguna Niguel, Valencia and Westlake Village in four important respects. First, its charter allows it to perform a broader array of functions. Second, it has the responsibility for actually financing and developing, as well as maintaining and operating, community recreational facilities and amenities. Third, because it can assess commercial and industrial as well as residential property located in the new town zone (at a rate of up to $0.75 per $100 of assessed valuation) and because its assessments are a first lien on property which take precedence over purchase money mortgages, it has a strong and secure financial base. Fourth, voting for association officers is not limited to property owners but includes renters as well.

In addition, the Columbia Association has a unique federal structure. Each village in Columbia has its own village association. These associations were formed to provide vehicles for citizens participation but to be dependent on the Columbia Association for financial support. While residents can be members of their village association, they are not legally members of the Columbia Association whose only members are its board of directors. For every 2000 dwelling units completed in Columbia, the residents are entitled to one-half vote on the board. However, the board of directors is not directly elected by the residents. Instead, residents elect village representatives to the Columbia Council, which in turn nominates members of the Columbia Association Board of Directors. The board of directors selects the residents' village representatives from the list of nominees.

Until 16,000 dwelling units are constructed in Columbia, the board of directors will be controlled by the developer. In 1973, official resident participation in the Columbia Association came from the Columbia Council, on which each village was entitled to one member. The Columbia Council acted in an advisory role by sitting in on meetings of the executive committee of the Columbia Association Board of Directors. Additional resident input to the decisions of the Columbia Association was provided by the Columbia Combined Board, an organization composed of representatives of each village association; by the individual village association boards of directors, and by various special interest committees formed by the Columbia Association's professional staff.

The basic genius of the Columbia Association, and the reason for its attractiveness to the developer, was the shifting of the capital costs of various community facilities from the land to the association. This avoided front-end loading of amenity costs onto home prices while insuring developer control of investments in community amenities. The construction of community facilities by the Columbia Association and its early operating deficits were financed through note agreements with the Howard Research and Development Corporation, Connecticut General Life Insurance Company and the Teachers Insurance and Annuity Association in the amount of $15 million, which was due in December 1975. In addition, a second loan for $7.5 million was secured from Chase Manhattan Bank, Teacher's Annuity and Connecticut General. The initial loan was repaid in 1973 when the association sold $15 million in bonds (based on an A rating at 7−7/8 percent) and placed $7.5 million in short-term 9 percent subordinated notes whose repayment was guaranteed by the developer. The bond sale was crucial to Columbia, since it proved that the association could finance its activities through private money markets. Such financing was essential, since the association had accrued a debt of $25.378 million through April 1974, and the total debt would continue to grow for a number of years.

Revenues to repay the association's bonded indebtedness and notes and to finance the costs of park and open space maintenance (which produced no revenue) were generated from the association's assessments on real property. Recreational programs and facility operating costs were financed by user fees. The financial condition of the Columbia Association was monitored, in part, through use of the Columbia Association Economic Model. As of 1973 the model provided a projection of all capital and operating costs and all expected revenue for twelve years into the future.

The Columbia Association was organized into three operating divisions, including the Division of Physical Planning, Division of Human Services and Division of Commercial Operations. Recreational programming was carried out by the Recreation Department in the Human Services Division. This department, with a 1973 budget of $350,000, operated a variety of programs at 22 recreational sites in Columbia, including each of the neighborhood centers. By employing registration fees and user charges, the department attempted to "break even" financially. The Division of Commercial Operations, with a 1973 budget of $1 million and expected revenues of $1.2 million, attempted to make a profit that could be used to subsidize other programs. The Commercial Division operated two golf courses, the Columbia Athletic Club, Columbia Ice Rink, Columbia Service Center, Columbia Tennis Club, Lake Kittamaquandi Boat Dock, Wilde Lake Boat Dock and eight neighborhood parks. Together, these facilities represented a capital investment by the Columbia Association of some $4.5 million.

Columbia Association officials estimated that the association provided 75 percent of the recreational opportunities in the community, with 20 percent provided by voluntary associations and commercial establishments and 5 percent by Howard County. Commercial establishments that provided recreational facilities in Columbia included the Tennis Barn, Merriweather Post Pavillion, and a putt-putt golf course. Active voluntary associations included the Columbia Youth Baseball Association, Optimists and open school programs at Phelps Luck and Longfellow elementary schools. Finally, the Howard County Park and Recreation Department operated an open school program at Wilde Lake High School.

Although Howard County allocated few resources for recreation in Columbia, it was at times critical of various Columbia institutions. In 1971 The Columbia Commission, an organization established by the county council to investigate the impact of Columbia on the county, called for greater county involvement in decisions regarding the allocation of open space in Columbia and recommended that, because of the public nature of the Columbia Association, the county council take legislative action to insure that at least one representative of county goverment serve as a member of the Columbia Association's board of directors (Columbia Commission 1971).

THE FEDERALLY ASSISTED
NEW COMMUNITIES

Passage of federal new communities legislation in 1968 and 1970 opened a new chapter in new community development in the United States. Through a public-private partnership the pace of new community development was to be significantly expanded. New communities for the first time were viewed as keystones in an emerging national urban growth policy. As important, in exchange for federal backing of their long-term debt and various other forms of assistance, new community developers and the communities they created were expected to contribute to the accomplishment of a broad range of economic, social, environmental and governmental objectives that were rarely emphasized in wholly private new community ventures. As noted by HUD Assistant Secretary Samuel C. Jackson:

> they are communities whose creators are sensitive not only to the need for diversity and innovation in the physical planning sense, but in social planning as well. This is as it should be; in the final analysis, social questions are the really important ones, for the final measure of new communities is not convenience or reduction in urban sprawl for their own sake but the quality of life they sustain (Samuel C. Jackson 1972, p. 7).

However, while the federal new communities program was begun with very high aspirations, it delivered few resources to assist in their realization.

In addition to guarantying developers' bonds and debentures, Title IV of the 1968 Housing and Urban Development Act authorized supplemental grants of up to 20 percent of the required local costs of federal grants for water, sewer and open space. The Urban Growth and New Community Development Act of 1970 greatly expanded the scope of potential federal assistance to approved projects. The secretary of Housing and Urban Development was authorized to loan developers up to $20 million for a period of fifteen years after the start of development so that they could make interest payments on their debts. Public service grants to enable local agencies to provide educational, health, safety and other services during the first three years of development were authorized. Up to two-thirds of the cost of special planning studies was authorized so that developers could plan programs that were fully responsive to social and environmental problems and that supported the use of new and advanced technology. The secretary of Housing and Urban Development was authorized to provide technical assistance to developers, and the 20 percent supplemental grants authorized by Title IV were extended to thirteen federal grants-in-aid programs.

Unfortunately, most of these provisions were never implemented. The Department of Housing and Urban Development never requested funds from Congress to make interest loans to developers, public service grants or to provide technical assistance. Although $168 million in supplementary grants for public facilities was authorized by Congress through 1973, only $25 million had actually been appropriated for this purpose. In June 1973 this provision of the new communities program was terminated by the administration. The new communities program also suffered when administration priorities resulted in delays in the release of funds for some categorical grant programs and the suspension of other federal aid programs such as the January 1973 moratorium on federally subsidized housing.

The paucity of federal support, internal management problems experienced by some federally assisted new communities and the crippling effects of the national economic recession that began in 1973 combined to produce a struggle for survival among the new generation of new communities participating in the federal program. Jonathan, the first federally assisted new community under Title IV, failed to make a $468,000 interest payment that HUD was forced to cover when it found that it had a two and one-half year inventory of lots and homes for sale. In 1975 a refinancing plan was being negotiated so that the Landtect Corporation could take over community development from the Jonathan Development Corporation. Park Forest South, another federally assisted new community, was placed in default on its loan guarantee when HUD had to make a $1.05 million interest payment. HUD subsequently allowed the developer to raise additional capital by selling land used as collateral for its federally guaranteed loans. However, during 1975 development was again stalled and the community's future growth was uncertain. Although both new communities were in financial trouble, each had achieved the nucleus of its community recreational system and was providing services to a combined total of some 7000 residents.

Jonathan, Minnesota

As part of its project agreement with the Department of Housing and Urban Development (1970), the Jonathan Development Corporation agreed to "develop and sell to a public or community body, dedicate or otherwise protect, for public or community use, 1705 acres of land within the Project for permanent recreation, conservation, or other open space uses." In a 1972 revision of the 1970 General Development Plan, the goals for the community and role of open space and recreation were discussed more fully. One goal that was to guide the development process was the desire "to make possible maximum opportunity for self-realization and development of individuals of all ages," and "to heighten the awareness of the individual as to his role within a working ecological system by preservation of natural features of the site and provision of an on-going environmental education program" (Jonathan Development Corporation 1972). To achieve this goal the plan reserved some 25 percent of the total site as open space for active and passive recreational use, pedestrian walkways and wildlife and ecological resources. In addition, a variety of specific recreational facilities were to be provided in a series of residential villages.

The Jonathan Development Corporation had to determine how to implement the provisions of this and earlier development plans. The corporation's first choice was to annex to the nearby city of Chaska, which was accomplished in 1967 shortly after the initial plans for Jonathan were announced to the public. The decision to become a part of Chaska was based on three primary considerations: (1) social and political structures already existed and would be immediately available to Jonathan residents; (2) existing municipal services were in place and could be expanded to serve Jonathan; and (3) it was financially expedient, since Chaska could receive state and federal infrastructure grants, issue municipal industrial development bonds and make available its water and sewer system. The alternative, creation of a homes association, was discarded because, as an official of the Jonathan Development Corporation noted, "Private associations with covenants running with the land are far too cumbersome and rigid for anything more than the delivery of an unsophisticated level of municipal services and maintenance" (Einsweiler and Smith 1971, p. 6). However, because of the unsophisticated service system that existed in Chaska (which had less than 5000 residents), the Jonathan Development Corporation found it impossible to proceed with development without establishing a homes association.

In fact, the primary means of providing recreational services in Jonathan was the Jonathan Association, a nonprofit, developer-controlled automatic membership association formed in 1971, to which all residential property owners belonged and paid annual assessments of $50 (which could be raised by 5 percent a year). As explained to its members, the association was designed to provide community services within Jonathan while the city of Chaska supplied municipal services. The Jonathan Association owned the common areas within the community, including greenways, walkways and recreational areas, and was responsible for their maintenance. It also supplied and supervised a variety of recreational programs. In 1973 the association had a recreation budget of over $41,000, of which 73 percent was contributed by the developer.

Several other organizations provided recreational services to the residents of Jonathan, though their facilities and programs were not located in the community. With a recreation budget of $38,000 in 1973, the city of Chaska operated a summer recreational program. Chaska had also secured two federal and one state grant for open space and recreational land acquisition and had passed a bond issue to finance its local share of the cost. However, although Jonathan was the primary instigator of Chaska's open space program, the first phase of open space land acquisition was to be in portions of Chaska lying outside of the Jonathan planning area. School District 112 had adopted a community school program and offered recreational activities and adult education programs at its schools, none of which had yet been built in Jonathan. Carver County contributed to an OEO-sponsored senior citizens' program in Chaska and had a county park in the city. Finally, several voluntary associations, including Little League, Babe Ruth League and a hockey association provided recreational services in Chaska, which also had a commercial bowling alley.

Park Forest South, Illinois

The project agreement between the federal government and the Park Forest South Development Company (1971) spelled out the details of an extensive developer commitment to open space and recreational facilities. The mature open space and recreational system was to be "a network of open space that will provide visual and physical enjoyment for the residents of the Project through scenic walks, trails, and leisure activity centers and through woods and valleys." In addition, each Park Forest South resident was to have "a number of options, including a nearby open space where he can relax and enjoy an outdoor setting; a variety of active areas, and equally important, a convenient and enjoyable movement system, enabling him to get nearly as much pleasure out of getting to his goal as he does from the goal itself."

Park Forest South was incorporated as a village in 1967, before actual development began and before the developer sought assistance from the federal government. The Village of Park Forest South, however, was financially and technically incapable of implementing the initial recreation and open space elements of the community plan. In 1973 the village recreation commission had a budget of only $3000, with which it provided a limited recreational program. To overcome the limitations of its local government, the developer attempted to establish the New Town Park and Recreation Association, modeled after the Columbia Park and Recreation Association described above. This effort failed when the village board of trustees indicated that it did not want to share its powers with a nonprofit community corporation and the Federal Housing Administration refused to let the association's assessments take precedence over purchase money mortgages, which had previously been approved on an experimental basis in Columbia. As a result, plans for the association were implemented on paper (and recorded in deeds) but not in fact. Instead, the developer organized a series of small automatic membership homes associations and multi-neighborhood recreational associations to operate and maintain the common open space, clubhouses and swimming pools that were to be provided.

In 1973 the developer controlled the homes and recreation associations and operated two major recreational facilities, a golf course and an ice rink, as commercial ventures. Most major open space in Park Forest South, including lakes and various wooded areas, were still owned by the developer but were made available for general public use pending public acquisition by the village after it had received federal open space grants. In addition, the developer had agreed to limit the extensive development that was originally planned for the Thorn Creek Woods in the northern sections of the community bordering Park Forest.

SUMMARY

Although community recreational service systems began in each of these new communities as spatially defined systems of parks and open spaces designated on master and concept plan maps, implementation of the plans led to the evolution of fifteen diverse and unique systems for providing community recreational resources and services. Because of differing local circumstances, new community developers and citizens used a number of different types of organizations, often in the same community, to provide services. In order of the number of new communities in which they were active, these included: voluntary associations; county park and recreation departments; new community developers; home associations; municipal park and recreation departments; independent park and recreation districts; school districts; commercial establishments; state agencies; and other county and municipal agencies. Overall, each new community had an average of 4.5 different organizations that provided major (as defined by local recreation professionals) recreational services. Surprisingly, the range of organizations providing recreational services in the paired conventional communities, though not described in this chapter, was little different from that found in the new communities. Thus, while new communities differed from typical suburban development in the degree and comprehensiveness of community planning, they did not limit the fragmentation of responsibility for public services that characterizes most metropolitan areas.

✱ *Chapter 3*

Key Decision Agents and Administrative Practices

The organization and administration of recreational services in new communities challenge the ingenuity of planners and developers. New communities are typically initiated on the peripheries of metropolitan areas, far from existing urban service systems. Yet, as Royce Hanson (1972, p. 1) has observed, "the imperatives of new community development which favor social diversity, balanced land use, and the serving of social purposes, imply a much higher level of public benefits and services for the community than has been normally assumed to be the obligation of the developer." Because traditional development organizations cannot effectively plan and provide all of the recreational services desired in a new community, developers have had to form new institutions and to enlist the aid and cooperation of other organizations.

The experiences of fifteen new communities in organizing the provision of recreational services were reviewed in Chapter 2. Particular attention was given to the behavior of new community developers and to identifying the public, quasi-public and privately operated organizations that participated in the provision of recreational services. In this chapter the orientations and actions of these key decision agents are analyzed in relation to the goal of providing a "higher level of public benefits and services" in new communities. In addition, three key administrative processes are examined, including the governance of recreation organizations and citizens participation, community planning for recreational areas and facilities and methods of financing capital improvements and recreational services.

KEY DECISION AGENTS IN RECREATION
SERVICE SYSTEMS

New community developers encountered a number of difficulties in breaking away from established patterns of recreational service delivery. In large part these difficulties stemmed from the lack of any clear agreement in the United States as to who should be responsible for public recreation and urban open space in newly developing areas (see Bollens and Schmandt 1965, pp. 335–338), what level of resources should be devoted to these purposes and how they should be financed. As a result, while the recreational and environmental goals and land use arrangements proposed by new community development schemes tended to be highly rational, implementation of the plans was often subject to a high degree of variability and unpredictability, depending on the orientations of the key decision agents involved. The following discussion attempts to explain why this was so by examining the roles of each of the key agents involved in providing recreational services in new communities.

New Community Developers

From the developer's point of view, the organizational structure for the provision of open space and recreational facilities and services should have three characteristics (see Institute of Government 1971). First, the structure should maintain, for as long as necessary, developer control of the quality of facilities and programs and the timing of their provision. Ideally, open space and recreational facilities should be provided prior to residential sales in each development increment and should be of high enough quality to be an asset in marketing the community. Without developer control of the organizational structure that provides facilities, it is impossible to assure that each of these objectives will be met. Second, the structure should allow the costs of open space and recreational facilities and programs to be shared by the residents of the community. In addition, in order to maintain reasonable residential price levels during the early years of development when there are few residents with whom to share heavy early capital costs, repayment of costs should be deferred for as long as possible. Third, the organizational structure should be satisfactory to the residents, so that resident discontent (and resulting adverse publicity) is kept to a minimum.

Unfortunately, these three goals for the organization of the recreational service system conflict with one another. If developers monopolize control of the recreational system, they may find it hard to share costs and maintain resident satisfaction (see Raymond J.

Burby, III 1974). If cost sharing is maximized through public provision of facilities and services, then control is sharply diminished. If resident satisfaction is sought, developers must choose between prospective and existing residents. That is, developers can probably do a better job of selling the community to prospective residents if they control the recreational system and develop it to further their marketing objectives. However, this risks dissatisfaction of existing residents whose views may be disregarded in decision making. If the satisfaction of existing residents is sought, this may damage marketing by delaying decisions while the residents decide what they want.

Viewed from this perspective, it is clear that the developers of pre-1960 new communities (Elk Grove Village, Forest Park, North Palm Beach, Park Forest and Sharpstown) chose to give up control in favor of sharing costs of the recreational system. Thus, they fostered incorporation of their communities and municipal provision of facilities. Given the strong interest in housing value and frequent lack of attention to environmental quality among consumers during that period, this was probably a rational course of action.

Developers of communities initiated since 1960, on the other hand, generally sought to achieve a balance among the three desirable characteristics of the recreational service system. This became feasible after the automatic homes association concept gained widespread acceptance among FHA and local government officials and among consumers. As used in Columbia, Reston and Jonathan, community-wide homes associations allowed their developers to control the character of the open space and recreational service systems while sharing the cost with the residents. However, as shown in Burby (1974), extensive developer control decreased residents' satisfaction with these communities as places to live. A similar approach by the developer of Foster City, but using a developer-controlled municipal improvement district, resulted in extreme resident discontent, which in turn caused severe delays in the pace of development, led to municipal incorporation and the eventual sale of the community to another developer.

An alternative use of homes associations characterized the Southern California new communities (Irvine, Laguna Niguel, Valencia and Westlake Village) and Park Forest South. In these communities developers tended to maximize their control over the provision of neighborhood amenities through developer provision of facilities and dedication to neighborhood homes associations but to share the costs of community-wide facilities with public agencies. This approach had the advantage of increasing residents' satisfaction with the community, since control of neighborhood associations was transferred to the residents after a short period of time. However, it may result in inadequate community-level open space and recreational facilities if public agencies are not in a position to provide them or if the residents prefer to use their tax dollars for other purposes.

In most new communities developers were willing to own and operate recreational facilities that had the potential to break even financially and to make a profit if they were managed carefully. Typically, these were facilities (such as golf courses and entertainment parks) that had a large enough regional clientele to become self-supporting well before a new community's population reached the critical mass needed for their support. In addition, developers often assisted community recreational groups and supported community-wide festivals, sponsored youth athletic teams, and dedicated or sold land at below market rates for recreational purposes. In these cases developers operated on a situational basis, evaluating their role and the extent of their commitment to support recreational activities as each opportunity to do so arose.

As part of the recreation professional survey (see Appendix A), respondents were asked to assess the adequacy of developers' attention to the recreational needs of people living in their communities. As shown in Table 3-1, about two thirds of the recreation professionals felt that developers' activities had been adequate. In all but three new communities, however, one or more recreation professionals felt that this was not the case. Professionals who rated developers' attention to the recreational needs of their communities as inadequate were asked to explain the reasons for this judgment.

Some of the reasons for professionals' disapproval of developer actions were in the form of blanket criticisms of the developer's role in community recreation, which was perceived as being nonexistent or minimal (Sharpstown and North Palm Beach). Several professionals felt that developers had taken care of basic needs only, ignoring larger responsibilities (Lake Havasu City) or that in concentrating on green space, the developer had not done anything about "recreation" (Jonathan). In Reston, professionals' comments reflected the change in the developer from Robert E. Simon, Jr. to Gulf-Reston, Inc. Gulf was said to have abandoned Simon's commitment to carry out recreational master plans. In the case of Elk Grove Village recreation professionals felt that in a recently developed area of the community the development company had abandoned its own commitment to recreation. Other comments cast doubt on developers' motivations—public relations and profit were believed to outweigh service to the community—and on their organizational ability, use of money and hiring practices (Columbia and Reston).

Table 3–1. Recreation Professionals' Rating of Developer Attention to Community Recreational Needs
(frequency distribution of respondents)

New Communities	"Do you feel (NAME OF COMMUNITY DEVELOPER) has given adequate attention to the recreational needs of people living in (NAME OF COMMUNITY)?"		
	Yes	*No*	*Sample Size*
Nonfederally Assisted New Communities			
Columbia	2	1	3
Elk Grove Village	1	1	2
Forest Park	3	1	2
Foster City	2	0	3
Irvine	2	1	3
Laguna Niguel	2	0	2
Lake Havasu City	1	1	3
North Palm Beach	a	1	2
Park Forest	2	a	1
Reston	0	2	4
Sharpstown	1	2	2
Valencia	1	0	1
Westlake Village	3	1	4
Total	20	11	31
Federally Assisted New Communities			
Jonathan	1	1	2
Park Forest South	1	0	1

[a] Respondent was not familiar with developer's contribution to community recreational needs.

In a number of new communities professionals felt that an insufficient amount of land had been set aside for recreation (Forest Park, Laguna Niguel, North Palm Beach and Sharpstown) or that specific facilities had been ignored, including a recreational center (Elk Grove Village), swimming pool (Forest Park) and cultural facilities (Irvine).

Finally, in four of the communities (Jonathan, Reston, Valencia and Westlake Village), administrators of public recreation organizations stated that private facilities or those operated by homes and community associations should be opened to the public. These administrators felt that new community developers are sometimes at fault for not making their facilities and activities sufficiently available to the general public and for not taking advantage of and supporting public recreational opportunities.

County Governments

Developers' ability to share the costs of open space and recreational systems have been severely constrained by the inability of existing governmental units to finance and staff high quality urban open space and recreational systems. During the initial phases of development, most new communities are served by county governments. As subdivisions of state governments, many counties are not legally authorized to provide urban-type services, including recreational services. In addition, as Hjelte and Shivers (1972, p. 143) have noted, state legislatures have been reluctant to provide counties with broader discretionary powers. Very few counties have a chief executive, and most are too poorly staffed to undertake new functions.

Where counties have become interested in open space and recreation, their efforts have often been devoted to the development of regional parks and recreational facilities. For example, the National Association of Counties adopted a resolution in 1964 which suggested that:

> ... the special role of the county is to acquire, develop, and maintain parks and to administer public recreation programs that will serve the needs of communities broader than the local neighborhood or municipality, but less than statewide or national in scope. (National Association of Counties 1964)

This focus of county action was beneficial to some new communities. County-owned regional parks were located in Forest Park, Irvine, Laguna Niguel and Sharpstown, and the residents of Elk Grove Village and Park Forest used the forest preserves of the Cook County

Forest Preserve District. However, it does not offer a means for developing or operating neighborhood and community recreational systems. In addition, because their staffs are oriented toward large-scale regional park facilities, county park officials often view with disdain the more intimate open space and recreational facilities planned for new communities.

Of course, some counties did provide urban recreational services. Although Columbia's developer did not rely on county services, the Howard County Park and Recreation Department provided some programs in the community, as did the Fairfax County Recreation Department in Reston. In both cases, however, greater county involvement was inhibited by the counties' inability to provide a higher than usual level of service in only a portion of their jurisdictions. This problem was overcome in Los Angeles County, where the county provided relatively high quality recreational services throughout its jurisdiction. As a result, Los Angeles County was able to develop and operate neighborhood parks in Valencia and Westlake Village. The problem may also be overcome by the use of special county service areas and taxing districts, which allow counties to provide a higher level of urban services to areas that are willing to pay for them. This approach was used by Los Angeles County and Orange County, California in providing recreational services to Irvine, Laguna Niguel and Valencia. It was also used in Reston, where a Fairfax County service district (Small District 5) was used to finance the construction of a $2.6 million community center adjacent to the Hunters Woods Village Center.

School Districts

While counties had an inconsistent record in providing recreational services to new communities, this was generally not the case for the school districts in which the study new communities were located. In the past fifteen years there has been a growing awareness among educational officials that recreational experiences are educational and that school facilities have the potential to serve as community recreational resources.

Hjelte and Shivers (1972, pp. 117–118) enumerated five reasons for the expansion of the functions of public schools to include some of the responsibility for recreational services: (1) schools have the physical facilities required for recreational activities, such as playgrounds and athletic fields; (2) schools are distributed according to the same plan generally used to locate neighborhood and community recreational centers; (3) schools have more contact with children and adults than any other public institution; (4) the aims and purposes of public education are becoming indistinguishable from those of public recreational service; and (5) the schools have the potential leadership required for a recreational program. Nevertheless, these arguments have not won unanimous approval from school officials. According to Hjelte and Shivers, many school officials feel that arguments for a fundamentalist approach to education, which excludes diversion of school resources to recreational services, are sound. Some school officials may feel that the use of school facilities after school hours will lead to excess wear and tear on the school plant and will decrease the efficiency of the school program. Also, some recreationists may feel that school-run recreational programs will have a regimented educational bias; that funds for recreation, *per se*, may be harder to obtain; that school programs will favor programs for children at the expense of adults; and that many recreational activities are not suitable for school grounds and buildings.

Notwithstanding the rationales for and against provision of recreational activities at new community schools, in every new community studied at least some of the public schools were used by community groups for recreational purposes. Among the public schools serving these communities, 56 percent had gymnasiums and 75 percent had multipurpose rooms that were used for community purposes. Eighty percent of the schools were used for outdoor recreational activities. Twenty-two percent of the new community household survey respondents (and 21 percent of the respondents who lived in the paired conventional communities) reported using community schools for recreational activities during the previous year.

In a number of new communities schools were designed in conjunction with a neighborhood or community park or recreational center. Community school programs (adult educational and/or recreational activities) were offered by 58 percent of the schools serving the study new communities. Also, 60 percent of the new community recreation organizations surveyed reported the existence of cooperative programs with local schools. Finally, community colleges and universities located in several new communities also provided recreational resources, including Howard Community College in Columbia, College of the Canyons, in Valencia and the University of California at Irvine.

In spite of the widespread use of schools in new community recreational systems, several factors limit the role they can potentially play in providing recreational services. The first limiting factor is state legislation. Most of the legislation authorizing wider use of the schools goes only so far as to permit agencies other than the school board to use the schools. Only a few states, including California,

Minnesota, Illinois, New York and Ohio, authorize school boards to conduct community school programs financed by the school district. Second, as noted above, school officials are not uniformly in favor of community use of school facilities. Often this decision is left to the discretion of individual school principals, so that uniform availability of a new community's schools for recreational purposes may be difficult to achieve. Third, school districts have not been immune from the financial problems that beset all efforts to pre-service public facilities in new communities (see Burby and Donnelly 1976). As a result, school construction in a new community may lag behind the pace of residential construction. For example, among the fifteen new communities studied, 55 percent of the high school students, 47 percent of the middle school students and 27 percent of the elementary school students attended schools outside of their home communities. In addition, in school districts with declining enrollments at existing schools, such as the districts serving Foster City and Reston, there was strong internal resistance to building new schools instead of busing children to existing schools. This attitude plays havoc with a community plan, such as Foster City's, that designates elementary and secondary schools as neighborhood and community recreational centers. In sum, because of state legislation, varying attitudes of school officials, financial problems in the timing of school construction and occasional excess capacity at existing facilities in a school district, schools have not been able to provide a consistent recreational resource for new communities even though they have augmented recreational services provided by other institutions.

Municipalities, Park Districts and Homes Associations

Because existing governmental units were not able to assume full financial and operating responsibility for new community open space and recreational systems, developers and residents had to establish new governmental arrangements to secure recreational facilities and services. New governmental arrangements that were adopted, in part, to provide recreational facilities and services included: annexation to neighboring municipalities and/or special districts (Jonathan, Sharpstown and Westlake Village); incorporation of a municipality (Elk Grove Village, Forest Park, Foster City, Irvine, North Palm Beach, Park Forest and Park Forest South); formation of multipurpose special districts (Foster City and Lake Havasu City); formation of an independent park and recreation district (Elk Grove Village); incorporation of private community-wide homes associations (Columbia, Jonathan and Reston); and incorporation of a series of private neighborhood homes associations (Irvine, Laguna Niguel, Park Forest South, Valencia and Westlake Village).

In a number of cases, the governmental unit formed to develop and operate the community open space and recreational service system was constrained by the same financial problems as the developer. One of the major hurdles new community developers have to overcome is the negative cash flows that are typical in new community projects during the first years of development. Governmental units face the same problem. During the first years of development the need for new recreational facilities and services is great, but property values and economic activity do not produce sufficient revenues to support such expenditures. As a result, new communities that established new governmental units to provide recreational resources usually had to wait until their populations and tax bases grew before they could pass bond issues for recreational land acquisition and capital improvements. For example, Forest Park waited sixteen years; Elk Grove Village, ten years; Foster City and Irvine, seven years; North Palm Beach, five years; and Westlake Village, four years after initial residential settlement before proceeding with bond referenda. Governments' inability to finance open space acquistion and recreational facilities during the early years shifted the burden of preservicing to the developer. If the developer was unable or unwilling to assume this burden, the result could only be an underdeveloped recreational system not much different from that which occurs in the normal course of suburban expansion.

As noted above, developers of new communities initiated after 1960 solved the preservicing problem by forming automatic homes associations to assume responsibility for neighborhood and community recreational areas and facilities. In a number of new communities (Irvine, Jonathan, Laguna Niguel, Park Forest South, Reston, Valencia and Westlake Village) developers financed the construction of facilities, recouped their costs through increases in lot prices and dedicated them to neighborhood and community-wide homes associations which assumed responsibility for operating and maintenance costs. In Columbia, the Columbia Park and Recreation Association financed the capital costs of facility development in addition to assuming responsibility for facility operation and maintenance.

Although homes associations were an effective means of providing recreational resources at an early point in the development process (see Chapter 4), a number of disadvantages of this approach should be noted. For example, Stanley Scott (1967) enumerated eight objections to the widespread use of automatic homes associations: First, Scott noted that homes associations bypass local governments that could more appropriately be designated as custodians for developer-financed and resident-paid-for (through increased lot prices) recreational property. Second, associations may have an upper-middle-class bias and may not adequately represent the interests of working-class residents. Third, associations' open space and recreational facilities are almost always designed by the developer, but the public interest in such facilities is so great that the public should have a role in their planning, even before the residents move to a community. Fourth, developer control of associations during their initial year(s) is paternalistic and thwarts residents' rights to participate in decision making (see also Godschalk 1973, and Twentieth Century Fund Task Force on Governance of New Towns 1971). Fifth, residents may be apathetic about their association, citizen participation may be low and management practices may be inefficient. Sixth, using homes associations for separate neighborhoods of homogeneous housing types may institutionalize segregated housing patterns. Seventh, association voting is usually based on ownership, so that (with the exception of the Columbia Association) renters have no official voice in the governance of common facilities that affect their lives and are supported, in part, by their rent payments. Eighth, residents' concerns with property values and developers' concerns with profitability may obscure other important goals to which open space and recreational facilities contribute.

To the eight problems identified by Scott, two additional sets of problems with the homes association concept must be added. One is the thinness of revenue sources that, with the exception of the Columbia Association, plagues almost all associations. In order to maximize the salability of their housing products, developers tend to peg mandatory assessments at a level barely adequate to maintain and operate the amenity package developed for the neighborhood or community. As a result, associations are usually unable to finance extensive recreational programs at their facilities or major capital improvements (a problem that took three years to solve at Reston, where the residents eventually used a special county service district to finance the construction of a needed community recreational center). If homes associations do borrow funds, because assessments (again, with the exception of the Columbia Association) are not a first lien on property superior to purchase money mortgages and are usually not levied on commercial and industrial property, high interest rates have to be paid. In addition, homes association assessments are not progressive, so that associations are a poor way in which to redistribute resources to low-income residents who cannot afford to pay assessments or use fees;[a] and associations are not usually eligible for a number of revenue sources, such as sales taxes, privilege license taxes and state shared revenues, which are available to municipalities.

An additional set of problems with homes associations is the difficulty in coordinating activities and programs with public agencies. Coordination may be particularly difficult in new communities with community-wide homes associations. Because of their size and the breadth of the functions they perform, community-wide associations take on the semblance of governmental bodies. However, because they are private in character, they experience two types of problems with surrounding governmental jurisdictions. First, community-wide associations lack standing with public agencies as coordinate governmental bodies and are often at a disadvantage in competition for attention to their community's needs and in negotiating cooperative programs. Second, because community-wide associations provide a high level of amenities and services in their communities in comparison with surrounding areas, public agencies often place a lower priority on expenditures in new communities in comparison with areas that are less well endowed with recreational services and amenities.

Voluntary Associations

Voluntary associations were the most pervasive institutions providing major recreational services in new communities. Herbert J. Gans (1967, pp. 52–66) observed that voluntary organizations may be started in a new community by outsiders or by insiders. In many new communities, voluntary associations that were branches of national associations, such as the Jaycees, Lions Club, Optimists, Little League and Babe Ruth League baseball and Pop Warner football, played a crucial role in providing recreational services during the early years of the development process before recreational programs were initiated by public or quasi-public institutions. A number of communities organized voluntary associations to coordinate youth-oriented sports activities. These included the North Palm Beach Youth Activities Association, Forest Park Recreation Association, Elk Grove Village Athletic Association, Lake Havasu City Recreation Association, Reston Youth Athletic Association and Westlake Village Athletic Association. Also, voluntary associations were occasionally formed to provide particular recreational facilities, such as the Aqua-

[a]This problem was recognized by some associations. In Columbia, the Columbia Association reduced use fees by one half for families whose gross income did not exceed Federal Housing Administration guidelines. The Columbia Association also had an "earn-a-membership" program that allowed residents to pay use fees by working for the association at $2 an hour.

center in Park Forest and the Swim Club in Forest Park. The ten new communities in which recreation professionals reported that voluntary associations were "very active" included Columbia, Forest Park, Laguna Niguel, North Palm Beach, Park Forest, Park Forest South, Reston, Sharpstown, Valencia and Westlake Village.

ADMINISTRATIVE PRACTICES OF RECREATION ORGANIZATIONS

Much of the concern expressed about the organization of public services in new communities has centered on three administrative processes: governance and citizen participation; community planning; and financing recreational facilities and programs. The final section of the chapter reviews the experience of the fifteen new communities studied with each of these aspects of recreation administration.

Governance of Recreation Organizations

The question of what roles citizens should play in new community development processes has resulted in a lengthy debate between proponents and opponents of developer-controlled service systems. For example, Albert A. Foer (1969, p. 394) suggested that, ". . . the planning and construction of a New Town is such an expensive, complicated process that there may be no feasible way to combine a developmental period with meaningful resident participation." From this point of view, which pervades much of the thought about new communities, the community is viewed as a market and the residents as consumers who vote with their money (their decisions to move to the community) whether to accept the developer's decisions regarding characteristics of the community recreational system. In the words of Richard Brooks (1971, p. 375) residents may choose to trade off some of their rights to political participation for the "rewards of enlightened despotism."

Arguments for executive control of new community recreational systems have been countered by those who see citizen participation as an essential component of the development process and the provision of community amenities and services. For example, Royce Hanson (1971, p. 57) argued that local self-government is not strictly necessary to provide services, which could be handled through administrative decisions by larger governmental units. However, Hanson noted that citizen participation is essential for three reasons. First, it helps convert residents into citizens by allowing them to gain civic experience through sharing responsibility for decisions. Second, participation legitimates authority. Third, participation inevitably influences the character of services provided and helps to determine the beneficiaries of public programs. In this way, according to Hanson, "authority is tempered and obligated to respond to local opinion." In addition to serving these higher goals, a degree of citizen participation has been advocated as a means of securing public support for the recreational system, assisting in the actual provision of recreational programs and as a means of gauging the demand for various recreational services.

Although community governance has aroused a large amount of interest and debate, little information has been available about the means that are being used in new communities to bring residents into decision-making processes. Information that is available refers almost exclusively to the experiences of Columbia and Reston (see David R. Godschalk 1972 and Royce Hanson 1972). To accurately gauge the extent and methods of citizen participation in governing new community recreational systems, a broader perspective is required.

Use of boards and commissions. One approach to involving the citizens in decisions about the recreational system has involved the use of boards and commissions. The organization of recreation agencies in most of the fifteen new communities included boards of directors or commissions to oversee the agencies' activities. However, the composition and power of these bodies varied from community to community.

In the three new communities with community-wide home associations (Columbia, Jonathan and Reston) the associations' boards of directors had full power to determine recreational policies, budget and staff levels, recreational programs and recreational and open space land acquistion and facility construction. As noted previously, these associations were controlled by the new community developers. Homes association boards in communities with smaller neighborhood homes associations had similar powers, but were usually controlled by the residents. In addition to homes associations, boards or commissions with full governing authority included the park districts serving Westlake Village and Elk Grove Village and the recreation commission in Lake Havasu City. In all other cases, recreation boards and commissions functioned as advisory bodies to assist city councils, county boards of supervisors or city recreation departments and to represent the recreational interests of community residents.

Methods of selecting board members also varied. The complicated procedure for selecting board members of the Columbia Park and Recreation Association was described earlier. In 1973 five of the seven board members represented the developer and lenders (and were appointed by them); a sixth, the president of the association, was appointed by the developer but viewed himself as representing the residents; and the seventh was a representative of the residents nominated by the Columbia Council. In Reston, Gulf-Reston, Inc. placed three residents on the nine-member board of directors of the Reston Home Owners Association; the other six members were appointed by and represented the developer. The residents' representatives were nominated through a nonbinding preference poll, with one vote allocated to each household in the community. In Jonathan, six of nine directors of the Jonathan Association were selected by the developer and three by the residents during the early period of development. In each of the communities with community-wide homes associations, developers' control of the associations' boards of directors was designed to decrease gradually as the number of residents in the communities increased. However, because the transfer of power from the developers to the residents was based on the proportion of lots or housing units sold in these communities, the exact dates when the residents would assume control could not be specified in advance. Estimates were that this would occur in 1977 in Columbia[b] (ten years after intial residential occupancy) and after 1980 in Jonathan and Reston (sixteen and twelve years after initial residential occupancy).

In the case of the smaller neighborhood associations, boards of directors were selected from among the residents at annual meetings of the associations (the initial directors, whose terms usually expired after one or two years, were appointed by the developer/builder). Park district boards were selected by the registered voters of the districts. Boards and commissions with only advisory powers were usually appointed by the legislative bodies of the jurisdictions they served.

An important aspect of board and commission membership is the extent to which blacks and other minority groups are represented on the governing bodies of recreation organizations. In seeking to provide services to all segments of the population, communities are likely to find that such representation is vital in assuring participation in recreational programs by all community groups. However, the presence of blacks on recreation boards and commissions was an extreme rarity in new communities. In 1973 no blacks were represented on recreation boards and commissions serving twelve of the fifteen new communities studied. The Park Forest South Park and Recreation Commission had one black member, as did the Westlake

[b]The Columbia Park and Recreation Association's articles of incorporation guaranteed that regardless of the number of completed housing units by 1981 the association would be governed entirely by the residents.

Village Athletic Association board and the board of the Reston Youth Athletic Association. This lack of representation could be attributed primarily to the relative scarcity of blacks in the study new communities.[c]

The methods by which boards and commissions interacted with the residents of new communities when an important decision had to be made is also of interest. When recreation organizations act unilaterally, extreme resident discontent can result. The interviews with recreation professionals revealed that numerous methods were utilized in determining the viewpoints of community residents. The most frequent were open meetings of recreation boards and commissions at which residents could present their views, and public hearings which were often held in connection with major public investments in new areas or facilities and in connection with bond issue campaigns. In addition, recreation advisory boards were often viewed as representing the citizens (and were sometimes selected to represent cross-sections of their community's population). Board members and recreation directors often maintained informal contacts with voluntary associations and other residents and used this means to secure residents' opinions. In addition, board and staff members were contacted on an individual basis by residents who wished to express a point of view. Finally, some recreation organizations directly solicited residents' views through the use of polls in newsletters and community newspapers and, in very rare instances, through household and phone interviews or special mailings.

Use of citizens' committees.   In addition to boards and commissions, some organizations providing recreational services used citizens' committees to establish and maintain contact with community residents. This device was used most often where the residents did not control the organization providing recreational services and where the organization was very large and distant from the citizens (as was true of some county park and recreation departments). In Columbia, the Columbia Park and Recreation Association used two types of committees to secure residents' input to decision making. Each of the villages in Columbia had a recreation committee that advised its village board and the recreation director of the Columbia Association about the recreational needs of the village's residents and responded to proposed activities of the association. In addition, a number of other resident advisory committees were used to provide an effective

---

[c]The proportion of nonwhite residents in each of the study new communities is summarized in Appendix B, Table B–1.

mechanism for broad-based resident participation in the Columbia Association's activities.[d]

In Reston, the Reston Home Owners Association secured citizens' views about recreational matters through the use of three types of organizations. Village councils were created in 1970 to represent their residents to the newly consolidated Reston Home Owners Association (RHOA). In 1972 they became autonomous but still advised the association of their residents' views. A second body, the RHOA Council, was designed to facilitate resident input to the RHOA board of directors and professional staff. A third device used in Reston was individual committees established to oversee the operation of various types of recreational facilities and open space. These included the Pools committees (one for each swimming pool), Reston Tennis Association's operating committees, Reston Riding Association's operating committee, and the Environmental Management Committee. Finally, mention should be made of the Reston Community Association, a voluntary group that monitored the developer's activities and represented the residents at public hearings of the Fairfax County Planning Commission and Board of Supervisors.

The Jonathan Association had a less elaborate structure of committees to represent residents' views to its developer-controlled board of directors. These included a Greenway Committee, which oversaw internal open space and paths in residential neighborhoods and an informal recreation committee whose make-up tended to change with the seasons (and the recreational activities associated with them).

Among the smaller neighborhood homes associations, recreation committees were less common. Fourteen of the 35 associations in the California and Illinois new communities had organized such committees. The majority of the neighborhood associations, however, relied on their resident-elected boards of directors to represent residents' views in recreational matters.

---

[d]A partial listing of some of the committees and advisory groups that were active in Columbia provides an indication of the breadth of residents' interests that were represented in this way: The Arts and Crafts Committee; The Ad Hoc Committee on Biking Policy; The Ad Hoc Committee on the Performing Arts; The Columbia Aquatic Association; The Columbia Bike Club; The Columbia Gardeners; The Columbia Tennis Committee; The Columbia Youth Baseball Association; The Golf Committee; The Petting Zoo Advisory Group; and The Soccer Association of Columbia. The committees' roles in the association included advising the Columbia Association staff about residents' needs and interests; advising the village boards about program and budget priorities; keeping the village boards informed about progress and problems in the committees' areas of interest; and working cooperatively with the association staff in addressing issues and problems and in planning for the future.

A minority of the public agencies, most of which had resident-elected or appointed advisory recreation boards or commissions, used citizens' committees. Those that did use committees had established one or more of four types of committees: (1) committees established by geographical area, such as Howard County's area recreation councils or the advisory councils of the Houston Park and Recreation Department; (2) committees established to assist in the operation of particular facilities, such as recreation centers, parks and playgrounds; (3) committees established on the basis of an activity, such as baseball and arts and crafts; and (4) *ad hoc* committees, which were often established for special projects or to help secure passage of recreation bond issues.

Use of volunteers.   A final means of resident contact with and participation in the governance of recreation organizations was through volunteer help in operating recreational programs. The use of volunteers in recreational programs varied among the study committees. In Columbia, Elk Grove Village, Foster City, Irvine and Lake Havasu City relatively few volunteers were used beyond the activities of voluntary associations, resident advisory committees and homes associations. In these cases recreational program operation by professional staff and paid summer help was preferred, in some cases because of citizen apathy, in others because of insurance difficulties and in others because volunteers were viewed as undependable.

On the other hand, volunteer help in running community recreational programs was essential in a number of new communities. As noted earlier, with only one full-time recreation leader, the Reston Home Owners Association relied extensively on volunteers to provide recreational programming. Volunteers were also used extensively in Forest Park, Jonathan, Laguna Niguel, North Palm Beach, Park Forest, Park Forest South, Sharpstown and Valencia. In Westlake Village volunteer help was used by the Conejo Park and Recreation District to develop a park facility. In most of these communities volunteers were used because there were an inadequate number of professionals to staff community recreational programs. Although recreational programs operated by volunteers were sometimes criticized by professionals as amateurish, they provided another avenue of participation for residents who wished to play an active role in their communities' recreational systems.

Community Planning for Recreational Areas and Facilities

Advocates of community master planning have long looked with approval on new communities as an opportunity to demonstrate the validity of this approach to guiding community development. As noted by Godschalk (1973, p. 307), "New communities appear to be one of the few places where the master plan still holds sway. . . . Even the federal guidelines for new community development require that a project seeking a federal guarantee 'must have a general plan and program for its ultimate development. . . .'" In fact, master planning had little impact on the development of new community recreational systems; and master plans, though common, were little more than window dressing. Instead, planning for open space and recreational facilities in new communities was a dynamic and evolutionary process constantly adapting to new conditions. Duhl (1966, p. 65) observed, "For a plan to be effective, the plan must change; for a planner to be effective, the planner must also change." The experiences of the new communities studied clearly demonstrate the application of this apparent truism and the need for more realistic mechanisms to insure that community goals for open space and recreational facilities are realized.

Use of master plans. Every new community studied had a master plan of some sort. These ranged from the rather vague concept plans adopted to guide development in Columbia, Irvine, Jonathan, Laguna Niguel, Park Forest South and Westlake Village, to plans that precisely located open space and recreational areas, such as those adopted for the development of Sharpstown, Lake Havasu City and Valencia. Both types of plans tended to indicate the location and boundaries of major open space and recreational facilities, including lakes, golf courses, regional-type parks and environmental corridors along streams and their flood plains. However, concept-type plans designated only the number and general location of community and neighborhood open spaces and recreational facilities, while precise plans were much more exact in locating such areas and facilities.

In addition to developer-initiated master plans, most of the other recreation organizations serving the new communities, with the exception of voluntary associations, had master plans of some sort to guide land acquisition and facility development (27 of 35 recreation organizations). Most of these plans dealt exclusively with designating land for the preservation of open space and the location and development of recreational areas, although several also stressed the need for a balance between recreational use of land and intelligent environmental management. A few, notably those for Howard County, Maryland and the Elk Grove Park District, delved into the specifics of program development, staffing, institutional organization and relations with other jurisdictions.

While many of the recreation professionals interviewed indicated that master plans were used to guide development, most stressed the fact that such plans provided general guidelines only, because of gaps in the plans or because portions of them gradually became outdated. Other respondents held the view that master plans were totally outdated, useless or did not apply to their organizations.

Policies for staging open space acquisition and recreational facility development.   Since most master plans provided only general guidelines for open space acquisitions and recreational facility development, planning that served as a real basis for action did not begin until developers initiated detailed village and neighborhood site plans. During this phase in the planning process the goal of preservicing facility development came to the fore, and the roles and responsibilities of developers and public agencies overlapped most. The key question was, of course, who was responsible for preservicing?

In Columbia, Jonathan and Reston the new community developers assumed complete responsibility for preservicing. Neighborhood and village planning for open space and recreational facilities was accomplished in great detail by the developers' planners. Since developer-controlled homes associations constructed (in Columbia) and operated and maintained facilities (in Columbia, Jonathan and Reston), the involvement of public recreation organizations in the planning process was limited to negotiations with county and city planning agencies and to hearings leading to the approval of particular subdivision plats. Developers' responsibility for the provision of open space and other common lands was generally spelled out in initial planning and zoning agreements between the developer and county or city officials and, in the case of Jonathan, federal officials who approved the plans for Jonathan's development. For example, 20 percent of Columbia was to be devoted to open space; 40 percent of Reston was to be in "common lands," half to be controlled by the Reston Home Owners Association and half by smaller cluster associations, and approximately 20 percent of Jonathan was to be devoted to open space land uses.

In the twelve other new communities studied, preservicing was a joint responsibility of the developers and public agencies. The share of responsibility assumed by each varied from community to community and changed over time. In the five older new communities, developers' plans reserved sites for public parks, and public agencies were given the responsibility of developing them. In new communities developed since 1960, developers tended to assume responsibility for preservicing neighborhood recreational facilities (including parks and walkways, buffer greenways, swimming pools, tennis courts and tot lots) and some commercial recreation (such as golf courses), while public agencies were expected to provide larger parks and community-wide recreational facilities. However, as mentioned earlier, public agencies were often unable to meet their share of the open space and recreation package because of inadequate revenue during the early years of development.

One way local officials encouraged preservicing and eased the financial burden of open space and recreational land acquistion was to require developers to dedicate land to the public for these purposes. Such regulations, enacted by counties, municipalities and park districts, existed for all but four of the new communities (Jonathan, Park Forest, Park Forest South and Sharpstown) according to the recreation professionals interviewed. The amount of land to be dedicated varied from one new community to another. Typical requirements included 5 percent of platted tracts of 40 acres or more (North Palm Beach); 9 acres per thousand population, half for parks and half for schools (Westlake Village); 4½ acres per thousand population (Irvine); 2½ acres per thousand population (Valencia and Laguna Niguel), and 10 percent of developer-owned land (Elk Grove Village). However, few communities clearly specified the type of land to be dedicated. A common complaint among the recreation professionals interviewed was that developers often dedicated land that was unsuitable for recreational use. While open space was preserved, professionals felt that there was little benefit to the community in terms of facilities and programs. Moreover, some professional respondents pointed out that since open space could include lakes and golf courses in communities where "percent of development acreage" guidelines were used (Columbia, Elk Grove Village, Jonathan and Reston), there could be relatively little space actually available for general community use. Finally, in at least one new community (North Palm Beach), professionals felt that the developer strongly resisted existing land dedication requirements.

Although requirements governing land dedication were helpful in preservicing open space and recreational areas, the requirements fell short of guarantying that a high standard would be maintained. The best hope for new communities would appear to lie in developers' commitments to standards which exceed legal requirements. While such commitments were apparent in a number of new communities and resulted in the preservation of large areas of open space, developers were inconsistent in their actions, especially regarding the type of land selected and its potential use for recreational facilities and programs.[e]

Citizen participation in recreational planning. Citizen involvement in planning for recreational areas and facilities may occur in several arenas and at several points during the planning and development process. These include: first, initial planning carried out by new community developers; second, joint planning and negotiations between developers and local regulatory bodies, such as county and city planning commissions; and third, in the formulation of plans by recreation organizations, other than the developer. In the first case, citizen-developer collaboration in the design of open space and recreational systems for new increments of community development was extremely rare. At Columbia, joint resident-developer teams were formed to plan the next village of Owen Brown. The Irvine Company conferred with neighborhood homes association leaders in formulating plans for nearby neighborhoods and villages. Most developers, however, followed the Reston approach, where the developer was highly secretive in developing plans for new areas of the community.

Nevertheless, most new communities were regulated under some type of a planned development ordinance. These ordinances gave the developer flexibility in mixing land uses in exchange for much greater public discretion in approving developers' proposed plans. So, while residents were usually excluded from developers' internal planning processes, they did have an opportunity to voice their opinions at public hearings and other meetings where plans were reviewed before final public approval. The effectiveness of this form of participation was limited by several factors. First, the basic format of a new increment of development was rarely changed through the public approval process; instead, only minor changes in land use distribution and other factors were likely to be made. Second, the process was extremely variable from one community to another, depending upon the political power of the developer and the responsiveness of regulatory agencies to the residents of a new community. For example, where the regulating agency's jurisdiction was coterminous with a new community, as in those new communities that had incorporated (Elk Grove Village, Forest Park, Foster City, Irvine, North Palm Beach, Park Forest and Park Forest South), citizen's interests carried

[e]Resolution of the problem through explicit regulations governing the land to be dedicated may not be desirable, since it would reduce the site design flexibility that encourages innovation and sensitivity to the natural environment in new communities. (See Frank S. So, David R. Mosena and Frank S. Bangs, Jr. 1973.)

more weight than in communities whose jurisdictions included a broader area (Columbia, Jonathan, Laguna Niguel, Lake Havasu City, Reston, Valencia and Westlake Village). Third, the ability of the residents to exert continuing oversight at public meetings that may occur over an extended period of time is notoriously inconsistent. In some cases, such as the Reston Community Association's oversight of Gulf-Reston's relationship with Fairfax County, a community's residents may be effectively represented. In most cases, however, citizen interest is likely to be aroused only when an issue or controversy arises, so that their participation in the planning process is episodic rather than continuing. Given this situation, whether residents' interests in proposed open space and recreational areas are recognized depends upon developers' sensivity to residents' needs and the responsiveness of various agencies which review developers' plans.

A third avenue of citizen participation is in the planning programs conducted by community recreation agencies. Most of these agencies, as noted above, developed master plans to guide land acquisition and facility development. Most of those agencies with plans (seventeen of 27 agencies) reported that citizens took part in the planning process. However, recreation professionals indicated a lack of specific arrangements for citizen involvement. For example, recreation boards composed of citizens, board meetings open to the public and informal consultations with civic and homeowners' groups were the methods most often employed. In no instances did professional respondents refer to citizen groups with clearly defined responsibilities in the planning processes of their organizations. Recreation professionals also differed in their views on the value of citizen participation in planning. Some, such as a recreation professional employed by the Columbia Association, felt that citizen participation in the community was excessive, so that "Columbia is too process-oriented, and not product-oriented enough." On the other hand, a recreation official in Reston, where citizen participation in planning by Gulf-Reston had been minimal, remarked that this was a very sore point and that Reston was a "company town," which would benefit from greater citizen involvement in the recreational planning process.

Financing Recreational Facilities and Programs

A variety of methods were used in the fifteen new communities to finance the provision of open space and recreational facilities and the operation of the recreational system. These included development and construction loans in expectation of lot and home-sales revenues, loans to community associations, community association dues and assessments, budget allocations from the general revenues of local governments, special recreation tax revenues, bond sales proceeds, federal and state grants-in-aid, user charges and donations.

Capital expenditures. New community developers' profit from the development process is influenced by four sets of variables: (1) capital appreciation resulting from value added to land by the development process; (2) cash flows generated by land sales and income-producing properties; (3) tax savings; and (4) the financial structure of the project, including the mix of debt and equity, term and interest of mortgages and marketability. Although each of these is important, capital appreciation is primary to the profitability of a new community undertaking. As Mahlon Apgar, IV (1971, p. 46) noted, "The primary financial objective in community development is to create urban values on nonurban land as quickly as possible." Investment in open space and recreational amenities helps create urban values through external benefits which accrue to property surrounding such investments. In addition, these investments improve the marketability of a project, and thus affect cash flow and in some cases, such as golf courses, may directly generate income for the developer. For all of these reasons, early investment in open space and recreational amenities is essential to a financially successful new community development process.

On the other hand, there are a number of other demands for the developer's cash at the start of a project, including planning and overhead costs, land acquisition expenses and the costs of basic infrastructure such as water and sewer systems, roads and utilities. Because of the scale and lead time required by a new community project, substantial leverage of the developer's cash investment is required. According to Apgar (1971), it is not unusual for the development costs of a new town to be fifteen to twenty times as great as the assets of the developer. Therefore, financing, most of which usually comes from large financial institutions through equity and debt financing arrangements, is required. The financial arrangements used by each of the developers in the study were too numerous and complex to be summarized here. However, it should be noted that because of the high leverage involved, developers were forced to carry very high debt-service costs. To get out from under some of this financial burden, it was advantageous for them to shift as much of the costs of open space and recreational amenities to other institutions as soon as possible.

One method of doing this was to shift the responsibility for developing amenities to a homes association. As noted earlier, creation of the Columbia Park and Recreation Association, which as initially financed by the developer and his lenders, shifted the financial burden of carrying Columbia's amenity package from the developer to the residents. Repayment of the developer's loans to the association, which became possible when the association floated its own bonds, provided additional capital for other development activities in Columbia. A second method of shifting some of the developer's share of the cost of open space and recreational amenities was to have merchant builders assume responsibility for developing and financing (through interim development and construction loans) neighborhood open space and recreational facilities. The builders' costs were recouped through the sale of homes to consumers, and maintenance of the common land and recreational facilities provided was accomplished through the establishment of automatic neighborhood homes associations. A third method of shifting the financial burden of open space and recreational facilities was to have local governments assume responsibility for the capital costs of their provision.

Capital improvements for public recreational facilities were typically not financed from annual operating funds. Instead, bond issues were used to finance land acquisition and capital construction above the immediate revenue capacity of a community. However, because most states regulate the ratio of local governmental bonded indebtedness to assessed valuation rather conservatively (this limit is typically about 3 percent of the assessed valuation of all taxable property), this was generally not an effective method of financing the capital costs of open space and recreational facilities during the early years of a new community's development, before assessed values had accumulated. As noted earlier in the chapter, new communities did not pass municipal bonds for recreational purposes until some years after initial residential occupancy had occurred.

Nevertheless, after a community has matured, public financing of the capital costs of open space and recreational facilities is feasible. Between 1968 and 1975, recreational bond issue elections were held in ten of the fifteen new communities, including four bond issues in Elk Grove Village and three in Sharpstown. The purposes of these bonds included land acquisition (Elk Grove Village, North Palm Beach and Westlake Village), park and open space development (Irvine, Jonathan and Sharpstown), general improvements in facilities (Elk Grove Village, Forest Park, Foster City, Sharpstown and Westlake Village), and community center development (Foster City and Reston). The amounts involved in these bond issues ranged from $130,000 in Forest Park to $16 million in Irvine. Of the three most recent bond issue elections in the new communities, eleven passed and only one failed to receive voter support (bonds for an ice rink in Elk Grove Village).

Current operations. The operating budgets of the principal recreation organizations serving the new communities varied greatly: eighteen agencies spent $100,000 or less annually on current operations; seven agencies spent from $100,000 to $250,000; four from $250,000 to $500,000; and two spent in excess of $500,000. Excluding park and recreation districts, whose entire budgets went to recreational purposes, recreation expenditures generally accounted for less than 25 percent of the operating budgets of the parent organizations (most often, counties and municipalities). Sources of revenue to finance current operations came from county and municipal budget allocations, special recreation taxes, member assessments, user charges and donations. User fees were relied on heavily by all types of recreation organizations. In public agencies, especially at the county level, user fees supplemented the special taxes that were the main basis of support for county park districts. Homes associations, especially those that operated on a community-wide basis, often charged fees for the use of their facilities in order to supplement membership assessments (in Columbia and Reston the operation of swimming pools, tennis courts and other facilities was financed almost exclusively from user fees). Programs offered by voluntary associations, such as youth sports, were financed primarily from registration fees and donations from the developer, commercial establishments and interested citizens.

Financial difficulties experienced by recreation organizations. In spite of the high per capita expenditures for recreational activities in the fifteen new communities (see Chapter 4) and the popular support revealed in park and recreation bond issue elections, many recreation professionals indicated that their organizations (18 of 32) faced financial difficulties of various kinds. Financial difficulties were reported most frequently by municipal and county recreation officials, many of whom indicated that funds were simply inadequate to provide the facilities and services needed for their communities. These officials were about equally divided as to whether facilities or programs were suffering the most. In some communities officials felt that there was not enough money to develop existing open space areas or to undertake needed renovations. On the program side, the most common problems were inadequate staffing and difficulty in securing an adequate budget to operate recent capital improvements.

The reasons that financial problems were being experienced varied from one community to another. For example, poor performance of prior personnel or developers was cited in three new communities. An official of the Columbia Association stressed the need for a more businesslike approach to the operation of recreational facilities; an official of Avco Community Developers, Inc. noted that an extensive backlog of needs was left by Laguna Niguel's previous developer, the Laguna Niguel Company; and a city official in Foster City noted that the inability of the Estero Municipal Improvement District to finance recreational facility development prior to incorporation had left a backlog of needed facilities. Legislative tax limits were a cause of difficulties experienced by the Conejo Park and Recreation District (Westlake Village) in securing funds to develop facilities and then to staff them. A tremendous increase in visitation to Lake Havasu State Park after completion of the London Bridge in that community could not be adequately accommodated within the park's existing budget. In Reston the Reston Home Owners Association's financial structure was not adequate to finance a needed community center, and the expense involved in operating the Reston Riding Association's equestrian facilities was causing problems. In Forest Park heavy expenditures to purchase land had left the city's recreation commission with an inadequate budget to develop facilities and offer recreational programs. Finally, several county agencies were squeezed between fixed budgets and the rising costs of maintaining existing parks and recreational facilities.

The financial difficulties experienced in these communities and the reasons they occurred illustrate that although recreation has enjoyed as much support as other types of public services, its continued success is not assured, even in the favorable climate of new communities. It is likely that as these communities grow, the advantages they have experienced as a result of preservicing and the overall emphasis placed on recreation will decline unless community residents and recreation agencies work to assure that sufficient public and private financial resources continue to be devoted to recreational purposes.

CONCLUSIONS AND POLICY IMPLICATIONS

The *ad hoc* organizational structures that characterize many new communities resulted from the interaction of conflicting developer goals for the provision of recreational services and the general inability of public agencies to assume complete responsibility for community recreational systems. Developer goals for the provision of recreational services included: (1) control of the recreational system; (2) cost sharing with residents and other institutions; and (3) maintenance of residents' satisfaction with recreational services and the community. The most rational approach to organizing recreational service delivery occurred where developers maximized control (and financial support) of recreational systems through the formation of community-wide homes associations and municipal service districts. Four of the fifteen new communities took this approach. However, in eleven new communities developers chose to trade off control of the recreational system for cost sharing with other agencies. Five developers took an intermediate approach based on developer control of neighborhood facilities through the use of small neighborhood homes associations, while six developers chose to rely more heavily on public and private institutions to provide recreational facilities and services. Because no single public or private agency was capable of assuming full responsibility for the operation of community recreational systems in those cases where developers chose not to do so, developers and residents were forced to patch together organizational structures for the provision of recreational services. The end result was a fragmentation of responsibility for the provision of services that was not much different from that which normally occurs in the course of less planned suburban development. Whether it also resulted in less effective recreational service systems is a question addressed in the following chapter.

The inability of many public institutions to form mutually beneficial partnerships with new community developers resulted from several characteristics of the organization of local public services in the United States. These characteristics include: (1) state legislation that limits the authority of counties, school districts and some municipalities to provide recreational services and that limits the bonded indebtedness of local jurisdictions; (2) the orientations of state, regional and county agencies toward regional rather than local recreational facilities and services; and (3) the inability of local governments to finance urban services in advance of demand and the financial base needed to support them. Municipal incorporation of a number of new communities provided an organizational framework for the rational joint development (developer-municipality) of community recreational systems. However, since bonded debt assessed value requirements of state legislation severely limited the ability of municipalities to play an effective role in the initial stages of the development process, a partnership of developers and local government was not effective until the development process was relatively far advanced and a diffuse, complex organizational structure had evolved to fill the gap left by local government's inability to act more promptly.

To overcome this problem, three alternative approaches to organizing for recreational service delivery are possible. One that was mentioned above involves developer assumption of control of the recreational system through the formation of developer-controlled community-wide homes associations. However, these associations have a number of shortcomings and have been the subject of very severe criticisms because of their private, undemocratic character and because of various characteristics of their financing.

A second approach involves developer provision of neighborhood open space and amenities, the cost of which can be recouped through additions to residential lot prices, together with the formation of neighborhood automatic homes associations to operate and maintain facilities and deferral of actions to meet community-wide recreational needs until the population base is adequate to support municipal or other public agency assumption of this responsibility. This approach suffers from the criticisms that have been leveled against homes associations, uncertainty as to when an adequate population base will be achieved, and the tendency of residents to formulate *ad hoc* approaches in the interim.

A third approach, which has yet to be tried, would involve a true partnership between developers and municipal or other local governments in the joint development of the recreational system. In this approach, developers and local governments would jointly plan recreational facilities and services, developers would dedicate land for recreational facilities and open space preservation (in return for greater freedom in mixing land uses and higher residential densities on remaining land) and public agencies would develop recreational facilities and operate recreational programs. However, for this approach to work, financial aid would have to be extended to local governments in the form of both grants-in-aid and loans from states and/or the federal government. Alternatively, state governments could waive debt to assessed value requirements and either state agencies or the federal government could guarantee bonds issued by local agenices to finance recreational infrastructure. Although this would involve some risk, since the only security for such bonds would be future revenues generated as a new community develops, it would provide a means to rationalize the organization of recreational and other service delivery systems in new communities and to insure that residents' needs are fully met at all stages of the development process.

In addition to achieving a rational means to organize and finance the provision of recreational services, attention should also be given to key administrative practices of recreation organizations. Although new communities have been occasionally pictured as paternalistic company towns, most new communities provided a number of avenues for citizen participation in the operation of recreational facilities and services. These mechanisms included citizen representation on the governing boards of recreation organizations and the use of citizen advisory boards, citizen committees and volunteer help in operating recreational programs. On the other hand, citizen participation in recreational planning has been frequently neglected by both new community developers and recreation organizations. This is a problem, since, contrary to popular belief, master plans have not been used extensively to guide detailed recreational planning in new communities. Thus, the notion of a citizen contract with developers based on the master plan is mostly a myth. If citizens' views are to be represented, improved procedures to involve the residents in recreational site and facility development planning are needed.

Medium- and long-range planning for recreational facilities by recreation organizations other than the developer, while common, did not consistently serve as an effective guide to actual land acquisition and facility development decisions. Instead, both developers and local recreation agencies followed incremental approaches to the development of new community recreational service systems. Given this situation, the requirements by local agencies and the federal government for traditional new community master plans have little to recommend them in terms of the actual exigencies of the development process. Rather than long-range planning, governments would probably be well advised to require a staged planning and development approach in which planning is limited to smaller community units, such as neighborhoods and villages, and governmental regulation is based on performance criteria for various community systems and experience gained in previous stages of the development process.

Chapter 4

Recreational Resources in New and Conventional Communities

A basic function of recreational service systems is to provide indoor and outdoor areas, facilities and activities to meet the recreational needs of a community. In the previous chapter the manner in which recreational systems were organized to perform this function in new communities was examined. This chapter evaluates how well new communities have performed in comparison with a paired sample of conventional suburban communities.

To evaluate the performance of new communities in providing recreational resources, data were collected through field inspections and inventories, map measurements and calculations and interviews with professional personnel associated with organizations providing recreational services. The recreational resource data are summarized in five sections. The first examines recreational and open space acreage in the new and conventional communities. The next two sections focus on recreational hardware, including the number and variety of recreational sites and facilities available and their location in relation to potential users. Recreational software is then considered in terms of recreational staff and leadership levels and the variety of recreational programs offered. In the fifth section community recreational operating expenditures are summarized. The chapter concludes with an analysis of the effectiveness of different approaches to organizing new community recreational service systems in providing community recreational resources.

RECREATIONAL AND OPEN
SPACE ACREAGE

New community recreational service systems succeeded in preserving and providing more open space and recreational acreage than the less planned conventional communities. As shown in Table 4−1, the thirteen nonfederally assisted new communities had 406 acres per 10,000 population in open space and recreational land uses versus 216 acres per 10,000 population in the conventional communities. The advantages of preservicing can be observed in the two federally assisted new communities—Jonathan and Park Forest South—whose relatively small populations had access to relatively large amounts of

Table 4−1.   Recreational and Open Space Acreage[a]

New and Conventional Communities	Recreational and Open Space Acreage	
	Acres per 10,000 Population	*Total Acres*
Nonfederally Assisted New and Conventional Communities		
Thirteen new communities	406	9048
Thirteen conventional communities	216	6123
New Communities		
Columbia	382	922
Elk Grove Village	437	2347
Forest Park	308	523
Foster City	86	129
Irvine	400	800
Laguna Niguel	518	435
Lake Havasu City	1174	1076
North Palm Beach	151	188
Park Forest	304	930
Reston	341	682
Sharpstown	119	285
Valencia	606	424
Westlake Village	236	307
Federally Assisted New and Conventional Communities		
Jonathan	1328	201
Chanhassen	193	98
Park Forest South	2076	671
Richton Park	48	23

[a]Recreational and open space acreage includes all land devoted to recreational use in a community and all open land held by public or quasi-public institutions. Land in recreational use includes land owned by both public and private agents, including golf courses and school yards.

open space. Other new communities with extensive open space acreage available to their residents included Lake Havasu City, Valencia, Laguna Niguel, Elk Grove Village and Irvine, all of which had 400 or more acres of open space and recreational land per 10,000 population. The extensive acreage devoted to open space land uses in new communities was a result, in part, of the success of a number of new communities (including Lake Havasu City, Laguna Niguel, Elk Grove Village, Irvine, Forest Park and Sharpstown) in securing state and regional parks and forest preserves and also to developers' readiness to preservice communities with one or more golf courses.

Community-by-community comparisons of each new community with its paired conventional community showed that many of the conventional communities were also successful in preserving open space and recreational land. In fact, among the nonfederally assisted new communities, for seven of the thirteen paired comparisons the conventional communities preserved somewhat more open space acreage per capita. The most notable conventional community in this regard was Sharonville, which was paired with Forest Park. Sharonville encompassed a large county regional park and included a stream valley open space system acquired by its town government. As a result it provided 719 acres of recreational and open space land per 10,000 population, which was more than any of the nonfederally assisted new communities except Lake Havasu City.

RECREATIONAL SITES AND FACILITIES

Measures of total open space and recreational acreage can be somewhat misleading, since they do not indicate how the land was used. This dimension of recreational resources was evaluated by gathering information about the actual number of different sites where recreational activities could take place in a community and the variety of recreational facilities that were provided. See Table 4–2.

The large amount of open space and recreational land in new communities, in comparison with the conventional communities, was matched by a greater number of recreational sites. Six new communities (Columbia, Elk Grove Village, Foster City, Irvine, Park Forest and Reston), but only two of the conventional communities, had 30 or more recreational sites. Including the two federally assisted new communities, Jonathan and Park Forest South, there was a strong rank order correlation ($r_s = .49$) between the population size of new communities and the number of recreational sites available. Larger communities tended to provide more sites. The two major exceptions to this generalization, Sharpstown and Forest Park, were older new

Table 4–2.   Recreational Sites and Variety of Facilities Available

New and Conventional Communities	Number of Recreational Sites[a]	Number of Different Types of Facilities Available			
		Active Outdoor[b]	Passive Outdoor[c]	Indoor[d]	Entertainment[e]
Nonfederally Assisted New and Conventional Communities					
Thirteen new communities (average)	30	10	4	3	3
Thirteen conventional communities (average)	18	9	4	3	3
New Communities					
Columbia	72	14	5	5	6
Elk Grove Village	36	8	5	6	5
Forest Park	10	f	5	1	2
Foster City	33	8	5	4	3
Irvine	34	10	4	2	1
Laguna Niguel	13	11	5	2	2
Lake Havasu City	19	12	5	6	4
North Palm Beach	12	9	1	3	5
Park Forest	40	11	5	4	4
Reston	44	13	4	5	3
Sharpstown	12	9	3	4	7
Valencia	19	8	5	2	2
Westlake Village	24	10	5	1	3
Federally Assisted New and Conventional Communities					
Jonathan	20	12	6	3	0
Chanhassen	9	f	6	2	5

Park Forest South	14	11	4	3	3
Richton Park	6	5	1	3	3

a Includes 63 sites owned by neighborhood homes associations, but excludes recreational sites at rental apartment complexes.

b Active outdoor recreational facilities inventoried included fifteen types of facilities: basketball courts, baseball diamonds, beaches, bicycle trails, boating facilities, playing fields, fishing lakes, golf courses, ice skating rinks, stables and bridle trails, tracks, playgrounds, swimming pools, tennis courts and tot lots.

c Passive outdoor recreational facilities inventoried included six types of facilities: bathing beaches, parks, picnic areas, playgrounds, tot lots and walking paths.

d Indoor recreational facilities inventoried included eight types of facilities: arts and crafts rooms, gymnasiums, health clubs, recreational centers, teen centers, billiard parlors, bowling alleys and roller skating rinks.

e Entertainment facilities inventoried included nine types of facilities: bars and taverns, dinner theaters, drive-in restaurants, indoor and outdoor movie theaters, night clubs, outdoor concert facilities, restaurants and stage theaters.

f Data not ascertained.

communities whose developers were not particularly concerned with recreational facilities. Jonathan and Park Forest South, the two youngest and smallest new communities studied, were also exceptions in that they provided many more recreational sites than would be expected solely on the basis of their populations.

Table 4−2 also summarizes data on the variety of active and passive outdoor recreational facilities and entertainment facilities that were available. In terms of the variety of facilities offered, new and conventional communities differed very little. In both settings communities were likely to offer a greater variety of active and passive outdoor facilities (averaging about two-thirds of the different types of facilities inventoried) than either indoor facilities (three of eight types of facilities inventoried) or entertainment facilities (three of nine types of facilities inventoried). Among new communities, Columbia offered the greatest variety of active outdoor facilities; Elk Grove Village and Lake Havasu City provided the greatest variety of indoor facilities and Sharpstown provided the greatest variety of entertainment facilities.

Additional data on the availability of recreational facilities are summarized in Table 4−3, which tabulates the number (per 10,000 population) of each of 21 different types of recreational facilities in the new and conventional communities. The supply of ten of these facilities was much greater in the new communities than in the less planned conventional communities. The facilities that were available in greater numbers in the new communities included: walking paths (other than sidewalks), tot lots, swimming facilities, bicycle trails, arts and crafts rooms, recreational centers, playing fields, teen centers, fishing lakes and boating facilities. For eight facilities there was little difference between the number of facilities per 10,000 population provided in the new and conventional communities. These facilities were: golf courses, gymnasiums, ice skating rinks, parks, picnic areas, playgrounds, tennis courts, stables and tracks. Finally, the conventional communities tended to have more basketball courts and baseball diamonds per 10,000 population.

The relative success of recreational service systems in supplying facilities to new community residents was significantly aided by facilities provided through neighborhood homes associations and multi-unit townhouse and apartment complexes. Of the ten types of facilities that were found in greater numbers in the new communities, neighborhood homes associations and multi-unit complexes provided 20 percent or more of six facilities—bicycle trails, fishing lakes, recreational centers, swimming facilities, tot lots and walking paths. Homes associations and multi-unit complexes also contributed 20

Table 4–3. Availability of Selected Recreational Facilities

Number of Facilities per 10,000 Population

Type of Facility	Thirteen Nonfederally Assisted New Communities			Thirteen Conventional Communities		
	Total	Community-wide[a]	Other[b]	Total	Community-wide[a]	Other[b]
Arts and crafts rooms	3.0	2.6	0.4	1.3	1.1	0.2
Basketball courts	9.5	9.1	0.4	11.5	11.4	0.1
Baseball diamonds	8.0	7.9	0.1	10.6	10.5	0.1
Bicycle trails	2.1	1.7	0.4	0.4	0.3	0.1
Boating facilities	0.7	0.6	0.1	0.2	0.2	<0.1
Fishing lakes	0.8	0.5	0.3	0.3	0.3	<0.1
Golf courses	0.7	0.7	<0.1	0.5	0.5	<0.1
Gymnasiums	2.1	2.1	<0.1	2.1	2.1	<0.1
Ice-skating rinks	0.8	0.8	<0.1	0.6	0.6	<0.1
Parks with benches	2.6	2.0	0.6	2.3	2.1	0.2
Picnic areas	2.8	2.0	0.8	3.3	2.8	0.5
Playgrounds	5.0	4.4	0.6	4.8	4.8	<0.1
Playing fields	4.3	3.9	0.4	3.2	3.2	<0.1
Recreational centers	1.8	1.3	0.5	0.6	0.4	0.2
Stables	0.1	0.1	<0.1	<0.1	<0.1	<0.1
Swimming facilities	5.3	3.8	1.5	2.5	1.4	1.1
Teen centers	0.7	0.6	0.1	0.1	<0.1	<0.1
Tennis courts	7.5	5.8	1.7	7.7	7.4	0.3
Tot lots	8.0	3.9	4.1	2.4	1.8	0.6
Tracks	0.4	0.4	<0.1	0.5	0.5	<0.1
Walking paths	7.0	1.8	5.2	1.2	0.6	0.6

[a]Includes facilities provided by public agencies (including school districts), commercial establishments, private membership clubs, and homes associations that were available (sometimes at a price) to all residents of a community.

[b]Includes facilities provided by neighborhood homes associations and at multi-unit townhouse and apartment complexes that were available only to members of the associations or complex residents.

percent or more of three other types of facilities in the new communities, including parks with benches, picnic areas and tennis courts. In contrast with the new communities, homes associations and multi-unit complexes played only minor roles in the conventional communities' recreational service systems.

National performance standards have long been a preoccupation of recreation administrators and planners (Hjelte and Shivers 1972, p. 372). As a result, there is a general consensus about the minimal number of facilities that are required to serve a community's recreational needs. As shown in Table 4-4, the number of recreational facilities provided in the new communities more than met accepted minimal standards for each of the facilities for which standards were available, except arts and crafts rooms. In comparison with minimal standards, new communities were most successful in providing swimming facilities, community recreational centers, recreational sites, golf course and gymnasiums, all of which were provided at more than twice the ratio to population suggested by minimal standards. The conventional communities also compared well with the minimal standards suggested by recreation professionals. In these settings minimal standards were exceeded for eight of the twelve facilities for which standards were available. The conventional communities, like the new communities, were least successful in providing arts and crafts rooms. In addition, they fell below minimal standards for playgrounds, teen centers and tot lots.

Although new communities as a whole performed well when judged against minimal standards for adequate facilities, there was a large amount of variation among individual communities. For example, over a third of the new communities failed to meet minimal standards for teen centers, arts and crafts rooms, gymnasiums and playgrounds. The difficulties encountered by new communities in providing arts and crafts rooms and teen centers reflect recreation directors' and homes association leaders' preferences regarding the use of neighborhood and community centers, since most new communities had an adequate number of centers. Difficulties in providing gymnasiums and playgrounds, which were most often provided at public schools, reflect the lag in school construction noted in Chapter 3.

Six nonfederally assisted new communities—Columbia, Irvine, Lake Havasu City, Park Forest, Reston and Valencia—and both federally assisted new communities met or exceeded nine or more of the twelve minimal site and facility standards. Only three new communities—Forest Park, North Palm Beach and Sharpstown—failed to meet

Table 4–4. Comparison of Recreational Sites and Facilities Provided in New and Conventional Communities with Selected Minimal Standards

Facility	Minimal Standard	Number of Sites/Facilities per 10,000 Population			
		Thirteen Nonfederally Assisted New Communities		Thirteen Conventional Communities	
		Number	Adequacy (%)	Number	Adequacy (%)
Recreational Sites	5.0[a]	17.5	350	8.3	166
Indoor Facilities					
Arts and crafts rooms	3.3[b]	3.0	91	1.3	39
Gymnasiums	1.0[b]	2.1	210	2.1	210
Community recreational centers	0.5[c]	1.8	360	0.6	120
Teen centers	0.5[c]	0.7	140	0.1	20
Outdoor Facilities					
Baseball/softball diamonds	5.0[c]	8.0	160	10.6	212
Golf courses	0.2[b]	0.7	350	0.5	250
Parks with benches	2.0[d]	2.6	130	2.3	115
Playgrounds	5.0[e]	5.0	100	4.8	96
Swimming pools/beaches	0.7[c]	5.3	757	2.5	357
Tennis courts	5.0[c]	7.5	150	7.7	154
Tot lots	5.0[f]	8.0	160	2.4	48

Sources: [a] Hjelte and Shivers 1972.
[b] National Recreation Association 1965a.
[c] National Recreation Association 1965b.
[d] Butler 1959.
[e] Meyer and Brightbill 1956.
[f] Lackawanna County Planning Commission 1963.

half or more of the standards. These three were the oldest new communities studied. They were initiated by developers who were less concerned with the provision of recreational facilities than other developers and each had a municipal recreational system that was not very effective.

Respondents in the recreation professional survey were asked what they felt were their community's greatest needs for recreational areas and facilities. They gave a wide range of answers, but there were a number of clear favorites. Several responded that there was a need for more open space generally (Sharpstown) or that existing areas of open space should be developed for recreational use (North Palm Beach and Park Forest South). A need for regional parks was noted in Sharpstown, Valencia and Westlake Village. Recreation professionals working in North Palm Beach and Reston saw a need for additional neighborhood parks.

A number of recreation professionals called for new or expanded neighborhood or community recreational centers or multipurpose buildings (Columbia, Elk Grove Village, Irvine, Jonathan, Lake Havasu City, Park Forest, Reston and Westlake Village), a town hall with meeting room facilities (North Palm Beach, Reston), and a teen center (Elk Grove Village), or a senior citizens' center (Westlake Village). Other facilities that were often mentioned included playing fields (especially lighted fields), swimming pools and beaches, tennis courts, gymnasiums, arts and crafts facilities and nature study centers. A survey of articles appearing in local newspapers in the new communities showed that local residents and citizens' groups were also interested in bicycle trails and walking paths.

Since the facilities named most often in the new and conventional communities were among those found most frequently already, it appears that the problem of providing recreational facilities was one of keeping up with demand in these popular areas rather than providing a set of entirely new types of facilities. However, the call for multipurpose recreational centers, as well as the range of interests expressed by professionals, indicates that recreational planning must take into account a diversity of needs.

It is also of interest that few recreation professionals felt that additional facilities were needed for small children; most of the facilities named were for teenagers and adults. It may be that new communities have stressed the needs of small children sufficiently in the past and will have to change their approach as these children, and the communities themselves, mature.

ACCESSIBILITY OF RECREATIONAL FACILITIES

Harry P. Hatry and Diana R. Dunn (1971, p. 25) observed that:

> The geographical accessibility of potential users is a principal factor in the adequacy of recreation opportunities in any community. Other things being equal, the further away a person lives from the service, the less likely is he to use it. Therefore, the distribution of a community's population in relation to the recreation facilities and activities is very important.

To gauge the accessibility of recreational facilities in new and conventional communities, two types of measures were used. First, the road distance from each of the sample clusters of household survey respondents (groups of five to seven dwelling units) was measured to the nearest of each of five types of recreational facilities, including parks and playgrounds for children under twelve years old, golf courses, swimming facilities, tennis courts and walking paths.

Second, the existence or nonexistence of eleven types of indoor and outdoor recreational facilities in each respondent's neighborhood was recorded.[a] The rationale for this measure stems from the widespread adoption of the neighborhood unit concept in new community planning (John B. Slidell 1972). According to the neighborhood unit concept, neighborhoods should be relatively self-contained areas that provide their residents with all of the basic necessities for daily life, including community centers, pathways, parks and playgrounds, within easy and safe reach of all the residents (Clarence A. Perry 1929; American Public Health Association 1948).

Although differences were not great, new community residents tended to live somewhat closer to each of the five facilities for which road distance accessibility measures were calculated. See Table 4—5.

However, the accessibility of these facilities varied somewhat among the new communities. The median road distance to the nearest park or playground ranged from a low of 500 feet in Jonathan to 6400 feet in Lake Havasu City, which had a very scattered development pattern.

Golf courses were the least accessible recreational facilities. The median road distances to the nearest course ranged from lows of 6600 feet in Irvine, Reston and Westlake Village to highs of 15,900 feet in Foster City (which did not have a community golf course)

---

[a]Respondents' neighborhoods were defined as the areas within one-half mile of their homes, or a lesser area if bounded on one or more sides by a major thoroughfare, body of water, undeveloped land or the community boundary.

Table 4–5. Median Distance to Selected Facilities from Sample Clusters

| | Median Road Distance to the Nearest Available Facility:[a] (feet) | | | | | |
	Park or Playground	Golf Course	Swimming Facility	Tennis Court	Walking Path[b]	Sample Size
New and Conventional Communities						
Nonfederally Assisted New and Conventional Communities						
Thirteen new communities	2,100	10,500	3,900	4,600	4,800	2,599
Thirteen conventional communities	2,700	11,900	5,000	4,900	7,900	1,298
New Communities						
Columbia	1,000	11,800	2,800	5,200	800	199
Elk Grove Village	1,600	12,800	6,000	4,400	6,000	200
Forest Park	2,200	13,900	7,200	4,300	8,300	202
Foster City	1,500	15,900	2,100	6,900	4,800	197
Irvine	600	6,600	900	1,200	600	200
Laguna Niguel	3,100	13,900	23,100	6,300	6,400	200
Lake Havasu City	6,400	15,200	15,200	9,200	16,400	200
North Palm Beach	3,300	7,800	3,600	5,400	3,300	201
Park Forest	1,200	12,200	6,000	2,600	1,200	200
Reston	1,600	6,600	2,700	3,300	600	201
Sharpstown	2,800	7,600	7,200	4,600	12,600	200
Valencia	1,600	8,600	1,800	4,600	1,300	200
Westlake Village	2,900	6,600	1,700	4,600	2,700	199

*Federally Assisted New
and Conventional Communities*

Jonathan	500	8,600	4,200	3,600	500	200
Chanhassen	2,000	21,800	6,100	13,200	5,400	100
Park Forest South	1,200	10,400	4,300	3,300	500	201
Richton Park	1,600	15,600	12,300	11,100	15,800	100

[a] Road distance measured over most direct route. Homes association and apartment facilities were assumed to be available only to their members and residents.

[b] Does not include sidewalks in front of homes; does include internal path systems in greenways behind homes.

and 15,200 feet in Lake Havasu City. Nevertheless, since most golf courses were designed to serve populations of 50,000 or more, the accessibility of the nearest courses was quite good in all of the new communities studied.

The median distance to the nearest available swimming facility was one mile or less in nine new communities (Columbia, Foster City, Irvine, Jonathan, North Palm Beach, Park Forest South, Reston, Valencia and Westlake Village) and was over two miles in only two new communities (Lake Havasu City and Laguna Niguel). Tennis courts were also highly accessible, with the median road distances to the nearest court ranging from 1200 feet in Irvine to 9200 feet in Lake Havasu City. Finally, median road distances to the nearest available walking path ranged from a low of 500 feet in Jonathan and Park Forest South (and less than 1000 feet in Columbia, Irvine and Reston) to 16,400 feet in Lake Havasu City. In general, communities in which residents lived closer to the nearest walking path had community-wide greenway path systems (Columbia, Jonathan, Park Forest South, Reston and Valencia), neighborhood path systems in at least some sections of the community (Elk Grove Village, Foster City, Irvine and Westlake Village), or extensive neighborhood parks (Park Forest). Distances to the nearest walking path tended to be greatest in those communities with none of these characteristics (Forest Park, Laguna Niguel, Lake Havasu City, North Palm Beach and Sharpstown).

Table 4−6 summarizes the results of the neighborhood inventories by indicating the proportion of the respondents in the new and conventional communities who had thirteen different recreational and entertainment facilities located within their neighborhoods. With the exception of a movie theater, each facility was more likely to exist in the neighborhoods of new community residents. For five facilities— parks/playgrounds, swimming facilities, walking paths, picnic areas and neighborhood/community centers—the difference is statistically significant. The most prevalent recreational facility found in new and conventional community neighborhoods was a park or playground. Sixty-one percent of the new community respondents and 49 percent of the conventional community respondents had a park or playground within their neighborhood. Other facilities found in 25 percent or more of the new community respondents' neighborhoods included swimming facilities (39 percent), walking paths (34 percent) and tennis courts (25 percent). Surprisingly, only 15 percent of the new community respondents had a neighborhood or community center within their neighborhoods. However, many of the functions of such centers may have been served by neighborhood

Table 4–6. The Existence of Recreational Facilities in New and Conventional Community Neighborhoods[a]

Facility	Percent of Respondents with Facility within Their Neighborhoods	
	Thirteen Nonfederally Assisted New Communities	*Thirteen Conventional Communities*
Outdoor Recreational Facilities		
Park or playground[c]	61[e]	49
Swimming facility[c]	39[e]	33
Walking paths[b, c]	34[e]	15
Tennis court[c]	25	24
Picnic area[d]	12[e]	2
Ice-skating rink[d]	<1	0
Indoor Recreational Facilities		
Billiard parlor[d]	2	0
Bowling alley[d]	2	0
Neighborhood or community center[d]	15[e]	2
Roller skating rink[d]	1	<1
Teen recreational center[d]	1	0
Entertainment Facilities		
Bar or tavern[d]	2	0
Movie theater[d]	2	3
Sample size	2,596	1,298

[a]The neighborhood was defined as the area within a one-half mile radius of the sample clusters of five to seven contiguous dwelling units or a smaller area if bounded on one or more sides by a major thoroughfare, a body of water, undeveloped land or the community boundary.

[b]Does not include sidewalks; does include walking paths in greenways behind dwelling units.

[c]Based on road distance map measurements of one-half mile or less from sample clusters to the nearest facility of a given type.

[d]Based on an exists/does not exist inventory of neighborhood facilities.

[e]Difference between new and conventional communities statistically significant at 0.05 level of confidence.

elementary schools, which were located in the neighborhoods of 35 percent of the new community and 24 percent of the conventional community respondents. Finally, Table 4–6 shows that residential density was not great enough to support neighborhood commercial entertainment and recreational facilities, such as bars, bowling alleys and movie theaters.

Although not shown in Table 4–6, data on neighborhood facilities in the two federally assisted new communities were similar to those for the nonfederally assisted new communities. Both Jonathan and Park Forest South tended to have more neighborhood recreational facilities than their paired conventional communities. The most prevalent neighborhood recreational facilities were parks and playgrounds, community and teen centers, swimming facilities, tennis courts and walking paths.

RECREATIONAL PERSONNEL
AND PROGRAMS

Recreational facilities provide places for people to go and equipment to use for their recreational pursuits. Many of these pursuits are self-directed and self-organized, so that very little supervision and leadership are required. Nevertheless, many people want opportunities to engage in a variety of activities that by their very nature must be organized. Children need places to play that are protected and activities that are guided. Young adults need to acquire new skills, and adults often want to pursue hobbies and engage in other activities that require organization and leadership. To offer these opportunities the recreational system must provide leadership personnel who can organize programs and activities for a community's residents.

Most of the recreation organizations serving the new and conventional communities had relatively small staffs with ten or fewer persons employed full time. Table 4−7 shows the total number of full- and part-time employees per 10,000 population that were working for the principal recreation organizations serving the sample communities. Ten of the thirteen nonfederally assisted new communities had a larger number of recreational employees than their paired conventional communities. Overall, new communities provided 55 full- and part-time employees per 10,000 population, more than double the recreational personnel per 10,000 population employed in the conventional communities. The superior number of personnel employed in the new communities was a result primarily of their greater use of part-time and seasonal personnel (47 versus 21 employees per 10,000 population). Five nonfederally assisted new communities had more than 50 full- and part-time recreational personnel per 10,000 population, including Columbia, Elk Grove Village, Foster City, Irvine, Reston and Valencia. New communities with the fewest personnel were Forest Park and Sharpstown, each of which had fewer than ten employees per 10,000 population.

In addition to their paid staffs, many recreation organizations made extensive use of volunteers (see Table 4−7). In some organizations volunteers were active primarily in specific types of activities, most notably baseball and softball leagues, arts and crafts programs and festivals and special events. Elsewhere, volunteers were involved in all aspects of an organization's work, from planning and management to advertising and coaching, and in some cases took primary responsibility for the entire program side of an organization's work. This was particularly true of voluntary and automatic homes associations, but several public agencies also gave far-reaching responsibilities to volunteers.

Volunteers also played an important role in administrative and supportive activities, such as fundraising, service on boards and committees, distribution of literature, and in maintenance, clean-up and environmental work. In two of the conventional communities, Norbeck-Wheaton and West San Mateo, volunteers were an important part of programs in which recreation agencies supervised wards of the court in park-work activities. Clearly, the participation of volunteers was an essential aspect of community recreation in both new communities and conventional suburban areas.

Table 4—8 shows selected program areas in which organized recreational activities were offered in the new and conventional communities. Baseball was the only organized activity available in more conventional than new communities. The most popular types of programs in new communities were arts and crafts, softball, swimming, tennis, tumbling and gymnastics and volleyball. They were offered in ten or more of the thirteen nonfederally assisted new communities. Programs offered in less than a third of these communities were boating, bowling, camping, ice skating and track.

The new and conventional communities placed somewhat greater emphasis on activities for children and young adults than on adult activites. New communities also provided a slightly greater variety of programs for each age group, on the average, than the conventional communities. Among individual new communities, the greatest variety of programming for children was offered in Foster City, Lake Havasu City, Park Forest and Reston, all of which offered two-thirds or more of the selected programs enumerated in Table 4—8. For young adults and adults, the greatest variety of programming was offered in Irvine, Park Forest and Reston. The federally assisted new community of Jonathan provided a variety of activities that was equivalent to the average for the more mature nonfederally assisted new communities. Park Forest South, however, provided significantly fewer organized activities for young adults and adults.

Although small neighborhood homes associations contributed significantly to the availability of recreational facilities in new communities, they were much less active in the area of programming. Only

Table 4—7. Number of Personnel Employed by Principal Recreation Organizations Serving New and Conventional Communities

New and Conventional Communities	*Number of Employees per 10,000 Population[a]*			*Estimated Total Number of Volunteers[b]*
	Total	*Full Time*	*Part Time/ Seasonal*	
Nonfederally Assisted New and Conventional Communities				
Thirteen new communities	55	8	47	1,533
Thirteen conventional communities	26	5	21	1,488
New Communities				
Columbia	155	22	133	d
Elk Grove Village[c]	118	9	109	0
Forest Park[c]	1	0	1	30
Foster City	52	17	35	45
Irvine	26	5	21	520
Laguna Niguel[c]	16	7	9	110
Lake Havasu City	42	16	26	10
North Palm Beach	29	3	26	24
Park Forest	36	1	31	35
Reston	85	7	78	500
Sharpstown	6	3	3	24
Valencia	57	6	51	115
Westlake Village	16	5	11	120

Federally Assisted New and Conventional Communities

Jonathan	133	13	120	22
Chanhassen	14	2	12	25
Park Forest South	22	0	22	20
Richton Park	38	0	38	1

[a] Includes employees of homes associations with recreational areas and facilities.
[b] Does not include volunteers working with voluntary associations, except sports federations nominated by recreation professionals as principal organizations providing recreational services in the community.
[c] Does not include employees at state or regional parks, beaches or forest preserves located in or adjacent to community.
[d] Information not provided by recreation professionals.

Table 4–8.   Availability of Supervised Recreational Programs in New and Conventional Communities

Type of Program	Number of Communities That Offered Program[a]	
	Thirteen Nonfederally Assisted New Communities	Thirteen Conventional Communities
Arts and crafts	12	8
Baseball	7	10
Basketball	10	10
Boating	4	3
Bowling	3	4
Camping	4	2
Dancing	9	7
Drama	7	6
Field trips	10	6
Football	8	8
Golf	8	6
Ice skating	4	4
Music	6	6
Nature study	7	5
Soccer	6	6
Softball	11	8
Swimming	10	7
Tennis	11	7
Track	4	4
Tumbling and gymnastics	12	7
Volleyball	11	7

[a]Does not include programs offered by voluntary associations, except sports federations nominated by recreation professionals as principal organizations providing recreational services in community.

about a third of these associations offered one or more supervised recreational programs, either for youth or adults. The difficulties homes associations experienced in providing recreational programs stemmed from their small size (the median number of dwellings served was only 180) and limited budgets (median annual operating expenditures were only $37,000). For the most part they were established by builders and developers to maintain property rather than to provide recreational programs.

Directors of the principal recreation organizations operating in the new and conventional communities were also asked whether they had developed any special programs designed for the elderly, low-income persons or handicapped persons.

Programs for the elderly were offered in twelve new communities and eight conventional communities. For the most part these programs centered on golden age clubs that gave elderly persons an opportunity to socialize with each other, go on field trips and outings and attend various entertainment activities.

Six new communities and seven conventional communities had special provisions for lower-income residents. The new communities were the five with subsidized housing (Columbia, Forest Park, Lake Havasu City, Jonathan and Reston) and Valencia. Because most recreational facilities and programs at Columbia were operated on a self-financing basis, the residents of Columbia's initial subsidized housing projects found themselves financially excluded from many facilities and activities. To solve this problem the Columbia Association instituted an "Earn-a-Membership" program, which allowed low- and moderate-income families to work for the association in exchange for use of the association's facilities. In addition, sliding fee scales were established for some activities, such as the Early Childhood Program, and fees were cut in half for others if a family's income met FHA guidelines. The Reston Home Owners Association attempted to accommodate low- and moderate-income subsidized housing residents by offering free programs and keeping fees at minimal levels. In addition, the Reston Youth Activities Association sought out the youth living in subsidized housing, offered free use of sports equipment, and waived fees for those residents who could not afford them. Lake Havasu City organized a Big Brother Program aimed primarily at youth from moderate-income households. Finally, recreational organizations in Forest Park, Jonathan and Valencia attempted to keep fees for their programs within the means of moderate-income persons and waived fees in cases of extreme hardship. Although these communities made special efforts to eliminate financial barriers that might have restricted participation by low- and moderate-income persons, no new communities and only one conventional community (Fountain Valley's playground program for Spanish-speaking children) offered special programming for lower income residents.

Special programs for the handicapped were offered in six new communities and eight conventional communities. Among the new communities, Columbia had a program for the mentally retarded and had developed barrier-free access to its major recreational facilities. The Elk Grove Village Park and Recreation District was operating special individualized recreational programs for the handicapped. Activities offered included swimming lessons, a softball league, motor-movement relay races, ball-coordination exercises, appropriate motor skill play and social games. The county park district serving Forest Park had a naturalist program for blind, retarded and mentally ill persons. The Conejo Park and Recreation District, which served

Westlake Village, had developed a summer camp and playground program for handicapped children. A special rehabilitation unit from Los Angeles County served Valencia on a regular basis, and the Foster City Recreation Department offered a program of adaptive physical education for children with motor skill problems.

The recreation professional survey also gathered information about the prevalence of racial misunderstanding and conflict in community recreational programs. However, very few professionals indicated that racial problems of any kind had occurred, in part because only six new communities (Columbia, Forest Park, Park Forest, Park Forest South, Reston and Sharpstown) had a significant number of black residents. Columbia had the highest proportion of black residents of any new community in the sample and experienced more racial conflict than other communities. Racial difficulties had occurred at Columbia's teen centers, which were reportedly used by 4 percent of the white youths and 45 percent of the black youths in the community. Fighting at the Wilde Lake Village Teen Center led to its closing and to the redistribution of programs among different teen centers. The Columbia Association subsequently employed three full-time persons to offer enriched programs for young adults.

RECREATIONAL EXPENDITURES

Total annual operating expenditures and expenditures per capita for recreation in the new and conventional communities are summarized in Table 4—9. Because of the diverse character of the recreational systems in these communities, the data in Table 4—9 must be interpreted with some caution. They represent the combined operating expenditures of the principal recreation organizations in each community, but with the exception of the commercial division of the Columbia Association, they do not include operating expenditures of commercial recreation enterprises, such as bowling alleys and golf courses (except courses operated by municipalities or community associations), private clubs (such as golf and tennis clubs) or rental apartment complexes that provided recreational facilities. Nevertheless, the data do provide an indication of the effort various communities were making to provide recreational services for their residents.

The total operating expenditures for recreational services by the thirteen nonfederally assisted new communities was $5,692,000 ($26 per capita) in 1972—73, more than double the $2,865,000 ($10 per capita) expended in their paired conventional communities. However, per capita operating expenditures varied among individual new communities. The greatest financial effort for recreational services was made by Columbia, which expended $52 per capita for this purpose. Other nonfederally assisted new communities that spent $25 or more per capita for recreational services included Laguna Niguel ($48), Reston ($41), Irvine ($39) and Foster City ($25). The lowest per capita annual financial effort for recreational services was made in Park Forest ($5), followed by Sharpstown ($10), North Palm Beach ($13) and Valencia ($14). Per capita operating expenditures for recreational services in the federally assisted new communities, Jonathan ($33) and Park Forest South ($32), were much greater than in their paired conventional communities ($2 and $5), and were also greater than those in nine of the thirteen nonfederally assisted new communities.

SUMMARY AND IMPLICATIONS
FOR ORGANIZING RECREATIONAL
SERVICE SYSTEMS

The ability of new community recreational service systems to marshal recreational resources has been evaluated in terms of eight measures of effectiveness. These measures included: (1) open space and recreational acreage; (2) recreational sites; (3) variety of facilities; (4) adequacy of facilities in relation to national recreational standards; (5) accessibility of facilities; (6) recreational personnel; (7) recreational programs; and (8) annual operating expenditures for recreational services. On seven of these eight measures new community recreational service systems were more effective than systems serving the less planned conventional communities. New communities provided more than twice the per capita open space and recreational acreage, recreational sites and recreational personnel as were provided in the conventional communities. Per capita operating expenditures for recreation were also more than twice as large in the new communities. New community recreational facilities were more likely to equal or exceed minimal national standards and also tended to be more accessible to potential users. The only measure of effectiveness in which new communities, taken as a whole, did not greatly exceed the conventional communities was the variety of facilities available for use by community residents.

Although new community recreational systems as a whole were more effective than those in the conventional communities, all new communities were not equally effective in providing recreational resources. To gauge the overall effectiveness of individual new community recreational service systems, an index was constructed by computing the average rank of each new community's recreational

Table 4–9.   Annual Operating Expenditures for Recreation by Principal Recreation Organizations Serving New and Conventional Communities[a]

New Communities	Total Annual (1972–73) Operating Expenditures	Expenditures per Capita
Nonfederally Assisted New and Conventional Communities		
Thirteen new communities	$5,691,000[a,b,c,d]	$26
Thirteen conventional communities	2,865,000[a,c,d]	10
New Communities		
Columbia	1,375,000	57
Elk Grove Village[c,d]	518,000	23
Forest Park[b]	315,000	19
Foster City	377,400	25
Irvine[c]	783,000	39
Laguna Niguel[c,d]	408,000	48
Lake Havasu City	148,000	17
North Palm Beach	162,000	13
Park Forest[d]	140,700	5
Reston	821,000	41
Sharpstown	249,000	10
Valencia[c]	95,000	14
Westlake Village[c]	299,100	23
Federally Assisted New and Conventional Communities		
Jonathan	49,340	33
Chanhassen	9,900	2
Park Forest South[c]	103,000	32
Richton Park	27,000	5

ªExcludes recreational expenditures by voluntary associations, except sports federations nominated by recreation professionals as principal organizations providing recreational services in community. Also, does not include operating expenditures of commercial recreational enterprises, except Commercial Division of the Columbia Association.

ᵇIncludes entire operating expenditures for Winton Woods Regional Park, only a portion of which was in Forest Park.

ᶜIncludes total operating expenditures of neighborhood homes associations with recreational facilities and/or programs: Elk Grove Village ($18,000); Foster City ($74,000); Irvine ($74,000); Laguna Niguel ($298,000); Park Forest South ($100,000); Valencia ($50,000); Westlake Village ($158,000); Fountain Valley ($150,000); Bouquet Canyon ($20,000); and Agoura-Malibu Junction ($27,000). These figures do not include operating expenditures of condominium associations and cooperatives, a large proportion of whose expenditures were devoted to building maintenance rather than common lands and recreational facilities.

ᵈDoes not include maintenance expenditures for: Cook County Forest Preserve properties in Elk Grove Village, Park Forest, and Lansing; Capistrano State Beach in Dana Point; and Orange County's Mile Square Park in Fountain Valley and Niguel Regional Park in Laguna Niguel.

service system over all eight effectiveness measures. The index is based on the assumption that each measure contributes equally to the overall effectiveness of a recreational service system. This of course, is debatable; but, lacking consensus about the relative contribution of individual resource indicators to the overall recreational resource base of a community, it does provide a crude indication of which recreational systems performed most effectively in providing recreational areas, facilities, and programs.

Table 4–10 presents the index values computed for each of the thirteen nonfederally assisted new communities in the sample and each community's rank relative to the other nonfederally assisted new communities. Index values have a possible range of 1 to 13, with 1 indicating that a community ranked first on all eight measures of recreational resources and 13 indicating the community ranked thirteenth on all measures. Because they were at very early stages in the development process, the two federally assisted new communities

Table 4–10. Index of Recreational Resources

New Communities	Index of Recreational Resources[a] (1 = high; 13 = low)	Rank of Community
Nonfederally Assisted New Communities		
Columbia	3.2	1
Reston	3.9	2
Lake Havasu City	4.8	3
Valencia	5.9	4
Elk Grove Village	6.2	5
Park Forest	6.3	6
Foster City	6.9	7.5
Irvine	6.9	7.5
Laguna Niguel	7.7	9
Westlake Village	8.7	10
North Palm Beach	9.3	11
Forest Park	10.2	12
Sharpstown	11.1	13
Federally Assisted New Communities	(1 = high; 2 = low)	
Jonathan	1.3	1
Park Forest South	1.7	2

[a]This index was computed by calculating the average rank of each new community over eight measures of recreational resources: (1) recreational and open space acreage per 10,000 population; (2) recreational sites per 10,000 population; (3) variety of selected recreational facilities; (4) number of facilities in relation to minimal standards; (5) accessibility of facilities; (6) recreational personnel per 10,000 population; (7) recreational programs for children; and (8) per capita annual operating expenditures.

in the sample were treated as a separate group and ranks were computed so that they could be compared with each other, but not with the sample of nonfederally assisted communities.

Three new communities had index values below 5.0 (Columbia, 3.2; Reston, 3.9; and Lake Havasu City, 4.8) indicating that they were most effective in providing recreational resources for their residents. Five new communities with index values ranging between 5.9 and 6.9 were somewhat less effective in this regard. These communities were Valencia (5.9); Elk Grove Village (6.2); Park Forest (6.3); Foster City (6.9); and Irvine (6.9). Laguna Niguel (index value of 7.7), Westlake Village (8.7), North Palm Beach (9.3), Forest Park (10.2), and Sharpstown (11.1) had the least effective recreational service systems. In the case of the two federally assisted new communities, Jonathan was somewhat more effective than Park Forest South.

Data describing community recreational resources also have implications for the organization and structuring of new community recreational service systems. In Chapter 3 it was noted that three aspects of the organization of recreational services—control, cost sharing and residents' satisfaction—were of critical concern to new community developers. Because optimum solutions to each of these concerns conflicted, developers had to make trade-offs among them. The various courses of action they took resulted in the achievement of differing levels of community recreational resources.

Where developers assumed more control and financial responsibility for community recreational service systems, the systems were more effective in providing recreational resources. The average combined index of recreational resources was 3.5 for the two new communities, Columbia and Reston, that had very high developer control of their recreational service systems.[b] Where developers exercised somewhat less financial responsibility and control, as in Irvine, Laguna Niguel, Lake Havasu City, Valencia and Westlake Village, the average combined index of recreational resources was also lower (6.8). In those communities where developers limited their involvement in their community's recreational service systems to designating sites and/or operating one or two facilities, as in Elk Grove Village, Forest Park, Foster City, North Palm Beach, Park Forest and Sharpstown, the average combined index of recreational resources was lowest (8.3).

[b]Comparing these two new communities, Columbia's community-wide homes association (Columbia Association), was more effective than the Reston approach (Reston Home Owners Association) on six of the eight indicators of recreational resources (the exceptions were accessibility of facilities and programs for children).

Differing levels of developer control and responsibility did not affect all aspects of recreational resources in the same way. For example, a high degree of developer control had little effect on the amount of recreational and open space acreage per 10,000 population preserved or on the provision of recreational programs. The differences resulting from medium and low amounts of developer control and responsibility reflected themselves most notably in recreational and open space acreage, sites and expenditures, each of which tended to be greater in communities with medium rather than low developer control. On the other hand, medium or low developer control resulted in little difference in the variety of facilities provided, recreational personnel per 10,000 population and the number of recreational programs offered for children. The reason for these differences, and lack of them, is related to the nature of a developer's involvement in the recreational system. As noted in Chapter 3, developers who opted for a medium level of control focused much of their attention on neighborhood open space and facilities and tended to leave the provision of community-wide recreational facilities to other institutions. Since most recreational programming originated from community-wide institutions, it is not surprising that there was little difference in recreational personnel and programming between communities with medium and low developer involvement in the recreational system.

The degree of developer control of and responsibility for a community's recreational service system was closely linked to the choice of institutions used to operate the system. Developer control and responsibility were maximized through the use of community-wide homes associations. Somewhat less developer control, and correspondingly less financial responsibility, characterized communities where neighborhood homes associations were used. The least amount of developer control and financial responsibility occurred when public agencies, such as municipalities, park districts, county governments and states, assumed primary control of and responsibility for community recreational service systems. Table 4–11 summarizes indexes of recreational resources for communities grouped according to the types of institutions that accounted for the largest proportion of annual recreational operating expenditures in each community. Overall, recreational service systems in which community-wide homes associations were most active were significantly more effective in providing recreational resources than other institutional approaches. Communities that relied most heavily on neighborhood homes associations and municipalities or community park districts fared less well, while communities where county or state agencies assumed major responsibility for the recreational system had the least success in providing recreational resources.

In terms of the eight recreational resource indicators used in the analysis, community-wide homes associations were most effective on six, including the number of recreational sites per 10,000 population, variety of recreational facilities, adequacy of facilities provided, accessibility of facilities, recreational personnel per 10,000 population and per capita community recreational operating expenditures. Communities that used the neighborhood homes association approach to the organization of the recreational service system were most effective in terms of one indicator, recreational and open space acreage per 10,000 population, while communities where municipalities or park districts spent more annually than other institutions were most effective in providing recreational programs for children.

Communities in which neighborhood homes associations expended the most money annually for operating the community recreational system were somewhat more effective than communities in which municipalities or park districts expended the most money in terms of open space and recreational acreage, recreational sites, adequacy of facilities, and per capita expenditures for recreation, but were notably less effective in terms of the variety of recreational facilities provided, accessibility to facilities, and the number of recreational personnel and programs. This reflects the previously noted weakness of neighborhood homes associations in tapping community-wide resources to provide a wider variety of facilities than those initially constructed by developer/builders (which were usually restricted to common open space, swimming pools, tennis courts and club houses) and in programming recreational activities. Only one new community, Irvine, had an extensive system of neighborhood homes associations and a municipal government that encompassed the entire community. However, because the community was incorporated for only a short period before field work for this study was undertaken, the effectiveness of this combination could not be properly evaluated.

Recreational service systems in which county or state agencies spent more for recreational services than other institutions were somewhat more effective than municipalities and park districts in terms of open space and recreational acreage; somewhat more effective than neighborhood homes associations in the variety of facilities offered; and somewhat more effective than both community-wide and neighborhood homes associations in the number of recreational programs for children. Overall, however, these systems were the least effective in securing recreational resources for a community.

Table 4–11. Key Institutions in Recreational Service System and Provision of Recreational Resources
(average indexes of recreational resources)[a]

Resources Indices	Key Institutions[b]			
	Community-wide Homes Associations (n = 2)	Neighborhood Homes Associations (n = 4)	Municipality/ Park and Recreation District (n = 4)	County/ State (n = 3)
Overall index	3.5	7.3	7.2	8.7
1. Recreational and open space acreage per 10,000 population	6.5	4.5	9.3	7.0
2. Number of recreational sites per 10,000 population	2.5	6.0	8.3	9.7
3. Variety of recreational facilities	2.0	9.9	6.6	7.0
4. Adequacy of number of recreational facilities	4.0	6.3	8.0	8.7
5. Accessibility of recreational facilities	2.8	7.9	5.5	7.3
6. Number of recreational personnel per 10,000 population	2.0	8.5	5.5	10.3
7. Variety of recreational programs for children	7.0	9.3	5.3	6.3

| 8. Community recreational expenditures per capita | 2.0 | 5.6 | 8.9 | 9.7 |

[a] Index value may range from 1 (high) to 13 (low).

[b] Allocation of communities to categories is based on the type of organization expending the largest proportion of total annual recreational expenditures (excluding commercial recreation enterprises, private clubs and developer donations) in each community. Communities were allocated as follows: community-wide homes associations (Columbia and Reston); neighborhood homes associations (Irvine, Laguna Niguel, Valencia and Westlake Village); municipality/community park and recreation district (Elk Grove Village, Foster City, North Palm Beach and Park Forest); and county/state (Forest Park, Lake Havasu City and Sharpstown).

To recapitulate briefly, the preceding analysis has shown that the degree of developer involvement in new community recreational service systems was strongly related to the effectiveness of these systems in providing most types of recreational resources (recreational programming was a possible exception). Developer control was maximized through the use of community-wide homes associations. In those cases where developers chose to share responsibility for recreational resources with other institutions, the use of neighborhood homes associations resulted in the provision of greater amounts of open space and recreational acreage per capita and more adequate facilities, while the use of municipalities and park districts resulted in a greater variety of facilities and more effective recreational programming. Although it could not be tested in this research, it may be that by combining a system of neighborhood homes associations with a municipal government, developers may achieve the effectiveness of the community-wide homes association approach to organizing the provision of recreational resources, while more fully sharing control of and financial responsibility for the recreational service system.

Chapter 5

Residents' Responses to
Recreational Service Systems

In addition to considering community recreational resources, an evaluation of new community recreational
service systems must also consider the outputs of these systems—their effects on individuals living in new communities. In this
chapter six types of individual responses to recreational service systems are evaluated. These include: (1) children's use of parks and
playgrounds; (2) adults' participation in bicycling, golf, swimming,
tennis, walking and hiking and their favorite out-of-home activities;
(3) distances traveled to participate in recreational activities and the
proportion of residents who participated within their own communities; (4) residents' satisfaction with the recreational facilities they
most often used; (5) residents' overall evaluations of the quality of
community recreational facilities; and (6) residents' satisfaction with
the use of their leisure time. The effectiveness of new community
recreational service systems is evaluated by comparing values for each
of these measures among new communities and between new communities and the sample of paired conventional communities.

CHILDREN'S OUTDOOR PLAY

Child play areas are one of the most ubiquitous features of mod-
ern new communities. The inventory of recreational resources (see
Table 4−3) indicated that new communities had more tot lots than
any other recreational facility except basketball courts and baseball
diamonds. New communities met or exceeded national standards for
tot lots, parks and playgrounds and provided more child play facili-

ties than the paired conventional communities. Were these facilities used?

Overwhelmingly, children in both new and conventional communities tended to play in their own or a neighbor's yard (73 percent and 77 percent, respectively). See Table 5-1. Parks and playgrounds were the usual place of play for only 9 percent of the new community respondents' children and for only 4 percent of the conventional community children. Among individual new communities, a higher than average proportion of parents in Irvine, Jonathan, Foster City and Reston said that their children usually played at a park or playground. These new communities also tended to provide more tot lots per 10,000 population than other new communities.

Additional data on the use of parks and playgrounds are reported in Table 5-2. One reason why more children did not usually play at parks and playgrounds may have been the lack of accessibility of children's homes to them. In both the new and conventional communities only 30 percent of the child play areas that parents could identify were within one-quarter mile (easy walking distance for a child) of their homes.[a] Although most new community children did not usually play at parks and playgrounds, these facilities were used from time to time. For example, 38 percent of the parents living in the thirteen nonfederally assisted new communities and 33 percent of the conventional community parents who were aware of a nearby park or playground reported that their children played there at least once a week.

Variation in the use of parks and playgrounds paralleled variation in the accessibility of the nearest facility. New communities with more accessible park and playground facilities tended to have a higher proportion of children who used them. New communities in which a majority of the parents said that their children played at a park or playground once a week or more often included Columbia, Foster City, Irvine, Jonathan, Lake Havasu City, Park Forest and Park Forest South.

Parents were also asked how they felt about places near their homes for children under twelve years old to play outdoors. As indicated in Table 5-2, a somewhat larger proportion of nonfederally assisted new community parents (75 percent) than conventional community parents (67 percent) rated places near their homes as

---

[a]Parents' perceptions of the availability of a park or playground were strongly associated with the distance to the nearest facility that was actually available. The rank order association (Spearman's r_s) between the mean distance to the nearest park or playground and the proportion of parents who were aware of a park or playground near their home was $r_s = .86$.

excellent or good. Among the federally assisted new communities, 92 percent of the Jonathan parents rated areas near their homes highly, but this was the case for only 50 percent of the parents interviewed in Park Forest South. In addition to Jonathan, play areas near home were evaluated very highly by parents in Elk Grove Village, Irvine, North Palm Beach, Reston, Valencia and Westlake Village. Much lower than average ratings were given play areas near children's homes in Laguna Niguel (67 percent excellent or good), Forest Park (66 percent), Sharpstown (53 percent) and Lake Havasu City (53 percent). In each of these lower rated communities the availability and accessibility of parks and playgrounds for children under twelve years old tended to be significantly worse than for the entire sample of new communities.

ADULTS' PARTICIPATION IN OUTDOOR ACTIVITIES

Adult respondents (heads of households and their spouses) were asked about their participation during the previous year in five outdoor recreational activities: golf, swimming, tennis, bicycling and walking and hiking. To evaluate adults' responses to recreational service systems, information was obtained about the frequency of their participation in these activities, where they went to participate, and how satisfied they were with the sites and facilities they most often used. Recreational service systems were assumed to be more effective if they facilitated more frequent participation in outdoor recreational activities; participation within rather than outside of a community; participation closer to residents' homes; and higher levels of satisfaction with the recreational sites and facilities that were used.

Golf

As indicated in Table 5–3, 25 percent of the respondents in the thirteen nonfederally assisted new communities and 18 percent of those living in the conventional communities reported that they had played golf one or more times during the previous year. Although there was a significantly larger proportion of golfers in the new communities, the proportion of very frequent golfers (50 or more times per year) was nearly identical in each setting (6 percent and 4 percent, respectively). The proportion of golfers varied very little among the sample new communities. There was a significantly higher than average proportion of golfers in only two new communities—Valencia and Westlake Village—and significantly lower than average proportions in only three new communities—Columbia, Lake Havasu City and Reston.

Table 5–1.   Where Children under Twelve Years Old Usually Played[a] *(percentage distribution of respondents)*

New and Conventional Communities	Own or Neighbor's Yard	Street or Parking Lot	Underdeveloped Open Space	Park or Playground	Other
Nonfederally Assisted New and Conventional Communities					
Thirteen new communities	73	9	6	9	3
Thirteen conventional communities	77	9	9	4	1
New Communities					
Columbia	55	11	20	8	7
Elk Grove Village	78	5	3	10	4
Forest Park	86	7	4	1	2
Foster City	61	13	4	21	1
Irvine	53	9	5	31	1
Laguna Niguel	74	13	10	3	1
Lake Havasu City	62	4	27	6	0
North Palm Beach	82	13	0	3	2
Park Forest	89	3	4	4	0
Reston	55	7	14	16	8
Sharpstown	89	1	1	6	3
Valencia	64	8	7	14	7
Westlake Village	65	17	5	12	2

Where Children under Twelve Years Old Usually Played

Federally Assisted New and Conventional Communities

Jonathan	59	3	10	25	2
Chanhassen	84	2	6	4	4
Park Forest South	81	6	8	5	0
Richton Park	65	2	10	20	2

[a] *Question*: When your child(ren)—those under twelve—play(s) outdoors where do(es) (they/he/she) usually play? (Multiple choice from: in your yard/apartment or townhouse grounds; neighbor's yard; park or playground; street/parking areas; vacant lots; woods or open space away from your yard/apartment grounds).

Table 5-2. Accessibility and Frequency of Use of Parks and Playgrounds and Parents' Evaluations of Play Areas Near Home
(percentage distribution of respondents)

New and Conventional Communities	Park or Playground Used by Respondents' Children Under Twelve Years Old		Parents' Evaluations of Places near Home for Outdoor Play[b]		
	Accessibility: Facility within ¼ Mile of Home	Frequency of Use[a]: Once a Week or More Often	Excellent/ Good	Average	Below Average/ Poor
Nonfederally Assisted New and Conventional Communities					
Thirteen new communities	30	38	75	14	11
Thirteen conventional communities	30	33	67	18	15
New Communities					
Columbia	49	51	76	11	13
Elk Grove Village	32	34	83	15	2
Forest Park	28	40	66	15	19
Foster City	39	54	74	14	12
Irvine	66	61	87	10	3
Laguna Niguel	17	22	67	16	17
Lake Havasu City	13	64	53	21	26
North Palm Beach	10	13	82	10	8
Park Forest	49	57	75	18	7
Reston	68	48	83	4	13
Sharpstown	23	17	53	27	20
Valencia	14	43	84	10	6
Westlake Village	17	36	90	5	5

Federally Assisted New and Conventional Communities

Jonathan	91	86	92	4	4
Chanhassen	34	22	76	20	4
Park Forest South	58	54	50	15	35
Richton Park	81	36	52	33	15

[a]*Question:* Is there a park or playground near here where young children can play? (IF YES) And when the weather is good, do(es) your child(ren)—those under twelve—play there every day, several times a week, once a week, once or twice a month, or less often? This question was used only for those respondents with children under twelve years old living in their household. In addition, the bases for the percentages are the number of parents who were aware of a nearby park or playground where their children might play. If all new community parents of children under twelve years old were used as a base for calculation of percentages, the proportion of respondents' children who played at parks at least once a week would be somewhat lower.

[b]*Question:* How do you feel about the places *right near your home* for children under twelve to play out of doors—would you say they are excellent, good, average, below average, or poor? This question was asked only of those respondents with children under twelve years old living in their households. It does not refer specifically to parks or playgrounds used by respondents' children.

Table 5-3. Golf: Participation Rates, Distances Traveled to and Satisfaction with Facilities Used

| New and Conventional Communities | Annual Participation[a] (percent) | | Facility Used Most Often (participants only) | | | Satisfaction[b] (percent of users) | |
| | 1 or More Times | 50 or More Times | Location in or outside of Community (percent) | | Median Distance Traveled (feet) | Satisfied | Neutral or Dissatisfied |
			In	Outside			
Nonfederally Assisted New and Conventional Communities							
Thirteen new communities	25	6	41	59	20,300	79	21
Thirteen conventional communities	18	4	33	67	31,700	85	15
New Communities							
Columbia	15	4	85	15	19,600	70	30
Elk Grove Village	27	1	0	100	30,200	69	31
Forest Park	21	2	0	100	19,900	71	29
Foster City	22	5	0	100	26,000	90	10
Irvine	24	3	42	58	37,600	72	28
Laguna Niguel	24	5	44	56	31,900	84	16
Lake Havasu City	20	6	100	0	21,000	95	5
North Palm Beach	27	11	49	51	9,900	69	31
Park Forest	21	1	18	82	25,200	76	24
Reston	16	2	82	18	13,800	93	7
Sharpstown	22	4	24	76	41,200	69	31
Valencia	31	5	72	28	10,600	77	23
Westlake Village	33	14	80	20	8,700	86	14

*Federally Assisted New and
Conventional Communities*

Jonathan	22	1	0	100	99,800	64	36
Chanhassen	36	6	0	100	73,400	76	24
Park Forest South	30	2	0	100	51,200	76	24
Richton Park	16	2	8	92	49,600	71	29

[a] *Question:* About how often did you play golf last year, not counting when you were on vacation?

[b] *Question:* Overall, how satisfied are you with that place as a place to play golf? Which number comes closest to how you feel? Completely Satisfied 1 2 3 4 5 6 7 Completely Dissatisfied. Respondents citing "1," "2" or "3" were tabulated as satisfied; those citing "4" through "7" as neutral or dissatisfied.

Although a majority of golfers in both the new and conventional communities traveled outside of their communities to the course they most often used (59 percent and 67 percent, respectively), new community golfers tended to travel shorter distances. The median road distance traveled by golfers from the thirteen nonfederally assisted new communities was 20,300 feet (3.9 miles), versus a median distance of 31,700 feet (6.0 miles) to the golf courses used most often by the conventional community golfers. Distances traveled to play golf varied significantly among the sample new communities, ranging from median distances of 10,600 feet or less among golfers in North Palm Beach, Valencia and Westlake Village, to over 30,000 feet among golfers in Elk Grove Village, Irvine, Laguna Niguel and Sharpstown. Golfers living in both federally assisted new communities traveled long distances to play. Among Jonathan golfers the median distance traveled was 99,800 feet (almost 19 miles) and among Park Forest South golfers, 51,200 feet (almost 10 miles).

Golfers living in the thirteen nonfederally assisted new communities were somewhat less satisfied with the golf courses they used than were golfers living in the paired conventional communities (79 percent versus 85 percent were satisfied with the golf courses they used), but the difference is not statistically significant. Over a quarter of the golfers living in seven new communities—Columbia, Elk Grove Village, Forest Park, Irvine, North Palm Beach, Sharpstown and Jonathan—were dissatisfied with the course they most often used. Thus, although new communities were relatively successful in providing golf courses (see Tables 4−3 and 4−4), there was a fairly large proportion of golfers who were not satisfied with the facilities they used.

Swimming

The proportions of respondents who swam one or more times a year and who swam frequently (50 or more times) were similar in the thirteen nonfederally assisted new communities and their paired conventional communities. As shown in Table 5−4, 58 percent of the new community respondents had participated in swimming during the previous year. Twenty percent could be classified as frequent swimmers. Among the conventional communities, 55 percent of the respondents had participated in swimming, with 15 percent participating 50 or more times during the previous year. Communities with the highest proportions of swimmers were Irvine, Lake Havasu City, Columbia, Valencia, Reston and Laguna Niguel, where 65 percent or more of the respondents reported that they had gone swimming. These communities also had the highest proportions of frequent swimmers (50 or more times per year). Among the two federally assisted new communities, Jonathan had a somewhat higher proportion of respondents who had participated in swimming (70 percent) than Park Forest South (62 percent).

Rates of participation in swimming were comparable to those found in other studies of outdoor recreational participation. John B. Lansing, Robert W. Marans and Robert B. Zehner (1970) found that 76 percent of the Columbia respondents and 69 percent of the Reston respondents interviewed for their study of planned residential environments had participated in swimming during 1968−69. Using data from a national household survey conducted in 1971, Lewis Mandell and Robert W. Marans (1972) reported that 66 percent of the household heads interviewed had participated in swimming during the previous year. The Outdoor Recreation Resources Review Commission's national survey found that 67 percent of the respondents with family incomes of $10,000 or more had engaged in outdoor swimming in 1959−60 (Eva Mueller and Gerald Gurin 1962). In the 1964−65 national survey conducted five years later by the Bureau of Outdoor Recreation (1967), 73 percent of those with family incomes between $15,000 and $25,000 had participated in swimming.

Participation rates were similar in the nonfederally assisted new and conventional communities, but new community residents were much more likely to swim inside rather than outside of their communities (72 percent versus 57 percent) and were also more likely to travel shorter distances to the swimming facilities they most often used (median road distances of 4600 feet versus 6200 feet). Four of the six new communities with high participation rates in swimming had a very high proportion of respondents who swam within the community: Reston (95 percent), Columbia (94 percent), Irvine (93 percent) and Valencia (85 percent). The design of each of these communities included the provision of neighborhood swimming pools. Lake Havasu City and Laguna Niguel had higher than average participation in swimming, but only an average proportion of swimmers who usually swam at a facility within the community. Lake Havasu City fronts on Lake Havasu, while Laguna Niguel fronts on the Pacific Ocean. Numerous swimming beaches were located within close proximity of each of these communities.

Overall, there was little difference in the levels of satisfaction with the swimming facilities used by new and conventional community swimmers (87 percent and 83 percent, respectively were satisfied with the facilities they used). Dissatisfaction with swimming facilities was relatively low in both settings, but was significantly higher

Table 5-4.   Swimming: Participation Rates, Distances Traveled to and Satisfaction with Facilities Used

| New and Conventional Communities | Annual Participation[a] (percent) | | Facility Used Most Often (participants only) | | | | |
| | | | Location in or outside of Community (percent) | | Median Distance Traveled (feet) | Satisfaction[b] (percent of users) | |
	1 or More Times	50 or More Times	In	Outside		Satisfied	Neutral of Dissatisfied
Nonfederally Assisted New and Conventional Communities							
Thirteen new communities	58	20	72	28	4,600	87	13
Thirteen conventional communities	55	15	57	43	6,200	83	17
New Communities							
Columbia	70	19	94	6	4,000	76	24
Elk Grove Village	47	6	69	31	9,000	89	11
Forest Park	54	15	57	43	7,100	83	17
Foster City	43	13	75	25	7,200	93	7
Irvine	73	22	93	7	1,000	92	8
Laguna Niguel	65	23	74	26	17,000	91	9
Lake Havasu City	72	39	71	29	20,100	98	2
North Palm Beach	60	25	51	49	8,700	70	12
Park Forest	39	7	70	30	7,800	66	24
Reston	67	25	95	5	3,900	62	25
Sharpstown	52	17	37	63	20,600	60	40
Valencia	67	23	85	15	1,700	72	9
Westlake Village	61	34	89	11	500	81	7

Federally Assisted New and Conventional Communities

Jonathan	70	17	72	28	4,800	71	29
Chanhassen	67	14	67	33	18,000	70	30
Park Forest South	62	8	77	23	4,300	82	18
Richton Park	43	10	79	21	5,800	78	22

[a] *Question*: About how often did you go swimming last year, not counting when you were on vacation?

[b] *Question*: Overall, how satisfied are you with that place as a place to swim? Which number comes closest to how you feel? Completely Satisfied 1 2 3 4 5 6 7 Completely Dissatisfied. Respondents citing "1," "2" or "3" were tabulated as satisfied; those citing "4" through "7" as neutral or dissatisfied.

than average for some new communities. For example, a fifth or more of the swimmers living in Sharpstown, Reston, Columbia and Park Forest were dissatisfied with the swimming facilities they most often used. Dissatisfaction with swimming facilities was also relatively high among Jonathan swimmers (29 percent) and those in Park Forest South (18 percent).

Tennis

As indicated in Table 5–5, there was virtually no difference in the proportions of nonfederally assisted new and conventional community respondents who had participated in tennis during the previous year (21 percent and 19 percent, respectively) or who participated very frequently in this activity (4 percent in each setting had played tennis 50 or more times). Irvine ranked first, with 31 percent of the respondents there having played tennis, followed closely by Reston (30 percent) and Westlake Village (29 percent). The proportion of the respondents who had participated in tennis was also relatively high in both federally assisted new communities—30 percent in Jonathan and 28 percent in Park Forest South.

The proportion of Columbia (23 percent) and Reston (30 per cent) respondents who reported playing tennis was similar to that found by Lansing, Marans and Zehner (1970) in their survey of these same communities four years earlier (Columbia, 19 percent; and Reston, 29 percent). Tennis participation rates of household heads were reported in Mandell and Maran's (1972) national survey of participation in outdoor recreational activities. Only 6 percent of the household heads from their national sample reported participating in tennis during the previous year. However, their data for household heads were not tabulated by family income of households, so that the much lower participation rates in the nation as a whole may have been in part a result of lower family incomes than those of the new community respondents. For example, Mandel and Marans reported that 12 percent of the persons age ten and over with incomes between $15,000 and $24,999 had participated in tennis. Even this rate of participation, however, was lower than that found for new community household heads and/or spouses (21 percent).

A somewhat higher proportion of tennis players in the conventional communities (71 percent) than in the new communities (63 percent) reported that the tennis courts they most often used were located within their own communities. Nevertheless, the proportion of tennis players who most often used courts in their own community was above 80 percent in five new communities: Lake Havasu City, Reston, Park Forest, Laguna Niguel and Irvine. The median distance traveled to tennis courts was about the same in both the new and conventional communities (7300 feet and 7600 feet, respectively). Respondents living in Irvine and Park Forest traveled the shortest median distances to the tennis courts they used. These communities had the largest number of tennis courts, 22 and 24 respectively, of any of the sample new communities. Among the federally assisted new communities, tennis players in Jonathan were more likely to use courts within their own community (78 percent) than was the case for tennis players living in Park Forest South (61 percent). The median distance to the courts used most often, however, was about the same (4500 feet in Jonathan and 4200 feet in Park Forest South).

As was true for participation rates and distances traveled to facilities, there was little difference between the nonfederally assisted new and conventional communities in terms of satisfaction with the tennis courts that were most often used. Seventy-six percent of the new community respondents and 82 percent of the conventional community respondents were satisfied with the tennis courts they used.

Dissatisfaction with tennis facilities was highest among tennis players living in North Palm Beach (34 percent) and Sharpstown (34 percent), followed closely by Columbia (32 percent). In addition, more than 25 percent of the tennis players in six other nonfederally assisted new communities were not satisfied with the tennis courts they used, including tennis players living in Forest Park, Foster City, Irvine, Laguna Niguel, Park Forest and Valencia. Jonathan tennis players were somewhat more satisfied with the tennis courts they used (but Park Forest South players were significantly less satisfied) than tennis players in the nonfederally assisted new communities as a whole.

Bicycling

Bicycling participation rates were somewhat higher in the nonfederally assisted new communities than in the paired conventional communities. Thirty-nine percent of the new versus 33 percent of the conventional community respondents (a significant difference) had bicycled one or more times during the previous year. See Table 5-6. Among individual new communities, 45 percent or more of the respondents reported bicycling during the previous year in Elk Grove Village, Irvine, Columbia, Westlake Village, Valencia and Reston. On the other hand, fewer than 30 percent of the respondents from three new communities reported bicycling, including Lake Havasu City, North Palm Beach and Laguna Niguel. These three new communities had significantly higher proportions of elderly (age 65+) respondents

Table 5–5.   Tennis: Participation Rates, Distances Traveled to and Satisfaction with Facilities Used

New and Conventional Communities	Annual Participation[a] (percent)		Facility Used Most Often (participants only)				
	1 or More Times	50 or More Times	Location in or outside of Community (percent)		Median Distance Traveled (feet)	Satisfaction[b] (percent of users)	
			In	Outside		Satisfied	Neutral or Dissatisfied
Nonfederally Assisted New and Conventional Communities							
Thirteen new communities	21	4	63	37	7,300	76	24
Thirteen conventional communities	19	4	71	29	7,600	82	18
New Communities							
Columbia	23	4	74	26	7,200	68	32
Elk Grove Village	15	1	76	24	7,200	88	12
Forest Park	18	2	70	30	6,000	73	27
Foster City	19	6	42	58	13,800	75	25
Irvine	31	9	82	18	2,100	74	26
Laguna Niguel	22	5	83	17	10,100	75	25
Lake Havasu City	15	3	100	0	15,000	92	8
North Palm Beach	14	1	41	59	9,900	66	34
Park Forest	20	1	87	13	3,600	73	27
Reston	30	9	87	13	6,000	85	15
Sharpstown	23	1	21	79	13,100	66	34
Valencia	25	8	41	59	5,000	74	26
Westlake Village	29	13	77	23	5,400	91	9

Federally Assisted New and Conventional Communities

Jonathan	30	3	78	22	4,500	79	21
Chanhassen	26	5	10	90	49,600	75	25
Park Forest South	28	2	61	39	4,200	55	45
Richton Park	15	0	65	35	6,300	74	26

[a] *Question:* About how often did you play tennis last year, not counting when you were on vacation?

[b] *Question:* Overall, how satisfied are you with that place as a place to play tennis? Which number comes closest to how you fell? Completely Satisfied 1 2 3 4 5 6 7 Completely Dissatisfied. Respondents citing "1," "2," or 3 were tabulated as satisfied; those citing "4" through "7" as neutral or dissatisfied.

Table 5—6.   Bicycling: Participation Rates, Distances Traveled to and Satisfaction with Facilities Used

| New and Conventional Communities | Annual Participation[a] (percent) | | Facility Used Most Often (participants only) | | | | |
| | 1 or More Times | 50 or More Times | Location in or outside of Community (percent) | | Traveled under One-eighth Mile | Satisfaction[b] (percent of users) | |
			In	Outside		Satisfied	Neutral of Dissatisfied
Nonfederally Assisted New and Conventional Communities							
Thirteen new communities	39	12	97	3	93	83	17
Thirteen conventional communities	33	7	95	5	88	73	27
New Communities							
Columbia	48	11	96	4	81	85	15
Elk Grove Village	52	14	98	2	97	87	13
Forest Park	33	8	100	0	95	64	36
Foster City	34	13	97	3	96	95	5
Irvine	51	14	96	4	83	90	10
Laguna Niguel	29	9	95	5	90	76	24
Lake Havasu City	20	4	100	0	99	86	14
North Palm Beach	26	5	100	0	100	90	10
Park Forest	41	11	100	0	94	81	19
Reston	46	13	96	4	72	90	10
Sharpstown	35	12	100	0	94	60	40
Valencia	47	19	97	3	94	85	15
Westlake Village	48	22	95	5	93	87	13

*Federally Assisted New and
Conventional Communities*

Jonathan	61	19	96	4	81	70	11
Chanhassen	63	25	92	8	77	66	24
Park Forest South	47	8	99	1	93	64	22
Richton Park	21	5	84	16	68	69	16

[a] *Question:* About how often did you go bicycling last year, not counting when you were on vacation?
[b] *Question:* Overall, how satisfied are you with that place as a place to bicycle? Which number comes closest to how you feel? Completely Satisfied 1 2 3 4 5 6 7 Completely Dissatisfied. Respondents citing "1," "2," or "3" were tabulated as satisfied; those citing "4" through "7" as neutral or dissatisfied.

than the other nonfederally assisted new communities. In the case of the federally assisted new communities, Jonathan had a higher proportion of bicyclists (61 percent) than any of the nonfederally assisted new communities and Park Forest South also had an above average proportion of residents (47 percent) who had participated in this activity.

The participation rate in bicycling in Columbia (48 percent) was significantly higher than the rate found by Lansing, Marans and Zehner (1970). Their 1969 survey of Columbia residents indicated that 31 percent participated in this activity during 1968−69. In the case of Reston, however, Lansing, Marans and Zehner reported that 44 percent of the Reston respondents had participated in bicycling during 1968−69, which is comparable to the 46 percent who reported participating in bicycling during 1972−73. In the Mandell and Marans (1972) national survey of recreational participation, 13 percent of the household heads reported participating in bicycling during 1970, much less than the 39 percent of the new community respondents who participated during 1972−73. However, their data for participation among persons ten-years old and older with family incomes in the $15,000−$24,999 income bracket (35 percent participated) were comparable to participation rates among new community household heads and spouses.

As shown in Table 5−6, most persons bicycled within their community and used a facility (usually the streets or pathways) that they could reach within one-eighth mile of their homes. This was particularly true in Elk Grove Village, Forest Park, Lake Havasu City and North Palm Beach where 95 percent or more of the bicyclists participated close to their homes. In the case of the federally assisted new communities of Jonathan and Park Forest South, a high proportion of the residents (96 percent and 99 percent, respectively) bicycled within their own communities. Eighty-one percent of the bicyclists in Jonathan and 93 percent in Park Forest South reported using a facility within one-eighth mile of their homes.

New community bicyclists were significantly more likely to be satisfied with the sites and facilities they used to pursue this activity than were bicyclists living in the conventional communities (83 percent versus 73 percent, respectively, were satisfied). The proportion of satisfied bicyclists was highest in Foster City, Irvine, North Palm Beach and Reston. Dissatisfaction with bicycling sites and facilities was generally low among new community bicyclists, though a high proportion of bicyclists were dissatisfied with the facilities they used in Sharpstown (40 percent) and Forest Park (36 percent). Jonathan bicyclists tended to be more satisfied with sites for bicycling in their community (70 percent were satisfied) than were bicyclists living in Park Forest South (64 percent satisfied).

Walking and Hiking

Walking and hiking for pleasure ranked second to swimming in the overall proportion of new and conventional community respondents who had participated during the previous year (56 percent and 52 percent, respectively, walked or hiked). As shown in Table 5-7, the highest proportion of nonfederally assisted new community respondents who had walked or hiked during the previous year was reported in Reston (81 percent). Columbia was second, followed by Valencia, Lake Havasu City and Westlake Village. Walking and hiking were also popular activities among respondents living in the two federally assisted new communities. Eighty-five percent of the Jonathan respondents and 63 percent of those living in Park Forest South had gone walking or hiking for pleasure during the previous year. Internal path systems located in greenways were available in four of the seven new communities with the highest rates of participation in walking (Columbia, Reston, Valencia and Jonathan). In addition, Westlake Village and Park Forest South had partial pathway systems that included some, but not all, neighborhoods in the community. The only community with high participation in walking and hiking that did not have a pathway system, Lake Havasu City, is located in a desert environment in which walking and hiking (in winter) are favored activities.

Walking and hiking participation rates reported by Lansing, Marans and Zehner (1970) for Columbia (72 percent) and Reston (86 percent) are similar to those found in the present survey (77 percent in Columbia and 81 percent in Reston). In comparison with national surveys of recreational participation, walking and hiking participation rates among new community residents (56 percent) were significantly higher. For example, Mandell and Marans (1972) reported that 40 percent of the household heads and 37 percent of all respondents age ten-years old and above in their 1971 national survey had walked or hiked during the previous year. When income was controlled, 48 percent of the respondents age ten and above with family incomes between $15,000 and $24,999 were found to have walked or hiked during the previous year.

Like those who bicycled, a large majority of new and conventional community respondents typically walked and hiked within the confines of their own communities (95 percent and 90 percent, respectively). Also, most persons (80 percent of the nonfederally assisted new community respondents and 74 percent of the conventional

Table 5—7. Walking and Hiking: Participation Rates, Distances Traveled to and Satisfaction with Facilities Used

New and Conventional Communities	Annual Participation[a] (percent)		Facility Used Most Often (participants only)					
			Location in or outside of Community (percent)		Traveled Under One-eighth Mile	Satisfaction[b] (percent of users)	
	1 or More Times	50 or More Times	In	Outside		Satisfied	Neutral or Dissatisfied
Nonfederally Assisted New and Conventional Communities							
Thirteen new communities	56	24	95	5	80	89	11
Thirteen conventional communities	52	20	90	10	74	85	15
New Communities							
Columbia	77	31	97	3	78	91	9
Elk Grove Village	42	7	96	4	58	94	6
Forest Park	56	17	97	3	65	84	16
Foster City	39	16	92	8	80	96	4
Irvine	58	28	92	8	86	92	8
Laguna Niguel	57	30	95	5	78	85	15
Lake Havasu City	65	27	95	5	90	96	4
North Palm Beach	47	24	99	1	95	90	10
Park Forest	52	18	99	1	70	84	16
Reston	81	41	97	3	73	90	10
Sharpstown	52	24	93	7	84	74	26
Valencia	72	34	90	10	86	93	7
Westlake Village	60	35	93	7	91	93	7

Federally Assisted New and
Conventional Communities

Jonathan	85	45	99	1	84	94	6
Chanhassen	77	26	96	4	70	92	8
Park Forest South	63	14	91	9	80	82	18
Richton Park	39	8	72	28	54	87	13

[a] *Question:* About how often did you go walking for pleasure or hiking last year, not counting when you were on vacation?
[b] *Question:* Overall, how satisfied are you with that place as a place to walk or hike? Which number comes closest to how you feel? Completely Satisfied 1 2 3 4 5 6 7 Completely Dissatisfied. Respondents citing "1," "2" or "3" were tabulated as satisfied; those citing "4" through "7" as neutral or dissatisfied.

community respondents) used a walking site or facility within one-eighth mile of their homes.

A somewhat higher proportion of new community respondents were satisfied with the walking sites and facilities they used (89 percent) than was the case for golf courses (79 percent), swimming facilities (87 percent), tennis courts (76 percent) or bicycling facilities (83 percent). Also, new community walkers and hikers were somewhat more satisfied with the facilities they used than were walkers and hikers living in the conventional communities (89 percent versus 85 percent were satisfied with the facilities they most often used). Ninety percent or more of the walkers and hikers living in nine new communities—Columbia, Elk Grove Village, Foster City, Irvine, Lake Havasu City, North Palm Beach, Reston, Valencia and Westlake Village—were satisfied with the facilities they most often used. In the case of Jonathan and Park Forest South, a higher proportion of Jonathan respondents were satisfied with walking and hiking facilities (94 percent) than respondents living in Park Forest South (82 percent).

Summary

To sum up the preceding discussion, it has been shown that non-federally assisted new community recreational service systems have not resulted in rates of adult participation in golf, swimming, tennis, bicycling or walking and hiking that are very different from those in the less planned conventional communities. Although somewhat higher proportions of new community residents participated in each of these activities, the margin of difference ranged from a high of only 7 percent for golf to a low of 2 percent for participation in tennis. Considering distances traveled to the facilities that were most often used, residents of the nonfederally assisted new communities were somewhat more likely than conventional community residents to use facilities within rather than outside their communities for golf, swimming and walking and hiking. New and conventional communities were equivalent in terms of bicycling within the community, and a somewhat higher proportion of conventional community residents chose to play tennis within their own communities. Recreationists' satisfaction with the facilities they used was also mixed. Somewhat higher proportions of new community than conventional community respondents were satisfied with the swimming, bicycling and walking facilities they most often used. However, higher proportions of conventional community respondents were satisfied with the golf courses and tennis courts they most often used.

Jonathan and Park Forest South consistently exceeded their paired conventional communities in rates of participation in recreational activities and in the accessibility of and recreationists' satisfaction with the facilities they used. The one major exception was Jonathan's poor performance relative to Chanhassen in golfing. Over all five activities analyzed, Jonathan compared favorably with the nonfederally assisted new communities and performed somewhat better than Park Forest South in terms of tennis, bicycling and walking and hiking but not swimming or golf. Park Forest South compared favorably with the nonfederally assisted new communities in terms of participation and accessibility, but Park Forest South recreationists were consistently less satisfied with the facilities they most often used than were recreationists in the nonfederally assisted new communities.

RESIDENTS' FAVORITE OUT-OF-HOME ACTIVITIES

In addition to the five outdoor activities discussed above, household heads and their spouses were asked about their favorite out-of-home activities. Although 30 activities were mentioned by 1 percent or more of the respondents living in the thirteen nonfederally assisted new communities (see Table 5−8), eleven activities accounted for 71 percent of the responses. In order of the frequency with which they were mentioned, these included: (1) golf; (2) swimming; (3) gardening; (4) walking and hiking; (5) bowling; (6) tennis; (7) boating; (8) fishing; (9) bicycling; (10) arts and crafts; and (11) playing cards. Each of the five activities discussed in the preceding section (bicycling, golf, swimming, tennis and walking and hiking) were among the most frequently mentioned favorite activities.

There were relatively few differences in the proportions of new and conventional community respondents who mentioned particular activities as their favorites. Somewhat higher proportions of new than conventional community respondents mentioned golf, swimming and walking and hiking, while somewhat higher proportions of conventional community respondents mentioned bowling and camping. In the case of the federally assisted new communities, Jonathan residents were more likely than the residents of the nonfederally assisted new communities to specify walking and hiking and bicycling as their favorite out-of-home activities and were less likely to mention golf and gardening. Park Forest South residents were somewhat more likely to prefer bowling and arts and crafts and somewhat less likely to prefer boating and fishing.

Table 5−9 illustrates participation rates among respondents who mentioned golf, swimming, gardening, walking and hiking, bowling

Table 5–8.   Adults' Favorite Out-of-home Activities[a] (percentage distribution of respondents)

Favorite Activities	Nonfederally Assisted New and Conventional Communities		Federally Assisted New Communities	
	Thirteen New Communities	Thirteen Conventional Communities	Jonathan	Park Forest South
Golf	12	9	5	12
Swimming	11	8	11	11
Gardening	9	8	3	10
Walking and hiking	7	5	20	5
Bowling	6	7	3	9
Tennis	6	5	5	7
Boating	5	3	4	1
Fishing	5	6	5	2
Bicycling	4	3	10	4
Arts and crafts	3	5	2	6
Playing cards	3	4	1	3
Camping	2	5	3	3
Driving/sightseeing	2	2	0	2
Movies/theater	2	2	4	3
Restaurants/bars	2	2	0	2
Skiing	2	1	7	1
Baseball	1	1	3	1
Basketball	1	1	1	2
Flying/skydiving	1	c	0	1
Gym/exercising	1	1	c	1
Handball	1	c	1	0
Horseback riding	1	2	1	3
Motorcycle riding	1	2	1	1
Picnicking	1	1	c	0
Shopping	1	1	0	1
Socializing/visiting	1	1	1	3

Spectator sports	1	1	c	1
Surfing/skin diving	1	1	0	0
Volunteer work	1	2	2	2
Water skiing	1	2	c	0
Other activities[b]	9	11	14	5
Sample size	2596	1298	200	201

[a]*Question:* We are also interested in what people do in their spare time. What is your favorite type of leisure or recreational activity to do outside the house?

[b] Activities mentioned by less than 0.5 percent of the new community respondents included: going to the beach (activity unspecified), ice skating, sledding, tobogganing, ice hockey, target shooting, volleyball, football, soccer, archery, rock hunting, car racing, "being outdoors," dancing, billiards, baseball, softball, squash, roller skating, attending lectures and going to amusement parks.

[c]Less than 0.5 percent.

Table 5-9. Participation Rates in Selected Favorite Out-of-Home Activities[a]
(percentage distribution of respondents)

Participation in Favorite Activity during the Past 12 Months[b]	Nonfederally Assisted New and Conventional Communities	
	Thirteen New Communities	*Thirteen Conventional Communities*
Golf		
Did not participate	*3*	*2*
Participated	*97*	*98*
1-9 times	21	17
10-19 times	11	16
20-49 times	24	22
50 or more times	41	43
Sample size	260	99
Swimming		
Did not participate	*1*	*4*
Participated	*99*	*96*
1-9 times	8	12
10-19 times	10	10
20-49 times	23	31
50 or more times	58	44
Sample size	219	86
Gardening		
Did not participate	*0*	*0*
Participated	*100*	*100*
1-9 times	1	4
10-19 times	5	1
20-49 times	9	8
50 or more times	85	87
Sample size	176	75
Walking and Hiking		
Did not participate	*1*	*0*
Participated	*99*	*100*
1-9 times	7	1
10-19 times	12	13
20-49 times	10	26
50 or more times	70	54
Sample size	136	56
Bowling		
Did not participate	*1*	*2*
Participated	*99*	*98*
1-9 times	13	17
10-19 times	14	12
20-49 times	30	32
50 or more times	42	38
Sample size	126	76

Table 5–9. continued

Participation in Favorite Activity during the Past 12 Months[b]	Nonfederally Assisted New and Conventional Communities	
	Thirteen New Communities	Thirteen Conventional Communities
Tennis		
Did not participate	3	3
Participated	97	97
1–9 times	9	6
10–19 times	7	8
20–49 times	26	20
50 or more times	55	63
Sample size	121	52

[a]*Question:* About how often did you (ACTIVITY) last year, not counting when you were on vacation?

[b]Includes only respondents who cited activity as their favorite out-of-home activity. Does not include respondents who gave nonquantitative responses, such as "a lot" or "numerous times."

or tennis as their favorite out-of-home activity. In comparison with participation rates for all household heads and spouses (Tables 5–3 through 5–7), participation rates were much higher among the respondents who cited an activity as their favorite. For example, while only 6 percent of all nonfederally assisted new community respondents were frequent participants in golf (50 or more times during the previous year), 41 percent of those who specified golf as their favorite activity participated that often. For other activities differences in frequent participation between all participants and those who mentioned an activity as their favorite were: swimming, 20 percent versus 58 percent; tennis, 4 percent versus 63 percent; bicycling, 12 percent versus 69 percent; and walking and hiking, 24 percent versus 54 percent. Thus, while frequent participation was relatively low in these activities when measured over all respondents, respondents who enjoyed them most participated at very high rates.

Higher proportions of the nonfederally assisted new community than conventional community respondents were frequent participants in swimming (58 percent versus 44 percent) and walking and hiking (70 percent versus 54 percent). However, for the other favorite activities summarized in Table 5–9 there were no significant differences in participation rates or in frequent participation between the new and conventional communities. This was also the case for several activities not tabulated in Table 5–9, including fishing, bicycling, arts and crafts and card playing. However, boating (which is

also not tabulated in Table 5-9) had a significantly higher proportion of frequent participants in the new communities (36 percent
versus 13 percent). Because of the relatively low proportion of respondents who specified any one activity as their favorite, there were
an insufficient number of cases available to make community-by-
community comparisons for each activity.

An important objective of community recreational service systems
should be the accommodation of residents' favorite out-of-home
activities. The effectiveness of these systems in meeting this objective
is illustrated in Table 5-10, which shows the proportions of respond-

Table 5-10. Participation in Selected Favorite Out-of-home Activities Within and Outside of the Community[a] *(percentage distribution of respondents)*

	Nonfederally Assisted New and Conventional Communities	
Location Where Respondents Participated Most Often[b]	*Thirteen New Communities*	*Thirteen Conventional Communities*
Golf		
Within community	47	39
Outside community	51	58
Location not ascertained	2	3
Sample size[c]	268	102
Swimming		
Within community	78	59
Outside community	21	40
Location not ascertained	1	1
Sample size[c]	246	88
Gardening[d]		
Within community	97	100
Outside community	3	0
Location not ascertained	0	0
Sample size[c]	200	83
Walking and Hiking		
Within community	72	69
Outside community	24	29
Location not ascertained	4	2
Sample size[c]	148	56
Bowling		
Within community	19	15
Outside community	81	79
Location not ascertained	0	4
Sample size[c]	128	79

Table 5–10.   continued

Location Where Respondents Participated Most Often[b]	Nonfederally Assisted New and Conventional Communities	
	Thirteen New Communities	Thirteen Conventional Communities
Tennis		
Within community	74	55
Outside community	25	45
Location not ascertained	1	0
Sample size[c]	125	55
Boating		
Within community	45	13
Outside community	54	86
Location not ascertained	1	1
Sample size[c]	106	33
Fishing		
Within community	17	13
Outside community	77	79
Location not ascertained	6	8
Sample size[c]	104	60
Bicycling		
Within community	92	81
Outside community	6	17
Location not ascertained	2	2
Sample size[c]	87	29
Arts and Crafts		
Within community	51	43
Outside community	45	52
Location not ascertained	4	5
Sample size[c]	57	49

[a]*Question:* Where do you go most often? (Name of facility; nearest intersection; town)?

[b]Includes only respondents who cited activity as their favorite out-of-home activity.

[c]The difference in the number of respondents between this table and Table 5–9 is due to the fact that some respondents did not indicate the number of times they participated in an activity or gave general responses, such as "a lot." These respondents were excluded from the tabulations in Table 5–9, but are included here.

[d]Between 92 percent and 100 percent of these respondents gardened in their own yards.

ents who usually participated in their favorite out-of-home activities within their own communities. A majority of the new community respondents usually participated within their own community in six of the ten favorite activities that are summarized in Table 5-10. In order of the proportion of respondents who participated within their communities, these activities included gardening (97 percent), bicycling (92 percent), swimming (78 percent), tennis (74 percent), walking and hiking (72 percent) and arts and crafts (51 percent). Favorite activities for which a majority of new community respondents most often did not participate within their own communities included fishing (17 percent), bowling (19 percent), boating (45 percent) and golf (47 percent). In most cases participation within the community was similar among all participants and just those participants who cited an activity as their favorite. The only exception was walking and hiking for pleasure. Although 95 percent of the persons who walked and hiked usually engaged in this activity within their own community, only 72 percent of those who cited walking and hiking as their favorite out-of-home activity participated within their own community.

A significantly greater proportion of new community than conventional community respondents most often participated within, rather than outside, their own communities in three of the ten activities summarized in Table 5-10. These were swimming (78 percent versus 59 percent), tennis (74 percent versus 55 percent) and boating (45 percent versus 13 percent). Although differences were smaller, and not statistically significant, new community respondents were also more likely than conventional community respondents to participate in each of the other activities considered, with the exception of gardening, within their own communities.

Table 5-11 summarizes respondents' reported levels of satisfaction with the facilities and sites they most often used to participate in their favorite out-of-home activities. Over 80 percent of the respondents living in the thirteen nonfederally assisted new communities were completely satisfied or satisfied with facilities they used for gardening, walking, arts and crafts, swimming, boating and bicycling. Somewhat lower satisfaction levels were reported for facilities used for tennis, golf, bowling and fishing. Conventional community respondents were less likely than new community respondents to be satisfied (including completely satisfied) with the facilities they used for six of the ten activities summarized in Table 5-11. These facilities included those used for swimming, gardening, walking, bowling, tennis and bicycling. On the other hand, new community respond-

Table 5–11. Satisfaction with Facilities Used for Favorite Out-of-home Activities[a] *(percentage distribution of respondents)*

	Nonfederally Assisted New and Conventional Communities	
Favorite Activities[b]	*Thirteen New Communities*	*Thirteen Conventional Communities*
Golf		
Completely satisfied	45	59
Satisfied	32	29
Neutral or dissatisfied	23	12
Sample size	259	99
Swimming		
Completely satisfied	62	53
Satisfied	25	31
Neutral or dissatisfied	13	16
Sample size	240	86
Gardening		
Completely satisfied	62	54
Satisfied	26	27
Neutral or dissatisfied	12	19
Sample size	190	79
Walking		
Completely satisfied	65	59
Satisfied	23	17
Neutral or dissatisfied	12	24
Sample size	108	42
Bowling		
Completely satisfied	35	34
Satisfied	36	31
Neutral or dissatisfied	29	35
Sample size	127	77
Tennis		
Completely satisfied	41	42
Satisfied	37	35
Neutral or dissatisfied	22	23
Sample size	125	54
Boating		
Completely satisfied	60	65
Satisfied	26	30
Neutral or dissatisfied	14	5
Sample size	160	31

Table 5–11 continued overleaf . . .

Table 5-11. continued

Favorite Activities[b]	Nonfederally Assisted New and Conventional Communities	
	Thirteen New Communities	Thirteen Conventional Communities
Fishing		
Completely satisfied	33	47
Satisfied	35	31
Neutral or dissatisfied	32	22
Sample size	98	54
Bicycling		
Completely satisfied	52	30
Satisfied	29	49
Neutral or dissatisfied	17	21
Sample size	83	29
Arts and Crafts		
Completely satisfied	61	64
Satisfied	27	26
Neutral or dissatisfied	12	10
Sample size	53	44

[a]*Question:* Overall, how satisfied are you with that place as a place to (ACTIVITY)? Which number comes closest to how you feel? Completely satisfied 1 2 3 4 5 6 7 Completely dissatisfied.

[b]Includes only respondents who cited activity as their favorite out-of-home activity. Respondents citing "1" were tabulated as completely satisfied; those citing "2" or "3" were tabulated as satisfied; and those citing "4" through "7" as neutral or dissatisfied.

ents were less satisfied (including completely satisfied) than conventional community respondents with facilities used for golf, boating, fishing and arts and crafts. It should be noted, however, that in both cases differences in satisfaction were not great—the most notable was the 12 percent more conventional community respondents who were not satisfied with walking facilities and the 11 percent more new community respondents who were not satisfied with the golf facilities they most often used.

While the results presented above are mixed, they indicate that, on the whole, new community recreational service systems performed somewhat better in accommodating residents' favorite out-of-home activities than recreational service systems in the conventional communities. Participation rates were significantly higher in new communities for swimming, walking and boating (for no activities were participation rates significantly higher in the conventional communities), and new community respondents were more likely to pursue their favorite activities within their own communities. In the case of satisfaction with the facilities used, however, only minimal differences between the new and conventional communities were apparent.

The data also suggest several recreational activities which probably deserve more attention from new community recreational service systems. For example, few new communities provided facilities for residents who liked to garden and for those who liked to bowl. Although much gardening takes place in individual yards, the increasing number of townhouses and apartments in new communities precludes opportunities for gardening for a significant proportion of their populations. Provision of public gardening space would probably be a highly beneficial recreational service. Only three new communities—Elk Grove Village, Lake Havasu City and Sharpstown—had bowling alleys, possibly because of the working class overtones associated with this sport. Nevertheless, bowling ranked fifth in the proportion of respondents who designated it as their favorite activity. Bowling should also receive more attention in the design and development of new community recreational systems. Other facilities that deserve more attention include lakes for boating and fishing and bicycle trails.

RESIDENTS' OVERALL EVALUATIONS
OF RECREATIONAL SERVICE SYSTEMS

In addition to gathering information about participation in recreational activities and use of particular facilities, respondents were asked to rate the overall quality of community recreational facilities. As shown in Table 5–12, respondents living in the thirteen nonfederally assisted new communities were significantly more likely to rate recreational facilities in their communities as excellent or good than were respondents who lived in the less planned conventional communities (77 percent versus 62 percent).

Among individual nonfederally assisted new communities, Columbia ranked first (92 percent of the Columbia respondents rated recreational facilities as excellent or good). Four other new communities—Irvine, North Palm Beach, Reston and Westlake Village—received excellent or good ratings from 85 percent or more of the respondents. The lowest rated nonfederally assisted new communities were Sharpstown (53 percent excellent or good), Foster City (67 percent) and Forest Park (69 percent). Both federally assisted new communities received significantly higher ratings than their paired conventional communities. Ninety-four percent of the Jonathan respondents rated community recreational facilities as excellent or good compared to

Table 5-12. Residents' Overall Evaluations of Community Recreational Facilities[a] *(percentage distribution of respondents)*

New and Conventional Communities	Overall Evaluation of Recreational Facilities		
	Excellent or Good	Average	Below Average or Poor
Nonfederally Assisted New and Conventional Communities			
Thirteen new communities	77	14	9
Thirteen conventional communities	62	21	17
New Communities			
Columbia	92	6	2
Elk Grove Village	82	13	5
Forest Park	69	16	15
Foster City	67	15	18
Irvine	85	10	5
Laguna Niguel	74	12	14
Lake Havasu City	75	16	9
North Palm Beach	88	9	3
Park Forest	75	20	5
Reston	85	9	6
Sharpstown	53	31	16
Valencia	81	16	3
Westlake Village	89	6	5
Federally Assisted New and Conventional Communities			
Jonathan	94	5	1
Chanhassen	51	36	13
Park Forest South	56	25	19
Richton Park	35	25	40

[a]*Question:* All things considered, how good would you say the recreational facilities in this community and its immediate vicinity are for the people who live here—excellent, good, average, below average or poor?

only 51 percent of the Chanhassen respondents. Although a lower proportion of Park Forest South respondents rated recreational facilities highly (56 percent excellent or good), much lower ratings were given recreational facilities in Richton Park, Park Forest South's paired conventional community (35 percent excellent or good).

Another perspective on residents' overall evaluations of community recreational facilities and services is provided by respondents' perceptions of recreational facilities as a community problem and their desires for greater community expenditures for outdoor recreation. As shown in Table 5–13, about the same proportion of new and conventional community respondents, 12 percent and 10 percent, indicated that recreational facilities were one of the most important problems facing their communities. Only two other aspects of these communities, the quality of the environment and the schools, were cited as major problems by a greater proportion of new community respondents. Recreational facilities were most likely to be perceived as a major community problem in North Palm Beach and Laguna Niguel. They were least often cited as a community problem in Irvine and Columbia. Among the federally assisted new communities, a much higher proportion of Park Forest South (16 percent) than Jonathan (1 percent) respondents mentioned recreational facilities as a major problem facing their community.

Residents' desires for increased community expenditures for outdoor recreational facilities were inversely related to their overall evaluations of the quality of community recreational facilities. Overall, 34 percent of the respondents living in the thirteen nonfederally assisted new communities, compared to 40 percent of those living in the conventional communities, said that more should be spent in their communities for outdoor recreational facilities. The proportion of respondents who desired increased expenditures for this purpose was greatest in the five new communities whose recreational service systems received the lowest proportion of excellent or good ratings. Between 35 percent and 50 percent of the respondents living in Forest Park, Foster City, Laguna Niguel, Park Forest and Sharpstown wanted to see more money spent on outdoor recreational facilities within their community. In contrast, a much lower proportion of respondents who lived in the top-rated new communities—Columbia, Irvine, North Palm Beach and Westlake Village—wanted to see more spent on outdoor recreational facilities. The one exception was Reston, where 85 percent of the respondents rated the recreational system as excellent or good, but 40 percent wanted to see more money expended on outdoor recreational facilities within the community.

SATISFACTION WITH THE USE OF LEISURE TIME

To many recreation professionals, recreational facilities and services are not ends in themselves, but are a means of enabling individuals to make personally productive and enjoyable use of their spare time. (See Hjelte and Shivers 1972, p. 15.) Respondents living in the thirteen nonfederally assisted new communities were more likely to be satisfied with the use of their leisure time than the conventional

Table 5-13. **Perception of Recreational Facilities as a Community Problem and Perception of Need for Additional Community Expenditures for Outdoor Recreation** *(percentage distribution of respondents)*

	Perceive Recreational Facilities As a Community Problem[a]	Believe Community Should Spend More for Outdoor Recreational Facilities[b]
New and Conventional Communities		
Nonfederally Assisted New and Conventional Communities		
Thirteen new communities	12	34
Thirteen conventional communities	10	40
New Communities		
Columbia	5	19
Elk Grove Village	9	27
Forest Park	12	48
Foster City	10	35
Irvine	4	23
Laguna Niguel	17	39
Lake Havasu City	9	28
North Palm Beach	18	25
Park Forest	14	36
Reston	9	40
Sharpstown	10	50
Valencia	11	28
Westlake Village	11	26

Federally Assisted New and Conventional Communities

Jonathan	1	21
Chanhassen	16	37
Park Forest South	16	55
Richton Park	10	62

[a]*Question:* In your opinion, what are the most important issues or problems facing the *community as a whole* at the present time?

[b]*Question:* Here is a list of facilities and services. Some we have talked about already, others we have not. For each, I want you to tell me whether you think about the right amount of money is now being spent on the facility or service in the community or whether there should be more money spent, or less money spent than there is now.

community respondents (72 percent versus 66 percent were satisfied). However, as shown in Table 5–14, new communities with the highest proportions of satisfied respondents were for the most part not those with the most recreational resources or even those in which respondents rated recreational facilities highly. Thirty-five percent or more of the respondents living in five new communities were completely satisfied with the use of their leisure time. Foster City ranked first, followed by Lake Havasu City, Westlake Village, North Palm Beach and Laguna Niguel. Of these communities, only Lake Havasu City rated among the top five new communities in terms of recrea-

Table 5–14. Adults' Satisfaction with the Use of Their Leisure Time[a]
(percentage distribution of respondents)

	Satisfaction with Use of Leisure Time		
New and Conventional Communities	*Completely Satisfied*	*Satisfied*	*Neutral or Dissatisfied*
Nonfederally Assisted New and Conventional Communities			
Thirteen new communities	31	41	28
Thirteen conventional communities	30	36	34
New Communities			
Columbia	21	46	33
Elk Grove Village	25	39	36
Forest Park	29	41	30
Foster City	42	35	23
Irvine	24	48	28
Laguna Niguel	35	46	19
Lake Havasu City	41	38	21
North Palm Beach	36	40	24
Park Forest	29	43	28
Reston	22	44	34
Sharpstown	27	44	29
Valencia	24	38	38
Westlake Village	38	36	26
Federally Assisted New and Conventional Communities			
Jonathan	17	53	30
Chanhassen	14	44	42
Park Forest South	24	44	32
Richton Park	22	48	30

[a]*Question:* Overall, how satisfied are you with the way you spend your spare time? Which number comes closest to how you feel? Completely satisfied 1 2 3 4 5 6 7 Completely dissatisfied. Respondents who cited "1" to the above question were tabulated as completely satisfied; those citing "2" or "3" as satisfied; and those citing "4" through "7" as neutral or dissatisfied.

tional resources, while Westlake Village and North Palm Beach rated among the top five communities in terms of respondents' overall ratings of recreational facilities. Columbia and Reston, which ranked first and second in terms of resources, and first and fourth in terms of overall respondents' ratings, ranked thirteenth and twelfth in terms of respondents' satisfaction with the use of their leisure time. Respondents' satisfaction with the use of their leisure time was no higher in the two federally assisted new communities. In Jonathan 70 percent of the respondents were satisfied (only 17 percent completely so) with the way they used their leisure time, while 68 percent of the Park Forest South respondents reported that they were satisfied, with 24 percent reporting complete satisfaction.

IMPLICATIONS FOR ORGANIZING RECREATIONAL SERVICE SYSTEMS

New community residents' responses to recreational service systems have been considered in terms of children's outdoor play, five outdoor recreational activities, residents' favorite out-of-home activities, their overall evaluations of community recreational facilities and their satisfaction with the ways in which they spent their leisure time.

In concluding the analysis of recreational resources (Chapter 4), it was shown that recreational service systems that centered on community-wide homes associations were more effective in providing recreational resources than systems that centered on neighborhood homes associations or municipalities and recreation and park districts, which, in turn, were more effective in providing resources than recreational systems in which county or state agencies played leading roles. To evaluate whether varying approaches to organizing recreational service systems were also associated with residents' responses to these systems, average residents' response indexes were computed for communities grouped according to the types of institutions that accounted for the largest proportion of annual recreational operating expenditures in each community.

As illustrated in Table 5–15, communities with community-wide (index value of 6.8) and neighborhood (6.5) homes associations performed somewhat better than communities with recreational service systems centered on municipalities and community park districts (7.5) or those centered on county and state agencies (8.1). In terms of the four residents' response indexes used in the analysis, community-wide homes associations (Columbia and Reston) were more effective than other institutional approaches in terms of children's

Table 5–15. Key Institutions in Recreational Service Systems and Residents' Responses
(average indexes of residents' responses)[a]

Response Indexes	Key Institutions[b]			
	Community-wide Homes Associations (N = 2)	Neighborhood Homes Associations (N = 4)	Municipality/Park and Recreation District (N = 4)	County/State (N = 3)
Overall Index	6.8	6.5	7.5	8.1
1. Children's outdoor play	4.6	6.2	7.2	9.5
2. Adults' recreational activities	6.1	6.1	7.7	8.1
3. Overall evaluations of community recreational facilities	3.9	6.3	7.4	9.4
4. Leisure satisfaction	12.5	7.3	5.1	5.5

[a]Index values may range from one (high) to 13 (low).

[b]Allocation of communities to categories is based on type of organization expending largest proportion of total annual recreational expenditures (excluding commercial recreation enterprises, private clubs and developer donations) in community. Communities were allocated as follows: community-wide homes associations (Columbia and Reston); neighborhood homes associations (Irvine, Laguna Niguel, Valencia and Westlake Village); municipality/community park and recreation district (Elk Grove Village, Foster City, North Palm Beach and Park Forest); and county/state (Forest Park, Lake Havasu City and Sharpstown).

outdoor play and residents' overall evaluations of community recreational facilities. They were equivalent to neighborhood homes associations in terms of adult activities, but performed poorly in terms of leisure satisfaction. Although a number of factors contribute to leisure satisfaction, it is noteworthy that recreational service systems that used community-wide homes associations were not very effective in providing organized recreational programs, which may have more effect on leisure satisfaction than any other community recreational resource.[b]

As a group, new communities with recreational service systems centered on neighborhood homes associations ranked first on the overall index. Communities with municipal- or park and recreation district-centered recreational systems ranked first in terms of residents' leisure satisfaction, but behind the groups of communities with community-wide and neighborhood homes associations on the other three summary indexes. Finally, county- and state agency-centered recreational systems ranked last on each index except leisure satisfaction, where they ranked second behind municipal- and park and recreation district-centered recreational service systems.

[b]It should be noted, however, that the rank-order association between the provision of recreational programs in new communities and residents' leisure satisfaction, though positive, is rather low ($r_s = .18$) and is not statistically significant.

 *Chapter 6*

The Recreational Experiences
of Population Target Groups

The idea of a complete community embodied in the new community concept implies that provision is made for a variety of population groups and for a variety of life styles. In Chapter 4, however, it was noted that in most cases new community recreational service systems were designed to meet the needs of the general population. Very few new communities developed recreational facilities or programs designed specifically for population target groups. In this chapter the recreational experiences of five population groups—young adults, elderly persons, women, blacks and subsidized housing residents—are evaluated. The analysis indicates how well new communities have performed in meeting their needs in comparison with those of other new community residents and in comparison with population target groups living in conventional suburban communities. In those cases where deficiencies in the performance of new community recreational service systems are apparent, potential remedial actions are suggested.

YOUNG ADULTS

One of the largest "minority" populations living in new communities is young adults in the fourteen to twenty-year age bracket. Almost a quarter (24 percent) of the households interviewed in the thirteen nonfederally assisted new communities had one or more young adult members. To evaluate how well new community recreational service systems are meeting the needs of this group of residents, data on young adults were collected through a self-administered questionnaire that was left by interviewers with a randomly selected person fourteen to twenty years old (excluding family heads and their spouses) in each sample household where such persons were residing. The young adult questionnaire was designed so that key comparisons between young adult and adult responses could be made.

Overall, there were very few differences between young adults' responses to the recreational service systems in nonfederally assisted new communities and their paired conventional communities. See Table 6–1. Although new communities tended to pay more attention to young adults' recreational needs than the conventional communities, young adults' awareness of teen centers and after school recreational programs was equivalent. Less than half of the young adult respondents were aware of neighborhood and community teen centers, while about two-thirds knew of teen recreational programs and activities in their communities.

Young adults' rates of participation in leisure activities were remarkably similar in the new and conventional communities. Relatively few young adults (20 percent and 15 percent) used teen centers at least once a week. However, higher proportions participated frequently (50 or more times a year) in their favorite out-of-home activities (41 percent and 38 percent). Frequent participation in favorite activities was much greater among new community young adults than among household heads and spouses living in the same new communities (41 percent versus 29 percent were frequent participants). This was also true of participation in bicycling (24 percent of the young adults versus 12 percent of the household heads and spouses participated frequently), and swimming (27 percent versus 20 percent frequent participation), but household heads and spouses participated more frequently in walking for pleasure and hiking (27 percent versus 15 percent). There were virtually no differences in participation rates in bicycling, swimming and walking and hiking between young adults living in the new and conventional communities.

One factor that may account for the relatively low use of teen centers by young adults was their rather low regard for the quality of these facilities. Only about a third of the young adults living in the new and conventional communities rated available teen centers as excellent or good places to go for people their age. Also, less than a majority reported that they were happy with organized recreational activities for young people in their communities or believed that there were enough good places in their communities for them to get together with their friends. However, when asked about specific recreational facilities they most often used, young adults reported much higher levels of satisfaction (over 80 percent were satisfied) with the facilities they used for their favorite out-of-home activities and for bicycling, swimming and walking and hiking. In this regard, young adults were about as satisfied as household heads and spouses.

In spite of high levels of satisfaction with some facilities, young adults' low regard for teen-oriented facilities and programs carried over to their overall evaluations of recreational facilities in their communities. Less than a third (32 percent and 30 percent) of the young adults living in the sample new and conventional communities rated community recreational facilities as excellent or good. In comparison, 77 percent of the household heads and spouses living in new communities rated recreational facilities that highly. Young adults were also significantly less satisfied than household heads and spouses with the ways in which they spent their leisure time. Only 17 percent of the young adults living in the new communities and 20 percent of those living in the conventional communities were completely satisfied, compared to 31 percent of the new community household heads and spouses interviewed.

In summary, these findings show that new community recreational service systems have performed rather poorly in meeting the leisure needs of young adults, though their performance was no worse than that of the less planned conventional communities. To provide one indication of what might be done to improve this situation, young adults who believed that their communities did not have enough good places for them to get together with their friends were asked to name the kinds of places that were needed in their communities. Apparently new communities have done an adequate job of providing indoor and outdoor sports facilities for young adults. Only 8 percent wanted more indoor and only 14 percent more outdoor recreational facilities. In contrast, a relatively high proportion of conventional community young adults, 28 percent, indicated a need for more outdoor facilities and 12 percent wanted more indoor facilities. Rather than sports facilities, a relatively high proportion (26 percent) of new community young adults expressed a need for teen centers and an equal proportion wanted more cultural, entertainment and shopping facilities in their communities, including theaters, places for dances and parties, shopping malls, fast food places and libraries. While some of these facilities, such as teen centers and libraries, can be provided relatively early in the development process, the "action" places many new community young adults want usually require a large population for their support. Thus, until new communities mature, they may be rather dull and unsatisfying places for young adults to live. To overcome this problem, new communities may find

Table 6–1. Young Adults' (Age 14 to 20) Responses to New and Conventional Community Recreational Service Systems[a]
(percentage distribution of respondents)

Indicator	Young Adults (Age Fourteen to Twenty)		Household Heads and Spouses
	Thirteen Nonfederally Assisted New Communities	Thirteen Conventional Communities	Thirteen Nonfederally Assisted New Communities
Perception of Teen Facilities and Programs			
Teen center available	45	48	d
Teen recreational activities and programs (outside school) available	66	62	d
Participation			
Use teen center (one or more times per week)	20	15	d
Favorite out-of-home activity (50+ times annually)	41[e]	38	29
Bicycling (50+ times annually)	24[e]	24	12
Swimming (50+ times annually)	27[e]	26	20
Walking and hiking (50+ times annually)	15	16	24[e]
Rating of and Satisfaction with Facilities and Programs			
Rate teen center excellent or good	33	37	d
Happy with teen recreational activities and programs[b]	47	45	d

Believe there are enough good places to get together with friends in community	47	48	d
Satisfied with facility used for favorite out-of-home activity	82	81	83
Satisfied with facility used for bicycling	84	83	83
Satisfied with facility used for swimming	83	80	87
Satisfied with facility used for walking and hiking	80	87[c]	89[e]
Overall Evaluation of Community Recreational Facilities			
Excellent or good	32	30	77[e]
Average	32[e]	35	14
Below average or poor	36[e]	35	9
Overall Satisfaction with Use of Leisure Time			
Completely satisfied	17	20	31[e]
Satisfied	49[e]	47	41
Neutral or dissatisfied	34[e]	33	28
Sample size	610	309	2838

[a]These data were collected by means of a self-administered questionnaire left by interviewers with a randomly selected person fourteen to twenty years old (excluding family heads and their spouses) in all sample households where such persons were residing.

[b]Thirty-nine percent of the young adults living in new communities and 42 percent of those living in the conventional communities responded that they could not evaluate these programs because they did not participate in them.

[c]Difference between new and conventional community young adults statistically significant at 0.05 level of confidence.

[d]Question is not applicable to adult respondents.

[e]Difference between new community young adult and adult respondents statistically significant at 0.05 level of confidence.

it advantageous to provide organized weekend transportation services to cultural and entertainment facilities in the surrounding region.

ELDERLY RESIDENTS

As of the 1970 census there were just over 20 million people age 65 and over in the United States. Elderly persons comprised almost 10 percent of the population. By the year 2000 the elderly are expected to increase to 28.8 million persons, or about 11.5 percent of the population. Since the elderly, as a group, have needs that are distinctly different from the general population that is likely to settle in new communities (see M. Powell Lawton and Thomas O. Byerts 1973), it is important to determine the extent to which new communities are meeting their needs. Also, since one of the most widely debated issues in environmental planning for the elderly is whether older people should live in proximity to other older people (age segregation) or in age mixtures approximating those found in the population at large (age integration), it is of interest to see how elderly residents respond to recreational service systems in age-integrated versus age-segregated new community environments. In order to make this comparison, elderly residents living in two retirement communities, Rossmoor Leisure World, Laguna Hills, California and Sun City Center, Florida, were interviewed.

Elderly persons (age 65+) comprised only 4 percent of the sample respondents from the thirteen nonfederally assisted new communities and only 2 percent of those living in the less planned conventional communities. They were also unevenly distributed among new communities. Over half of the elderly respondents lived in three new communities that were located in warmer climates: Lake Havasu City, Laguna Niguel and North Palm Beach. As a group, elderly residents of both the new and conventional communities were relatively affluent. Less than 50 percent had annual incomes of under $10,000; 32 percent of the new community elderly and 40 percent of those living in the conventional communities had incomes of $15,000 or more per year. Elderly persons living in the two age-segregated retirement new communities, Rossmoor Leisure World and Sun City Center, were also relatively affluent. Less than 50 percent had incomes of under $10,000 and 26 percent had incomes of $15,000 or more.[a] However, there were some notable differences in the characteristics

---

[a]Sun City Center elderly respondents tended to be significantly more affluent than the elderly respondents living in Rossmoor Leisure World. Thirty-nine percent had annual incomes of $15,000 or more versus only 16 percent of the Rossmoor Leisure World respondents.

of elderly persons living in the sample new, conventional, and age-segregated retirement communities. The heads of elderly new and conventional community households were more likely to be over age 75 (50 percent and 55 percent) than the heads of elderly households in the retirement communities (39 percent in Rossmoor Leisure World and 21 percent in Sun City Center), and were more likely to have either the household head and/or spouse still working for pay (25 percent and 20 percent in the new and conventional communities versus 9 percent and 3 percent in Rossmoor Leisure World and Sun City Center). In terms of social class, however, elderly households in each of these settings were predominantly middle class. Only 20 percent or fewer of the household heads were employed in blue collar occupations.

Recreational resources in the new and conventional communities were described in Chapter 4. In both types of communities, recreational facilities designed specifically for the elderly had not been developed nor were recreational programs for the elderly, other than an occasional golden age club, in evidence. In contrast, the age-segregated retirement communities each had recreational service systems and programs designed specifically for older persons. In addition to golf courses, swimming pools and tennis courts, which are also available in the age-integrated new communities, Rossmoor Leisure World provided its residents with an internal transportation system (mini-buses) to get around the community; numerous arts and crafts facilities with instructors; boccie, lawn bowling and shuffle board courts; stables; library; garden plots (since the community consisted entirely of apartments); and a movie theater. An extensive array of recreational programs was offered residents throughout the year. Sun City Center, which was smaller (3000 residents versus 15,000 residents in Rossmoor Leisure World), had a more limited array of recreational facilities and services. Nevertheless, in addition to golf and swimming facilities it provided shuffle board and lawn bowling courts, four lakes for fishing and boating and a large recreational center with arts and crafts and card rooms. Sun City Center also offered extensive year-round recreational programs to accommodate the leisure interests of its residents.

Table 6−2 compares elderly residents' responses to recreational service systems in the new, conventional and retirement communities. A much lower proportion of elderly respondents participated in selected outdoor activities than was true of the general population of the sample new and conventional communities. For example, comparison of data presented in Tables 5−3 through 5−7 with Table 6−2 indicates that while 25 percent of the general population of the

Table 6–2. Elderly Residents' (Age 65+) Responses to New and Conventional Community Recreational Service Systems

Indicator	Thirteen Nonfederally Assisted New Communities	Thirteen Conventional Communities	Two Retirement Communities[a]
Selected Activities			
Participation (percent one or more times annually)			
Golf	14[b]	12	3
Swimming	24	27	27
Tennis	3	2	1
Bicycling	7	10	9
Walking and hiking	27	27	20
Evaluation of facilities used most often (percent satisfied)			
Golf	71	89	89
Swimming	82	92	98[b]
Tennis	d	d	d
Bicycling	74	73	100[b]
Walking and hiking	91	77	99
Distance traveled to facility used most often			
Golf (median miles)	2.4	1.7	1.1
Swimming (median miles)	0.2	0.1	0.1
Tennis (median miles)	d	d	d
Bicycling (percent within one-eighth mile)	100	100	100
Walking and hiking (percent within one-eighth mile)	93	94	94
Favorite Activities			
Mentioned most (percent)			
Gardening	19[b]	15	3

Walking and hiking	19[c]	6	21
Golf	16	20	20
Swimming	15[c]	4	11
Playing cards	8	16	15
Bowling	3	1	7
Arts and crafts	1	9[c]	6
Participation (percent 50+ times) All favorite activities	48[c]	26	54
Evaluation of facility used most often (percent satisfied) All favorite activities	75	85	97[b]
Location of facility used most often (percent in community) All favorite activities	75	69	84
Overall Evaluation of Community Recreational Facilities (percent)			
Excellent or good	82[c]	66	96[b]
Average	12[b]	23[c]	3
Below average or poor	6	11	1
Satisfaction with Use of Leisure Time (percent)			
Completely satisfied	42	44	66[b]
Satisfied	36[b]	32	22
Neutral or dissatisfied	22[b]	24	12
Sample size	179	111	165

[a] The retirement communities are Rossmoor Leisure World, Laguna Hills, California and Sun City Center, Florida.
[b] Difference between new and retirement community elderly residents statistically significant at 0.05 level of confidence.
[c] Difference between new and conventional community elderly residents statistically significant at 0.05 level of confidence.
[d] Insufficient number of respondents to tabulate (fewer than ten).

thirteen nonfederally assisted new communities had participated in golf during the previous year, only 8 percent of the elderly (age 65+) had done so. Similarly, the older persons living in new communities were less likely than the general population to have participated in swimming (24 percent versus 58 percent), tennis (3 percent versus 21 percent), bicycling (7 percent versus 39 percent) or walking and hiking (27 percent versus 56 percent). There were no significant differences in participation rates in these activities between older persons living in new communities and the less planned conventional communities. Compared to older persons living in the age-segregated retirement communities, those living in the age-integrated new communities were significantly more likely to have participated in golf and somewhat more likely to have gone walking and hiking during the previous year.

On the other hand, elderly respondents living in the retirement communities were more likely to be satisfied with the facilities they most often used for outdoor activities. Differences between new and retirement communities in the proportions of respondents who were satisfied with the facilities they used included golf (71 percent versus 89 percent satisfied), swimming (82 percent versus 98 percent) and bicycling (74 percent versus 100 percent). Elderly persons living in the conventional communities were more satisfied than new community elderly persons with the facilities they used for golf and swimming, but were less satisfied with the facilities they used for walking and hiking. Differences in the distances traveled to participate were not great, though for each activity retirement community residents tended to travel the same or shorter distances than new or conventional community elderly residents.

The most frequently mentioned favorite out-of-home activities of the elderly were much the same as for the general populations of the new and conventional communities. For example, among the new community respondents, gardening, walking and hiking, golf and swimming were among the top five favorite activities of both the elderly and the general population. Nevertheless, there were some notable differences. A higher proportion of new community elderly respondents than the general population mentioned gardening, walking and hiking and playing cards as their favorite activities. Compared with older persons living in new communities, a higher proportion of elderly persons living in the retirement communities mentioned playing cards (15 percent versus 8 percent), bowling (7 percent versus 3 percent) and arts and crafts (6 percent versus 1 percent). As noted above, community facilities for each of these activities were available in the retirement communities. On the other hand, older persons living in the retirement communities were much less likely to mention gardening as their favorite out-of-home activity (3 percent versus 19 percent). This may have been due to the high proportion of apartment dwellers in Rossmoor Leisure World and the availability of a number of less solitary activities for older persons in both retirement communities.

Elderly persons living in new communities participated significantly more often in their favorite activities and somewhat more often in their own communities than elderly persons living in the conventional communities, but they were somewhat less satisfied with the facilities they most often used for these activities. Elderly persons living in the retirement communities participated in their favorite activities much more often than those living in the less planned conventional communities and somewhat more often than new community elderly persons. Also, they were much more satisfied with the facilities they used for their favorite activities than were elderly persons living in either the new or conventional communities. In addition, elderly persons living in the retirement communities were the most likely to participate in their favorite out-of-home activities within their own communities.

In terms of overall evaluations of community recreational facilities and overall satisfaction with the use of leisure time, the retirement communities ranked first. Ninety-six percent of the elderly residents of the retirement communities rated recreational facilities excellent or good, compared to 82 percent of the elderly persons living in new communities and only 66 percent of those living in the less planned conventional communities. In the case of leisure satisfaction, 88 percent of the elderly who lived in the retirement communities were satisfied with the ways they spent their leisure time, compared to 78 percent of the elderly persons living in the new communities and 76 percent of those who lived in the conventional communities.

In summary, these data indicate that age-segregated retirement communities provide viable alternative environments for the middle class, affluent, elderly represented in the samples. Age-integrated new communities appear to provide somewhat better leisure and recreational environments for older persons than do less planned suburban communities. However, to maximize choices available to older persons and to provide a large enough population base to provide economically recreational services for the elderly, new communities may wish to experiment with the development of age-segregated, retirement-oriented neighborhoods and villages in otherwise age-integrated communities. This, in fact, is occurring at Sun City Center, where an age-integrated new community is being developed around what was

originally a retirement community. Other retirement-oriented neighborhoods and villages are being developed as part of two age-integrated new communities—Laguna Niguel and Mission Viejo—located
in California.

WOMEN

Table 6—3 summarizes women's responses to nonfederally assisted
new and conventional community recreational service systems. As
expected, women living in new communities were much less likely
than men to have participated in golf during the previous year (14
percent versus 34 percent). In the case of other selected outdoor
recreational activities, however, there were no significant differences
in participation rates between women and men. In comparison with
women living in the less planned conventional communities, new
community women were more likely to have participated in golf and
tennis during the previous year, but there were no significant differences in participation in swimming, bicycling and walking and hiking.

New community women tended to be satisfied with the sites and
facilities they most often used for recreational activities. There were
no significant differences in satisfaction between women and men
living in the thirteen nonfederally assisted new communities. In comparison with conventional community women, women living in the
new communities were somewhat more satisfied with the facilities
they used most often for bicycling and walking, but were somewhat
less satisfied with the tennis facilities they used.

Eight out-of-home activities were mentioned as their favorites by
5 percent or more of the women living in the nonfederally assisted
new communities. In order of the number of times that they were
mentioned, these included: swimming, gardening, bowling, golf,
tennis, walking and hiking, bicycling and playing cards. New community women were more likely than men to mention swimming,
bowling, bicycling and playing cards as their favorite activities. Nevertheless, half of the favorite activities mentioned by 5 percent or
more of the new community women were also mentioned by 5 percent or more of the men interviewed, including swimming, gardening,
golf and walking and hiking. In comparison with women living in the
conventional communities, new community women were somewhat
more likely to have mentioned swimming, golf and tennis as a favorite out-of-home activity.

Although there were few differences in participation rates over
all favorite activities, frequent participation in individual activities

Table 6–3. Women's Responses to New and Conventional Community Recreational Service Systems

Indicator	Thirteen Nonfederally Assisted New Communities		Thirteen Conventional Communities
	Men	*Women*	*Women*
Selected Activities			
Participation (percent one or more times annually)			
Golf	34[a]	14[b]	9
Swimming	55	52	49
Tennis	19	19[b]	14
Bicycling	33	36	32
Walking and hiking	45	49	48
Evaluation of facility used most often (percent satisfied)			
Golf	77	81	82
Swimming	88	86	83[b]
Tennis	78	75	85[b]
Bicycling	82	83[b]	72
Walking and hiking	88	89	84
Distance traveled to facility used most often			
Golf (median miles)	4.0	3.7	7.9
Swimming (median miles)	1.3	0.8	1.3
Tennis (median miles)	1.7	1.3	1.4
Bicycling (percent within one-eighth mile)	92	94	89
Walking and hiking (percent within one-eighth mile)	77	82	78

Table 6–3. continued overleaf . . .

Table 6–3. continued

Indicator	Thirteen Nonfederally Assisted New Communities		Thirteen Conventional Communities
	Men	*Women*	*Women*
Favorite Activities			
Mentioned most (percent)			
Swimming	7	15[a,b]	10
Gardening	8	10	9
Bowling	4	8[a]	10
Golf	18[a]	8[b]	5
Tennis	5	7[b]	4
Walking and hiking	7	7	5
Bicycling	2	6[a]	4
Playing cards	1	5[a]	6
Participation (percent 50+ times)			
All favorite activities	27	31	30
Swimming[c]	28	41[a]	27
Gardening[c]	82[a]	61	64
Bowling[c]	42	34	36
Golf[c]	25	18	4
Tennis[c]	31	26	34
Walking and hiking[c]	40	56	33
Bicycling[c]	22	43	31
Playing cards[c]	21	46[a]	59
Evaluation of facility used most often (percent satisfied)			
All favorite activities	81	84	83
Swimming[c]	86	88	82
Gardening[c]	95[a]	81	81
Bowling[c]	72	71	70
Golf[c]	74	83	90

Tennis[c]	83	74	71
Walking and hiking[c]	66	91[a]	73
Bicycling[c]	82	81	75
Playing cards[c]	93	97	92
Location of facility used most often (percent in community)			
All favorite activities	46	58[a,b]	43
Swimming[c]	77	79[b]	61
Gardening[c]	97	97	100
Bowling[c]	10	23	13
Golf[c]	47	50	71
Tennis[c]	73	75	56
Walking and hiking[c]	85	83	80
Bicycling[c]	85	97[b]	76
Playing cards[c]	83	81	86
Overall Evaluation of Community Recreational Facilities (percent)			
Excellent or good	77	77[b]	61[b]
Average	14	15	22[b]
Below average or poor	9	8	17[b]
Satisfaction with Use of Leisure Time (percent)			
Completely satisfied	29	33[a]	30
Satisfied	41	40[b]	34[b]
Neutral or dissatisfied	30	27	36[b]
Sample size	1127	1421	706

[a] Difference between new community men and women statistically significant at 0.05 level of confidence.
[b] Difference between new community and conventional community women statistically significant at 0.05 level of confidence.
[c] Data refer to only those respondents who mentioned activity as their favorite out-of-home activity.

varied among women and men living in new communities and between women living in the new and conventional communities. In
the first instance, women whose favorite activities were swimming,
walking, bicycling and playing cards were more likely to participate
frequently (50 or more times during the past year) in these activities
than men who mentioned them as their favorites. Men, on the other
hand, were somewhat more likely to be frequent participants in gardening, bowling, golf and tennis. For three out of the four favorite
activities in which new community women were more likely to be
frequent participants than men, they also participated more frequently than conventional community women (swimming, walking
and bicycling). In the case of the fourth, playing cards, conventional
community women were most often frequent participants, as they
also were in playing tennis. New community women were much
more likely to play golf frequently if it was their favorite activity
than were conventional community women.

Satisfaction with the facilities that were used for favorite activities
and facility locations varied among men and women and between
new and conventional community women. In comparison with men,
a higher proportion of women living in new communities were satisfied with the facilities they used for golf and walking and hiking, and
a higher proportion were more likely to swim, bowl, play tennis and
bicycle within their own communities. Men, on the other hand, were
more satisfied with the sites they used for gardening and tennis.
There were no favorite activities in which men were significantly
more likely than women to participate within their own communities.

Fewer conventional than new community women participated in
golf frequently. However, conventional community women were
more likely to participate in their own communities and to be satisfied with the golf courses they used. For most other favorite activities, new and conventional community women were equally satisfied
with the facilities they used for their favorite activities. The most
notable difference was for walking facilities. Ninety-one percent of
new community women were satisfied versus only 71 percent of the
women living in the conventional communities. In the case of the
location of facilities used most often, new community women were
much more likely than conventional community women to bowl,
play tennis and bicycle within their own communities.

In sum, the data show that in terms of recreational participation
and the facilities used, women fared as well as men living in new
communities. While differences in participation and satisfaction were
evident, they were not consistently in favor of either group. In comparison with women living in the conventional communities, women

in new communities fared much better. They participated more frequently in more different activities, were as satisfied with the various types of facilities they used, and were more often able to participate in their favorite activities within their own communities. In terms of overall evaluations of community recreational facilities, new community women and men were equally likely (77 percent each) to rate facilities as excellent or good. New community women were much more likely than conventional community women to rate community recreational facilities as excellent or good (77 percent versus 61 percent) and were less likely to be neutral or dissatisfied with the use of their leisure time (27 percent versus 36 percent).

BLACK RESIDENTS

Contrary to the hopes of many planners (see American Institute of Planners 1968), racial integration has not been characteristic of new communities in the United States. Black respondents comprised just over 3 percent of the respondents from thirteen nonfederally assisted new communities. In addition, the distribution of black people living in new communities was not even. Blacks comprised 19 percent of the population of Columbia and had settled in significant numbers in four other nonfederally assisted new communities (Forest Park, 9 percent; Park Forest, 6 percent; Sharpstown, 5 percent, and Reston, 4 percent). In the remaining eight nonfederally assisted new communities in the sample, the proportion of blacks ranged between 1 percent and 3 percent in Foster City, Irvine, North Palm Beach, Valencia and Westlake Village, while virtually no blacks lived in Elk Grove Village, Laguna Niguel and Lake Havasu City. In the case of the two federally assisted new communities, Jonathan had attracted few black households (2 percent), but matched the Twin Cities metropolitan racial profile. Park Forest South had attracted a significantly higher proportion of black residents (9 percent) than Jonathan and was one of the few suburbs south of Chicago with a racially mixed population.

Although not many blacks lived in new communities, achievement of racially balanced communities is an important goal of federal new community policy. The Urban Growth and New Community Development Act of 1970 provided federal assistance for new community development, in part, to "increase for all persons, particularly members of minority groups, the available choices of locations for living and working, thereby providing more just economic and social environments" (Section 710 (f)). To achieve this objective, federally assisted new communities not only must provide housing opportunities for blacks, they must also be more attractive places for blacks to live than alternative suburban communities.

In order to evaluate black residents' responses to new community recreational service systems, supplementary samples of black residents were interviewed in five new communities—including Columbia, Forest Park, Park Forest, Park Forest South and Reston. Because an insufficient number of black respondents were obtained from the regular conventional communities (0.6 percent), two predominantly black, less planned suburbs, Markham, Illinois and Seat Pleasant, Maryland, were selected to provide a basis for comparison with blacks living in the five highly planned new communities.

Black respondents who lived in the five new communities and two conventional communities had comparable incomes (the conventional community blacks were sampled on the basis of housing prices and types), but new community black household heads tended to be younger (71 percent versus 48 percent were under age 40), better educated (32 percent versus 9 percent had graduate or professional training) and were more likely to be employed in a professional or managerial position (57 percent versus 30 percent). Recreational resources provided in the two conventional communities were much inferior to those provided in the five new communities. The conventional communities had only 58 acres of open space and recreational land per 10,000 population and had annual community recreational operating expenditures of only $2 per capita. In comparison, the five new communities in which subsamples of black residents were interviewed had between 304 and 2076 acres of open space and recreational land per 10,000 population and spent between $5 and $57 per capita annually on community recreational operating expenditures.

Table 6–4 summarizes new community black residents' responses to recreational service systems in comparison with nonblacks living in the same new communities and blacks living in the two suburban conventional communities. In terms of children's play areas and parks, there were no significant differences between black and nonblack new community residents in ratings of areas near home for children's play, or perceptions of nearby parks and playgrounds. Black parents were more likely to report that their children "usually" played at a park or playground, but the proportions of parents who said that their children played at a park or playground once a week or more often were not significantly different. New community black parents were significantly more satisfied than conventional community black parents with areas near their homes for children's outdoor play. New community black parents were also more likely to be aware of a park or playground within one-eighth mile of their

Table 6-4. Black Residents' Responses to New and Conventional Community Recreational Service Systems

Indicator	Five New Communities[a]		Two Conventional Communities[b]
	Nonblacks	Blacks	Blacks
Child Play			
Rating of area near home for children's play (percent excellent or good)	71	69[e]	47
Perceive park or playground within one-eighth mile of home (percent)	31	31[e]	3
Children "usually" play at park or playground (percent)	6	13[d]	5
Children play once a week or more often at park or playground (percent)	49	52[e]	35
Selected Activities			
Participation (percent one or more times annually)			
Golf	21[d]	9	4
Swimming	58[d]	40[e]	11
Tennis	23[d]	16[e]	5
Bicycling	40	39[e]	8
Walking and hiking	47	48[e]	13
Evaluation of facility used most often (percent satisfied)			
Golf	76	96[d]	85
Swimming	78	82	81
Tennis	71	70	82
Bicycling	82	77	88
Walking and hiking	90[d]	79	79

Table 6-4. continued overleaf . . .

Table 6–4. continued

Indicator	Five New Communities[a]		Two Conventional Communities[b]
	Nonblacks	Blacks	Blacks
Distance traveled to facility used most often			
Golf (median miles)	4.5	2.9	7.4
Swimming (median miles)	0.9	1.1	7.4
Tennis (median miles)	0.9	2.0	1.0
Bicycling (percent within one-eighth mile)	87	88	83
Walking and hiking (percent within one-eighth mile)	76	85[d,e]	64
Favorite Activities			
Mentioned most (percent)			
Bowling	8	17[d]	14
Basketball	1	9[d,e]	1
Gardening	10	7	10
Walking and hiking	9	7[e]	2
Tennis	6	7[e]	2
Movies, theater	3	6	4
Bicycling	5	5[e]	0
Swimming	10	5	8
Participation (percent 50+ times)			
All favorite activities	27	31	21
Bowling[c]	30	32	14
Basketball[c]	f	10	f
Evaluation of facility used most often[c] (percent satisfied)			
All favorite activities	80	75	87[d]

Bowling[c]	74	81	70
Basketball[c]	f	47	56
Location of facility used most often (percent in community)			
All favorite activities	45	50	49
Bowling[c]	22	6	4
Basketball[c]	50	58	56
Overall Evaluation of Community Recreational Facilities (percent)			
Excellent or good	26	67[e]	76[d]
Average	27	19	15
Below average or poor	47[e]	14	9
Satisfaction with Use of Leisure Time (percent)			
Completely satisfied	30	24	25
Satisfied	35	38	43
Completely dissatisfied	35	38	32
Sample size	177	245	1184

[a] Respondents living in five new communities with 4 percent or more black population only: Columbia, Forest Park, Park Forest South and Reston. Includes special nonrandom subsample of black respondents. See Appendix A.

[b] Because of an insufficient number of black respondents in the regular conventional communities, two suburban conventional communities with predominantly black residential areas were selected. Respondents with family incomes equivalent to new community black residents were interviewed in Markham, Illinois and Seat Pleasant, Maryland.

[c] There were an insufficient number of respondents (fewer than ten) to tabulate participation, satisfaction and location data for other individual favorite activities. Data refer only to those respondents who mentioned activity as their favorite out-of-home activity.

[d] Difference between black and nonblack new community respondents statistically significant at 0.05 level of confidence.

[e] Difference between black new community and black conventional community respondents statistically significant at 0.05 level of confidence.

[f] Insufficient number of respondents (fewer than ten) to tabulate.

homes and to report that their children played at parks and play-grounds once a week or more often.

In comparison with nonblacks living in new communities, black respondents were as likely to have participated in bicycling and walking, but were less likely to have played golf, tennis or to have gone swimming during the previous year. However, they were more likely to have participated in each of these activities, except golf, than black respondents living in the two conventional communities. New community black respondents' satisfaction with the facilities used for the activities varied. They were most satisfied with the golf courses they used (96 percent were satisfied) and least satisfied with the facilities they most often used for tennis (70 percent were satisfied). Compared to nonblacks living in new communities, blacks were more satisfied with golf courses used, equally satisfied with swimming, tennis and bicycling facilities and significantly less satisfied with the places where they walked and hiked. Compared to blacks living in the two conventional communities, new community blacks tended to be more satisfied with golf courses, were equally satisfied with swimming and walking facilities, but tended to be less satisfied with the tennis and bicycling facilities they most often used.

Black respondents who lived in new communities were more likely than black respondents who lived in the two conventional communities to travel shorter distances to each of these facilities, except those used most often to play tennis. Compared to nonblacks living in new communities, black respondents traveled somewhat shorter distances to play golf but went further to play tennis.

Black respondents' favorite out-of-home activities differed from those of new community nonblacks in three instances. Blacks were more likely to mention bowling and basketball as their favorite activities and were less likely to mention swimming. Compared to the black respondents living in the two conventional communities, new community blacks were much more likely to mention active sports, including basketball, tennis and bicycling, as their favorite out-of-home activities. New community blacks tended to participate as often as nonblacks in their favorite activities and somewhat more frequently than blacks living in the two conventional communities. However, new community blacks were much less satisfied than either nonblacks or blacks living in the conventional communities with the facilities they used for their favorite activities.

In addition, only 50 percent of the black respondents participated in their favorite out-of-home activities within their own communities. In this case, however, nonblacks were no more likely to participate in their favorite activities within their communities, although both new community blacks and nonblacks participated in their own communities slightly more often (50 percent and 49 percent versus 45 percent) than blacks living in the conventional communities.

Overall, new community black respondents were significantly less likely than nonblacks to rate community recreational facilities as excellent or good (67 percent versus 76 percent); but they gave much higher ratings to facilities in their communities than did black respondents who lived in the conventional communities (67 percent versus 26 percent excellent or good). Satisfaction with the use of leisure time, however, was another matter. There were no significant differences between the leisure satisfaction of blacks and nonblack respondents living in new communities, nor between black respondents living in new communities and blacks living in the conventional communities.

In summary, new community recreational service systems appeared to meet many of the needs of black residents more adequately than recreational systems serving the predominantly black residential areas of the two conventional suburban communities. However, new community recreational service systems were less responsive to the needs of black residents than they were to nonblack residents. Geared to golf and swimming, they did not respond to the sizable black interest in bowling and basketball, or in entertainment facilities, such as movie theaters. As a result, blacks were less satisfied than nonblacks with the facilities most often used for their favorite out-of-home activities and were less likely to rate community recreational facilities as excellent or good. A sizable proportion of black respondents (38 percent) were either neutral or dissatisfied with the ways in which they spent their leisure time. Thus, the data show that while new communities served black residents' recreational needs more effectively than alternative suburban communities available to black families, new community planners and developers should give much greater attention to the needs of blacks in planning and developing recreational facilities and services.

SUBSIDIZED HOUSING RESIDENTS

Like racial integration, economic integration of families with low and moderate incomes had not occurred in a number of new communities. Some new community developers had not even considered the possibility, while others encountered various stumbling blocks, including difficulties in getting housing projects approved by the federal government and by new community residents (see Raymond J. Burby, III, Shirley F. Weiss and Robert B. Zehner 1974, and Helene V. Smookler 1976). When the field work for this research was undertaken in 1973, five of the fifteen sample new communities had completed one or more housing projects for moderate-income families (in addition, subsidized housing for the elderly had been constructed in Park Forest and Reston and was contemplated in Forest Park). Economic integration, however, was required of new community development projects approved for federal assistance under the Title VII program. In fact, the Urban Growth and New Community Development Act of 1970 specifically stated that assisted projects should "make substantial provision for housing within the means of persons of low and moderate income" (Section 712 (a) (7)).

To determine whether new community recreational service systems were meeting the needs of low- and moderate-income residents, special subsamples of subsidized housing residents were interviewed in the five new communities—Columbia, Forest Park, Jonathan, Lake Havasu City and Reston—which had occupied FHA Sections 221(d)(3) (rental), 235 (ownership) and 236 (rental) subsidized housing projects. For purposes of comparison with the subsidized housing residents who were living in new communities, residents of subsidized housing projects in two conventional suburban communities were interviewed. These included an FHA Section 235 (ownership) project located in Chicago Heights, Illinois, which was entirely occupied by moderate-income black residents, and three racially integrated FHA Section 236 rental housing projects located just outside of Laurel, Maryland.

With the exception of race (17 percent of the new community subsidized housing residents versus 61 percent of those in the two conventional communities were black) subsidized housing residents in the new and conventional communities had generally similar characteristics. Sixty-two percent and 68 percent, respectively, had annual family incomes of less than $10,000 a year and 79 percent and 77 percent of the household heads were under age 40. Subsidized housing residents living in new communities had somewhat more formal education (33 percent versus 27 percent had attended college) and were somewhat more likely to be employed in white collar occupations (42 percent versus 37 percent). The recreational service systems in the five new communities with subsidized housing were much more effective in providing recreational resources than the systems in either of the two conventional communities. For example, recreational and open space acreage per 10,000 population ranged from 308 acres to 1328 acres in the five new communities versus 169 acres per 10,000 population in Laurel and 117 acres per 10,000 population in Chicago Heights. Per capita community recreational operating expenditures ranged from $17 to $57 in the five new communities versus only $3 in Laurel and $2 in Chicago Heights.

Table 6–5 summarizes new community subsidized housing residents' responses to recreational service systems in comparison with the responses of nonsubsidized housing residents living in the same new communities and the responses of subsidized housing residents living in the two conventional communities.

In the case of children's play areas and facilities, subsidized housing residents living in the new communities gave about the same ratings to areas near their homes for children's outdoor play as were given by nonsubsidized housing residents (73 percent and 77 percent, respectively, excellent or good) and much higher ratings than subsidized housing residents living in the conventional communities (73 percent versus 29 percent excellent or good). New community subsidized housing residents were more likely to be aware of a park or playground near their homes than either of the comparison groups (94 percent versus 36 percent for nonsubsidized new community residents and 94 percent versus 55 percent for residents of the conventional communities. They also were more likely to report that their children used such facilities frequently.

New community subsidized housing residents' participation rates in selected outdoor activities were comparable to those of residents of nonsubsidized new community housing and much higher than subsidized housing residents living in the conventional communities. Subsidized housing residents were less likely to play golf than nonsubsidized housing residents (8 percent versus 19 percent had played golf the previous year) and were also somewhat less likely to have played tennis (16 percent versus 22 percent). However, they were equally likely to have gone swimming (65 percent versus 63 percent) and to have walked for pleasure or hiked (64 percent versus 66 percent), and were somewhat more likely to have gone bicycling (48 percent versus 36 percent). Subsidized housing residents living in new communities were much more likely to have participated in all of these activities, except tennis, than subsidized housing residents living in the conventional communities.

In terms of satisfaction with the facilities used for recreational activities, new community subsidized housing residents tended to be as satisfied as the residents of nonsubsidized housing, although there were some differences. Subsidized housing residents were somewhat less satisfied with the golf and swimming facilities they used, were equally satisfied with walking and hiking facilities and somewhat more satisfied with tennis and bicycling facilities. In comparison with

Table 6–5. Subsidized Housing Residents' Responses to New and Conventional Community Recreational Service Systems

Indicator	Five New Communities[a]		Two Conventional Communities[b]
	Nonsubsidized Housing Residents	Subsidized Housing Residents	Subsidized Housing Residents
Child Play			
Rating of area near home for children's play (percent excellent or good)	77	73[e]	29
Perceive park or playground within one-eighth mile of home (percent)	36	94[e]	55
Children "usually" play at park or playground (percent)	11	16	8
Children play once a week or more often at park or playground (percent)	55	76[e]	54
Selected Activities			
Participation (percent one or more times annually)			
Golf	19[d]	8[e]	3
Swimming	63	65[e]	25
Tennis	22	16	12
Bicycling	36	48[d,e]	23
Walking and hiking	66	64[e]	30
Evaluation of facilities used most often (percent satisfied)			
Golf	81	67	88
Swimming	82	74	71
Tennis	78	89	78
Bicycling	83	88[e]	46
Walking and hiking	91	91[e]	61

Distance traveled to facility used most often			
Golf (median miles)	4.6	4.8	13.3
Swimming (median miles)	1.1	1.3	3.2
Tennis (median miles)	1.2	1.0	5.3
Bicycling (percent within one-eighth mile)	82	89	80
Walking and hiking (percent within one-eighth mile)	77	90[e]	60
Favorite Activities			
Mentioned most (percent)			
Swimming	10	17[d,e]	5
Walking and hiking	12	17[e]	6
Bicycling	5	9[e]	2
Fishing	3	7[d]	11
Gardening	7	5	5
Bowling	6	5	15[e]
Baseball, softball	2	5	7
Participation (percent 50+ times)			
All favorite activities	28	29[e]	16
Swimming[c]	14	20	f
Evaluation of facility used most often (percent satisfied)			
All favorite activities	83	80	77
Swimming[c]	86	80	f
Location of facility used most often (percent in community)			
All favorite activities	57	58[e]	47
Swimming[c]	86	71	f

Table 6–5 continued overleaf . . . .

Table 6—5. continued

Indicator	Five New Communities[a]		Two Conventional Communities[b]
	Nonsubsidized Housing Residents	Subsidized Housing Residents	Subsidized Housing Residents
Overall Evaluation of Community Recreational Facilities (percent)			
Excellent or good	83	83[e]	26
Average	10	10	22[e]
Below average or poor	7	7	52[e]
Satisfaction with Use of Leisure Time (percent)			
Completely satisfied	27	20	22
Satisfied	44	46[e]	19
Neutral or dissatisfied	29	34	59[e]
Sample size	973	274	187

[a]Respondents living in five new communities with subsidized housing: Columbia, Forest Park, Jonathan, Lake Havasu City and Reston. Includes special subsamples of subsidized housing residents.

[b]Because of an insufficient amount of subsidized housing in the regular conventional communities, residents of subsidized housing in two suburban conventional communities, Chicago Heights, Illinois and Laurel, Maryland were interviewed.

[c]There were an insufficient number of respondents (fewer than ten) to tabulate participation, satisfaction and location data for other individual favorite activities. Data refer to only those respondents who mentioned activity as their favorite out-of-home activity.

[d]Difference between new community subsidized housing and nonsubsidized housing respondents statistically significant at 0.05 level of confidence.

[e]Difference between new community and conventional community subsidized housing respondents statistically significant at 0.05 level of confidence.

[f]Insufficient number of respondents (fewer than ten) to tabulate.

subsidized housing residents living in the conventional communities, the most notable differences in satisfaction with facilities used were for bicycling and walking facilities. In both cases new community subsidized housing residents were significantly more likely to be satisfied (bicycling, 88 percent versus 46 percent; walking and hiking, 91 percent versus 61 percent) than were the conventional community subsidized housing residents.

In terms of distances traveled to the recreational facilities that were most often used there were no major differences between residents of new community subsidized and nonsubsidized housing. New community subsidized housing residents, on the other hand, traveled shorter distances to participate than the residents of the less planned conventional communities: golf (4.8 versus 13.3 median miles); swimming (1.3 versus 3.2 median miles); tennis (1.0 versus 5.3 median miles); walking and hiking (90 percent one-eighth mile or less versus 60 percent); and bicycling (88 percent one-eighth mile or less versus 46 percent). Thus, new community development may help to solve the often noted problem of poor people's isolation from outdoor recreational opportunities (see Lawrence Houston 1974).

Table 6-5 also indicates the favorite out-of-home activities mentioned by 5 percent or more of the new community subsidized housing respondents. Compared with residents of nonsubsidized housing living in new communities, subsidized housing residents were more likely to have mentioned swimming, walking and hiking, bicycling and fishing as their favorite activities. Participation rates for favorite out-of-home activities were equivalent among subsidized and nonsubsidized housing residents of new communities and both groups engaged in their favorite activities more frequently than subsidized housing residents who lived in the conventional communities. There was little difference between new and conventional community subsidized housing residents' satisfaction with the facilities they most often used for their favorite activities, but new community subsidized housing residents were more likely to have participated within their own communities.

The differences in recreational resources between the sample new and conventional communities were reflected in respondents' overall ratings of community recreational facilities. Eighty-three percent of both the new community subsidized and nonsubsidized housing respondents rated community recreational facilities as excellent or good. In contrast, only 26 percent of the subsidized housing respondents living in the conventional communities rated recreational facilities in their communities that highly. Also, although new community subsidized housing residents were somewhat less satisfied with the use of their leisure time than nonsubsidized housing residents (66 percent versus 71 percent were satisfied), they were much more likely to be satisfied than subsidized housing residents who lived in the conventional communities (66 percent versus 41 percent were satisfied).

To recapitulate these findings, the data clearly show that new community recreational service systems were meeting the needs of subsidized housing residents as well as they were meeting the needs of residents not living in subsidized housing. Compared to alternative suburban environments available to persons who qualified for subsidized housing, new community recreational service systems were far superior, whether gauged by recreational resources or by residents' participation in recreational activities, travel behavior and evaluations of facilities.

SUMMARY

This chapter has evaluated new community recreational service systems from the perspectives of five population target groups: young adults, elderly persons, women, blacks and subsidized housing residents. New community recreational service systems met the needs of each of these groups as well as or better than recreational service systems in less planned conventional suburban communities. Women and subsidized housing residents' responses to recreational service systems were equivalent to those of men and nonsubsidized housing residents. However, the findings for young adults, elderly persons and blacks suggest several areas which should be given greater attention in new community development.

Young adults (age 14 to 20) were much less satisfied with recreational facilities provided in new communities than were adult residents and did not rate highly or even use teen recreational facilities. In part, their discontent with recreational facilities in new communities stemmed from a perceived lack of urban activity places, such as entertainment facilities, restaurants catering to young adults and shopping facilities. Young adults used, and were satisfied with, selected outdoor recreational facilities provided in new communities, but the data clearly show that a recreational service system geared to the needs of adults and children will not be rated highly by young adults.

Elderly residents (age 65+) rated new community recreational facilities higher and were more satisfied with the use of their leisure time than were younger residents. However, age-segregated retirement new communities with elderly populations that were adequate to support recreational facilities and programs geared to older persons provided better leisure environments for the elderly than were available in new communities. Compared with the elderly residents living in the new communities, those who lived in age-segregated retirement communities were much more likely to participate in their favorite out-of-home activities in their own communities and to be more satisfied with the facilities they used. In addition, they gave much higher ratings to community recreational facilities and were more satisfied with their use of leisure time. These findings suggest that new communities would be justified in experimenting with neighborhoods and villages designed exclusively for older persons as component parts of otherwise age-integrated new community development projects.

Although new communities met black residents' needs more effectively than less planned, predominantly black sections of conventional suburban communities, blacks tended to be less satisfied with new community recreational service systems than nonblack residents. Blacks reported lower levels of satisfaction with facilities used for their favorite out-of-home activities, gave lower overall ratings to community recreational facilities and were more often dissatisfied with the ways in which they spent their leisure time. Like young adults, blacks appeared to desire more action-oriented leisure facilities, such as commercial entertainment and also expressed interest in activities such as bowling and basketball which most new community recreational service systems did not emphasize. It may be, however, that as the sample new communities mature and become better able to financially support commercial recreational and entertainment facilities, blacks will be better able to satisfy their leisure interests.

✼ *Chapter 7*

Planning New Community
Recreational Service Systems

To be most effective recreational facility and service planning in new communities should be based on a thorough
understanding of residents' recreational behavior and their
attitudes toward recreational resources. This chapter adds to our
knowledge of these subjects by analyzing the influences of residents'
characteristics and the characteristics of recreational facilities on
recreational participation and satisfaction with facilities used for outdoor activities. In the first section of the chapter, children's use of
parks and playgrounds is examined. The chapter then proceeds with
analyses of three outdoor activities: golf, swimming and tennis. For
each activity attention is first devoted to explaining residents' participation (versus nonparticipation) in them. Next, for those new
community residents who engaged in each activity, the analysis examines factors associated with the frequency of participation over a
twelve-month period. In particular, attention is devoted to evaluating
the relative influence of residents' and facility characteristics on participation rates and to identifying facility characteristics that are
associated with greater rates of participation. The analysis of each
activity concludes with an examination of the relationship between
various facility characteristics and participants' reported satisfaction
with the facilities they used.

Recreational planning for new communities must consider not
only residents' use of and satisfaction with various facilities, but also
their evaluation of the recreational system as a whole. In particular,
planners need to know which aspects of the recreational system are
most important to new community residents before they can make

intelligent decisions about ordering priorities and phasing the development of recreational facilities and programs. The final section of the chapter examines four questions related to residents' overall evaluations of new community recreational facilities. First, as presently developed, are recreational facilities rated more highly by some types of residents than others? In other words, whose needs are best being met by new community recreational systems? Second, are higher ratings of recreational facilities given by those residents who most often participate in particular recreational activities? Third, are higher overall ratings of recreational facilities more strongly associated with satisfaction with some recreational facilities than with others? Fourth, which objective characteristics of community recreational resources are most strongly associated with higher overall ratings of recreational facilities? Answers to these questions should provide useful guidelines for planning recreational service systems.

PARKS AND PLAYGROUNDS

In Chapter 5 it was noted that although new community children most often played in their own or a neighbor's yard, a significant proportion of parents (38 percent) reported that their children played at a nearby park or playground once a week or more often. As shown in Table 7–1, household characteristics and both the accessibility and availability of parks and playgrounds were associated with the frequency of children's use of these facilities. For example, children living in households with three or more children between the ages of six and eleven were likely to play more often at parks and playgrounds than other children (62 percent did so once a week or more often). This was also true of children who lived in townhouses and rental units. In these latter cases, parks and tot lots were likely to be included in the design of multi-unit projects, so that they were more accessible. Also, children living in multi-unit projects were the least likely to have individual yard space in which to play. As a result, their use of parks and playgrounds was much higher than for children who lived in single-family detached ownership units.

The strongest influence on children's use of parks and playgrounds was the relative accessibility of these facilities. Sixty-seven percent of the children who lived within one-eighth mile of the park or playground they most often used and 61 percent of those who lived within one-eighth mile of the nearest park or playground played there once a week or more often. As the distance between children's homes and the nearest available park or playground increased, the frequency of their use decreased. For example, among children who

Table 7–1. Measures of Association between Household Characteristics, Characteristics of Community Recreational Facilities and Children's Use of Parks and Playgrounds[a]

Variables	Measures of Association		Direction
	Chi-square Significance Level	*Gamma*	*Children were more likely to play once a week or more often at a park or playground if: (percent who played once a week or more often)*
Household Characteristics			
Race	NS	.006	all households (38%
Family income	NS	-.01	—
Children under six years old	NS	-.07	—
Children age six to eleven years old	.001	.20	three or more (62%)
Type of dwelling unit	.004	.22	townhouse (58%)
Tenure	NS	.15	rent (46%)
Accessibility of Parks and Playgrounds			
Distance to nearest park or playground	.001	-.38	under one-eighth mile (61%)
Distance to park or playground most often used	.001	-.34	under one-eighth mile (67%)
Availability of Parks and Playgrounds			
Number of playgrounds in community	.001	.17	eight or more (47%)
Number of tot lots in community	.001	.24	eight or more (46%)
Sample size	846		

NS = Not significant at 0.05 level of confidence.

[a]These analyses were performed with data from respondents living in thirteen nonfederally assisted new communities who had children under age twelve living in their households and who were aware of nearby parks and playgrounds.

lived between one-eighth and one-fourth mile of the nearest park or playground, 48 percent played there once a week or more often. Among those who lived more than a fourth of a mile from the nearest park or playground, only 28 percent played there at least once a week.

In the case of distance to the parks and playgrounds that parents reported their children used, children living up to one-half mile from a facility tended to use it frequently. Sixty-seven percent of the children who lived within one-eighth mile of the park or playground they used played there once a week or more often, while 49 percent of those who lived between one-eighth and one-half mile from the park or playground used played there that often. However, only 26 percent of those who had to travel more than one-half mile played at parks and playgrounds once a week or more often. The accessibility and availability of park and playground facilities were closely related. As shown in Table 7–1, communities which had more playgrounds and more tot lots had a higher proportion of children who frequently played at these facilities.

GOLF AND GOLF COURSES

Participation versus Nonparticipation

Table 7–2 summarizes the relationships between respondents' personal and household characteristics, community characteristics and participation in golf. Overall, 25 percent of the new community respondents participated in golf. However, participation was significantly greater among males (34 percent), persons who had graduated from college (29 percent), and those who had family incomes of $25,000 a year or more (32 percent). As noted in the previous chapter, black residents of new communities were much less likely than nonblack residents to participate in golf (8 percent versus 25 percent). This also tended to be true for younger residents under 25 years old (18 percent participated) and elderly residents age 65 and over (14 percent participated). Although these findings indicate that golf is an activity of residents with higher socioeconomic status, it should be noted that variations in the proportion of participants among most population groups living in new communities were not large.

Participation in golf was also associated with two community characteristics. Participation was greater among residents who lived within one mile of the nearest golf course (30 percent of these respondents reported playing golf), and a slightly higher proportion (27 percent) of the residents living in communities with more hours of sunshine reported playing golf during the previous year. Communities whose recreational agencies offered supervised golf activities had a somewhat lower than average proportion of residents who reported participating in this sport.

Frequency of Participation

Twenty-five percent of those respondents who reported participating in golf had done so frequently (50 or more times) during the previous year. Although blacks participated in golf less than whites, blacks who did participate were more often frequent golfers (38 percent). See Table 7−3. Frequent golfers also tended to be older (66 percent of the golfers over age fifty-five were frequent participants), not employed (70 percent were frequent participants), with family incomes between $15,000 and $24,999 (70 percent were frequent participants), and with no children in their household (31 percent were frequent participants). In sum, golf is a sport that attracted the most frequent participation from new community residents who were in later stages of their life cycle, affluent and who did not have to be concerned with the time this sport took away from family life and children.

By looking at just those respondents who participated in golf, it is possible to test the association between frequent participation and the characteristics of the golf courses golfers reported using. Distance traveled to play golf had a strong influence on frequent participation up to one mile from a golfer's home. Forty-five percent of the golfers who lived within a mile of the course they used were frequent participants. After one mile the proportion of frequent golfers dropped, but there was little relationship between additional distances traveled to play golf and the proportion of golfers who played golf frequently. The location of the golf course used also had an influence on participation. Frequent golfers were somewhat more likely to use courses within rather than outside of their own communities.

Several characteristics of the golf courses used were associated with frequent participation. The proportion of frequent participants was higher for those golfers who played at shorter golf courses (5000 to 5999 yards, 35%); courses with longer operating hours (12 hours a day or more, 33 percent); and at private golf clubs (39 percent) which had organized social activities, locker rooms, club houses, wet bars, driving ranges and night lighting. Of these golf course characteristics, courses with night lighting had the strongest association with frequent participation (37 percent of the golfers who used such courses were frequent participants). There was also an association

Table 7-2.   Measures of Association between Respondents' Personal and Household Characteristics, Characteristics of Community Recreational Facilities and Participation in Golf[a]

Variables	Measures of Association		Direction
	Chi-square Significance Level	Gamma	Respondents were more (less) likely to participate in golf if: (percent who participated)
Personal and Household Characteristics			all respondents (25%)
Race	.001	-.65	white (25%); black (8%)
Sex	.001	-.49	male (34%)
Age	.007	-.01	(under 25, 18%); 65+, 14%)
Education	.001	.21	college graduate (29%)
Marital status	NS	-.08	—
Employment of respondent	.001	-.35	full time (31%)
Family income	.001	.25	higher ($25,000+, 32%)
Number of children in household	.05	-.09	none (27%)
Children under six years old	NS	-.03	—
Children age six to eleven	NS	-.07	—
Type of dwelling unit	NS	.03	—
Tenure	NS	.04	—
Length of residence in community	NS	-.06	—

Community Characteristics

Distance to nearest golf course	.02	−.08	under one mile (30%)
Supervised golf program offered by community recreation agency	.04	−.10	no program (26%)
Climate	.003	.14	more hours of sunshine (3000+, 27%)[b]
Sample size	2,564		

NS = Not significant at 0.05 level of confidence.

[a]These analyses were performed with data from respondents who lived in thirteen nonfederally assisted new communities.

[b]Communities with 3000+ hours of sunshine in 1972 included: Foster City, Irvine, Laguna Niguel, Lake Havasu City, North Palm Beach, Valencia and Westlake Village.

Table 7–3. Measures of Association between Participants' Personal and Household Characteristics, Characteristics of Golf Courses Used and Frequent Participation in Golf[a]

Variables	Measures of Association		Direction
	Chi-square Significance Level	Gamma	Participants were more likely to be frequent participants (50+ times) in golf if: (percent frequent participants)
Personal and Household Characteristics			all participants (25%)
Favorite out-of-home activity is golf	NS	−.01	—
Race	NS	.59	black (38%)
Sex	NS	−.01	—
Age	.001	.38	55+ (66%)
Education	NS	−.001	—
Marital status	NS	.007	—
Employment of respondent	.001	.29	not employed (40%)
Family income	.002	.16	$15,000–$24,999 (40%)
Number of children	.001	−.25	none (31%)
Children under six years old	.001	−.25	none (26%)
Children age six to eleven years old	.001	−.26	none (25%)
Type of dwelling unit	.001	.27	apartment (31%)
Tenure	NS	−.03	—
Length of residence of community	NS	.01	—
Characteristics of Golf Course Used			
Location within or outside of community	.001	−.26	within community (29%)
Distance to golf course used	.001	−.14	under one mile (45%)

Ownership	.001	.23	private club (39%)
Operating hours	.08	.21	12+ hours per day (33%)
Length of course	.01	.10	5000–5999 yards (35%)
Organized social activities	.03	−.21	yes (28%)
Facilities at site:			
Locker room	NS	−.17	yes (25%)
Club house	NS	−.24	yes (25%)
Snack bar	NS	−.10	—
Wet bar	.04	−.33	yes (25%)
Restaurant	NS	.03	—
Driving range	NS	−.17	yes (25%)
Night lighting	.05	−.21	yes (34%)
Swimming pool	NS	−.06	—
Tennis courts	.001	−.39	yes (37%)
Landscaping of site	NS	−.23	generous (25%)
Maintenance of site	NS	.001	—
Satisfaction with Golf Course Used			
Satisfaction with golf course	.03	−.12	completely satisfied (52%)
Climate			
Hours of sunshine	.001	.27	more hours of sunshine (3000+, 28%)
Sample size	639		

NS = Not significant at 0.05 level of confidence.
[a] Data from golfers living in thirteen nonfederally assisted new communities.

between more generous landscaping of the golf course used and frequent participation in golf. Climate affected the frequency of participation as well as participation versus nonparticipation, although its influence was not great. In those new communities with the most hours of sunshine (3000+ hours), 28 percent of the golfers were frequent participants. Finally, golfers who were completely satisfied with the facility they most often used tended to participate frequently (52 percent).

In order to evaluate the relative contributions of golfers' personal and household characteristics, satisfaction with the golf course used and characteristics of the golf course used to frequent participation, a multiple regression analysis was performed. Overall, the variables listed in Table 7−3 explained 25 percent of the variance in the frequency of participation among golfers. Variables were entered into the regression equation sequentially by type of variable to test the importance of each set of variables listed in Table 7−3. Of the 25 percent of the variance in participation explained, golfers' personal and household characteristics accounted for 16.2 percent, satisfaction with the golf course used most often, 0.6 percent, and characteristics of the golf course used, 8.2 percent. The five variables with the strongest influence on frequent participation, as gauged by the amount of change in participation produced by a standardized change in a variable (beta coefficients), were: (1) ownership of the course used most often (private); (2) availability of a club house at the course used most often (available); (3) employment status of the golfer (retired); (4) location of the course used most often (in the community); and (5) availability of a driving range at the course used most often (available).

Satisfaction with Golf Courses Used

Table 7−4 summarizes the associations between characteristics of the golf courses used by golfers and their reported level of satisfaction with these courses. Overall, 45 percent of the golfers interviewed were completely satisfied with the golf courses they most often used. Complete satisfaction was lower among those golfers who used publicly owned courses (24 percent were completely satisfied) than among those who used commercial or private courses. Also, golfers were more likely to be completely satisfied if the course they most often used was within their community, if the course had green fees of $5 or more, sponsored social activities for members and if it was generously landscaped and well maintained. However, there was very little relationship between the types of support facilities at the golf courses used and reported levels of satisfaction. Although it was

Table 7–4. Measures of Association between Characteristics of Golf Courses Used and Satisfaction with Courses[a]

| Characteristics of Golf Course Used | Measures of Association | | Direction |
	Chi-square Significance Level	Gamma	Participants were more likely to be completely satisfied with the golf course used if: (percent completely satisfied)
All participants			45% completely satisfied
Location within or outside of community	NS	.14	within community (50%)
Distance to course	NS	.05	—
Ownership of course	.001	−.25	commercial (55%); private (50%); public (24%)
Greens fee	.03	−.35	$5 or more (52%)
Length of course	NS	.004	—
Organized golf activities	NS	.07	—
Organized social activities	NS	−.24	yes (54%)
Facilities at site:			
Locker room	NS	.05	—
Club house	NS	.10	—
Snack bar	NS	−.33	no (62%)
Wet bar	.02	.10	yes (47%)
Restaurant	NS	−.0001	—
Driving range	NS	.09	—
Night lighting	NS	−.02	—
Swimming pool	.001	−.34	no (48%)
Tennis courts	NS	.06	—
Landscaping of site	.04	.43	generous (47%)
Maintenance of site	NS	.44	well maintained (47%)
Climate			
Hours of sunshine	.03	−.19	more hours of sunshine
Sample size		639	

NS = Not significant at 0.05 level of confidence.

[a]These analyses were performed with data from golfers living in thirteen nonfederally assisted new communities.

hypothesized that satisfaction would be greater at golf courses that offered facilities for other activities besides golf (which could be used by other members of a golfer's family), the association between courses with swimming pools and tennis courts and satisfaction with the course was either not significant (tennis courts) or in an opposite direction than hypothesized (swimming pools).

A multiple regression analysis of satisfaction with the golf course used most often indicated that golfers personal and household characteristics together with the golf course characteristics enumerated in Table 7−4 explained 19 percent of the variance in satisfaction. However, personal characteristics accounted for only 2 percent of the variance, while golf course characteristics accounted for 17 percent. When personal and household characteristics of golfers were controlled in the regression analysis, the five variables that contributed most to explaining satisfaction were: (1) the availability of a swimming pool at the course used (unavailable); (2) length of the course (longer); (3) landscaping of the site (generous); (4) distance traveled to the course (longer); and (5) availability of a wet bar (available).

SWIMMING AND SWIMMING FACILITIES

Participation versus Nonparticipation

As illustrated in Table 7−5, participation in swimming, as with golf, was associated with race. Fifty-eight percent of the new community respondents participated in this activity, including 59 percent of the white but only 38 percent of the black respondents. In addition, the other two personal and household characteristics that had the strongest influence on participation in swimming were age (70 percent of the respondents under twenty-five years old versus only 24 percent of those over age sixty-five participated) and the presence in the household of children in the six to eleven age bracket (69 percent of these respondents reported going swimming). Participation in swimming was also reported by a significantly higher proportion of respondents who had attended graduate school, worked part time, had high family incomes, rented their homes and who had lived in the community three years or less.

Participation in swimming was moderately associated with the accessibility of swimming facilities. Sixty-three percent of the respondents who lived within one-half mile of the nearest available swimming facility, versus 58 percent of all respondents, reported swimming during the previous year. The availability of a supervised swimming program offered by a community recreation agency was associated with somewhat greater participation (60 percent). Climate had a very slight effect on the proportion of respondents who went swimming.

Frequency of Participation

Thirty-four percent of the respondents who reported that they went swimming during the previous year had done so frequently (50 or more times). As shown in Table 7−6, the swimmers' characteristic with the strongest association with frequent swimming was the level of preference for this outdoor activity. Fifty-eight percent of the swimmers who reported that swimming was their favorite out-of-home activity participated frequently. The proportion of frequent swimmers was also higher among participants with two or more children living in their household (46 percent), family incomes between $15,000 and $24,999 (45 percent), persons who were retired or unemployed (43 percent), apartment residents (39 percent) and single persons (37 percent). As was not the case with frequent participation in golf, a higher proportion of white swimmers (35 percent) participated frequently than did black swimmers (24 percent).

The accessibility of the nearest swimming facility had a strong effect on frequent participation for facilities up to one-eighth mile from swimmers' homes. Fifty-three percent of the swimmers who lived that close to a swimming facility were frequent swimmers. After one-eighth mile the proportion of frequent swimmers dropped sharply to 39 percent of the swimmers who lived between one-eighth and one-quarter mile, 28 percent of those who lived between one-quarter and one-half mile, and 42 percent for those who lived between one-half and one mile of the nearest available swimming facility. After one mile the proportion of frequent swimmers dropped steadily to only 21 percent of the swimmers who lived five or more miles from the nearest facility. In addition a higher proportion (38 percent) of swimmers who used a facility within their own communities swam frequently during the previous year.

Frequent participation in swimming was moderately associated with the ownership and type of swimming facility most often used. Swimmers who used quasi-public homes association or multi-unit project swimming facilities tended to be more frequent swimmers (41 percent), than swimmers who used public, private or commercial swimming facilities. Also, the proportion of frequent swimmers was higher for those who used lake bathing beaches (49 percent) and outdoor swimming pools (39 percent) than for those who most often used ocean beaches or indoor pools.

A number of characteristics of individual swimming facilities were also associated with frequent participation. A higher proportion of

Table 7-5. Measures of Association between Respondents' Personal and Household Characteristics, Characteristics of Community Recreational Facilities and Participation in Swimming[a]

Variables	Measures of Association		Direction
	Chi-square Significance Level	Gamma	Respondents were more likely to participate in swimming if: (percent who participated)
Personal and Household Characteristics			all respondents (58%)
Race	.001	-.38	white (59%); black (38%)
Sex	NS	-.03	—
Age	.001	-.33	younger (under age 25, 70%; 65+, 24%)
Education	.001	.26	graduate school (67%)
Marital status	NS	-.07	—
Employment of respondent	.001	-.12	part time (67%)
Family income	.001	.09	higher ($25,000+, 62%)
Number of children in household	.001	.20	two or more (64%)
Children under six years old	.001	.19	one or more (65%)
Children age six to eleven years old	.001	.32	one or more (69%)
Type of dwelling unit	NS	.03	—
Tenure	.001	.17	rent (64%)
Length of residence in community	.001	-.13	three years or less (61%)
Community Characteristics			
Swimming facility available in neighborhood[b]	.001	-.17	yes (62%)

Distance to nearest available swimming facility	.001	−.08	under one-half mile (63%); 5+ miles (58%)
Supervised swimming program offered by community recreation agency	.02	.09	supervised program (60%)
Climate[c]	.001	.11	more hours of sunshine (3000+, 61%)
Sample size	2488		

NS = Not significant at 0.05 level of confidence.

[a] These analyses were performed with data from respondents who lived in thirteen nonfederally assisted new communities.

[b] Residents' neighborhoods were defined as the area within a half-mile radius of their homes, or a smaller area if bordered on one or more sides by a major thoroughfare, body of water, undeveloped land or the community boundary.

[c] Communities with 3000+ hours of sunshine in 1972 included: Foster City, Irvine, Laguna Niguel, Lake Havasu City, North Palm Beach, Valencia and Westlake Village.

Table 7–6. Measures of Association between Participants' Personal and Household Characteristics, Characteristics of Swimming Facilities Used and Frequent Participation in Swimming[a]

| Variables | Measures of Association | | Direction |
	Chi-square Significance Level	Gamma	*Participants were more likely to be frequent participants (50+ times) in swimming if: (percent frequent participants)*
Personal and Household Characteristics			
Favorite out-of-home activity is swimming	.001	–.52	all participants (34%)
Race	NS	–.19	yes (58%)
Sex	.001	.30	white (35%); black (24%)
Age	.001	.11	men (27%); women (40%)
Education	NS	.005	65 or older (61%)
Marital status	.05	.11	—
Employment of respondent	.001	.22	single (37%)
Family income	.002	.08	not employed (43%)
Number of children in household	.008	–.11	$15,000–$24,999 (45%)
Children under six years old	.001	–.16	two or more (46%)
Children age six to eleven years old	NS	.03	none (36%)
Type of dwelling unit	.03	.14	—
Tenure	NS	.07	apartment (39%)
Length of residence in community	NS	–.05	—

Characteristics of Swimming Facility Used

Location within or outside of community	.001	-.34	within community (38%)
Distance to swimming facility used	.001	-.07	under one-eighth mile (53%)
Ownership	.001	.19	quasi-public homes association/ multi-unit project (41%)
Type of facility	.001	-.17	lake bathing beach (49%); outdoor pool (39%)
Operating season	.001	.29	over six months (42%)
Operating hours	NS	-.05	—
Swimming instruction	.003	.22	no (42%)
Organized swimming activities	.001	.24	no (41%)
Organized social activities	NS	-.07	yes (37%)
Facilities at site:			
Wading pool	.001	.26	no (42%)
Diving pool	.003	.22	no (39%)
Heated pool	NS	-.11	yes (40%)
Night lighting	NS	.04	—
Bath house	.03	.20	no (42%)
Club house	NS	-.08	yes (37%)
Snack bar	.001	.13	no (36%)
Wet bar	.001	-.36	yes (56%)
Golf course	.001	-.26	yes (36%)
Tennis courts	.02	-.11	yes (42%)
Landscaping of site	.04	-.05	minimal (38%)
Maintenance of site	NS	.23	inadequate (49%)

Table 7–6 continued overleaf . . .

Table 7–6. continued

Variables	Measures of Association		Direction
	Chi-square Significance Level	Gamma	Participants were more likely to be frequent participants (50+ times) in swimming if: (percent frequent participants)
Satisfaction with the Swimming Facilities Used			
Satisfaction with swimming facility	.001	–.20	completely satisfied (38%)
Climate			
Hours of sunshine	.001	.26	more hours of sunshine (40%)
Sample size	1439		

NS = Not significant at 0.05 level of confidence.

[a]These analyses were performed with data from swimmers living in thirteen nonfederally assisted new communities.

swimmers swam frequently if the facility they most often used was open six months a year or more, if the water was heated, if a club house was available, if a wet bar was available and if the site included a golf course or tennis courts. On the other hand, more frequent swimmers tended to use facilities that did not have wading or diving pools, bath houses and, surprisingly, where landscaping and maintenance were low. In part this may have been due to the tendency of some frequent swimmers to use lake bathing beaches, which might account for the lack of relationship between landscaping, maintenance and frequent participation. Homes association and multi-unit project pools were likely to be heated and to have an adjacent club house.

The sociability function of frequent participation in swimming is also indicated by the findings reported in Table 7-6. While the availability of swimming instruction and organized swimming activities at the swimming facilities that were used most often were associated with less frequent participation, the availability of organized social activities had an opposite effect. The proportion of frequent swimmers was somewhat greater (37 percent) among those who most often used swimming facilities that sponsored social affairs for their users.

As with frequent participation in golf, swimmers who were completely satisfied with the facilities they used most often tended to swim somewhat more frequently. This was also true for hours of sunshine. Again, the highest proportion of frequent swimmers (40 percent) were found in communities with 3000 or more hours of sunshine.

The relative contribution of each of the variables listed in Table 7-6 to an explanation of variation in the frequency of swimming was evaluated by means of a multiple regression analysis. Twenty-four percent of the variance in participation was explained, 5 percent by participants personal and household characteristics, 2 percent by satisfaction with the facilities they used most often and 17 percent by facility characteristics. The six most important variables in explaining frequent participation in swimming, as gauged by their beta coefficients, were: (1) distance traveled to the facility most often used (shorter); (2) type of facility (lake beach); (3) operating season (longer); (4) number of children between the ages of six and eleven in the household (more); (5) age of the swimmer (younger); and (6) satisfaction with the swimming facility used (higher).

Satisfaction with Swimming Facilities Used

Among all new community swimmers interviewed, satisfaction with the swimming facilities they used was very high. Sixty-three percent of the swimmers reported complete satisfaction. Swimmers who used pools within their community were somewhat more likely to be completely satisfied with the facilities they used than were swimmers who used facilities outside of their communities. See Table 7—7. Also, a higher proportion of swimmers who lived closer (within one-eighth mile) of the swimming facility they most often used were completely satisfied. While frequent participation in swimming was most common among swimmers who used homes association and multi-unit project pools, the highest level of satisfaction was reported for commercial swimming facilities (94 percent completely satisfied) and swimming facilities operated by private clubs (70 percent completely satisfied).

Swimmers were most satisfied with swimming facilities that provided organized social activities, while the provision of swimming instruction and organized swimming activities were not related to satisfaction. Swimmers were also somewhat more satisfied with the facility they most often used if it included a diving pool, heated water, night lighting, bath house, club house, snack bar, wet bar and if the site was generously landscaped. Again, climate made a difference. A much higher proportion of swimmers who lived in communities with more hours of sunshine (3000+ hours) reported complete satisfaction with the swimming facilities they used.

Multiple regression analysis of satisfaction with swimming facilities used indicated that these variables together with swimmers' personal and household characteristics explained 15 percent of the variance in satisfaction. Five percent of the variance was explained by personal and household characteristics (swimmers who lived in households without children under six years old and who owned their homes were most satisfied) and 10 percent was explained by the characteristics of facilities and climate. The five variables that contributed the most to explaining variation in satisfaction with swimming facilities, after controlling for swimmers' personal and household characteristics, were: (1) climate (more hours of sunshine); (2) distance traveled to facilities (shorter); (3) heated water (available); (4) indoor or outdoor facility (indoor); and (5) ownership of the facility (commercial).

TENNIS AND TENNIS FACILITIES

Participation versus Nonparticipation

Twenty-one percent of the new community respondents had participated in tennis during the previous year. The strongest personal characteristic influencing participation in this sport was age. See Table 7—8. Thirty-nine percent of the respondents under twenty-five years old had played tennis versus only 3 percent of those who were fifty-five years old or older. As with golf and swimming, a much higher proportion of white respondents (21 percent) than black respondents (11 percent) had participated in tennis. Tennis players also tended to have higher socioeconomic status characteristics than non-tennis players. Higher proportions of tennis players were found among respondents who had attended graduate school (30 percent) and who had family incomes of $25,000 or more (27 percent). Corresponding to their younger age and stage of life, a higher proportion of respondents with children under six years old in their household (28 percent), who lived in apartments (25 percent), who rented their homes (29 percent), and who had lived in their community three years or less (26 percent) reported participating in tennis.

Participation in tennis was associated with community characteristics as well as respondents' personal and household characteristics. For example, 40 percent of the respondents who lived within one-eighth mile of the nearest tennis court reported participating in this sport. In contrast, 27 percent of those who lived between one-eighth and one-fourth mile of the nearest court participated, while participation among respondents who lived farther from the nearest court ranged from a high of 20 percent among those who lived between one-half and one mile to 18 percent of those who lived more than five miles from the nearest available court. Greater participation was also associated with the availability of a tennis court within the respondents' neighborhoods, but not with the availability of supervised tennis programs offered by community recreation agencies. As was not the case with golf and swimming, there was no association between climate (hours of sunshine) and the proportion of respondents who reported playing tennis.

Frequency of Participation

Table 7–9 summarizes the associations between tennis players' personal and household characteristics, characteristics of the tennis facilities used and frequent (50 or more times during the previous year) participation in tennis. As with swimming, frequent participation in tennis was strongly associated with tennis players' preferences among recreational activities. While 22 percent of all tennis players reported participating frequently during the previous year, 57 percent of those who said that tennis was their favorite out-of-home activity participated that often. Although younger persons were more likely to have participated one or more times in tennis, the highest proportion of frequent participants was among tennis players in the forty-five to fifty-four age bracket (36 percent). Reflecting

Table 7–7. Measures of Association between Characteristics of Swimming Facilities Used and Satisfaction with Facilities[a]

Characteristics of Swimming Facility Used	Measures of Association		Direction — Participants were more likely to be completely satisfied with the swimming facility used if: (percent completely satisfied)
	Chi-square Significance Level	Gamma	
All participants			60% completely satisfied[b]
Location within or outside of community	.001	.33	within community (63%)
Distance to facility	.001	.20	within one-eighth mile (74%)
Ownership	NS	-.12	commercial (94%); private club (70%)
Type of facility	NS	-.03	—
Operating season	NS	-.12	seven to twelve months (63%)
Operating hours	.001	-.47	12+ hours per day (76%)
Swimming instruction	NS	-.11	no (63%)
Organized swimming activities	.03	-.18	no (65%)
Organized social activities	.04	.15	yes (63%)
Facilities at site:			
Wading pool	NS	-.04	—
Diving pool	NS	.08	yes (62%)
Heated water	NS	.13	yes (64%)
Night lighting	.007	.21	yes (65%)
Bath house	NS	.13	yes (61%)
Club house	.001	.27	yes (67%)
Snack bar	NS	.14	yes (65%)
Wet bar	NS	.20	yes (68%)
Golf course	NS	.09	—
Tennis courts	NS	.02	—

Landscaping of site	NS	.14	generous (62%)
Maintenance of site	NS	.01	—
Climate	.001		
Hours of sunshine		−.34	more hours of sunshine (3000+, 68%)
Sample size		1519	

NS = Not significant at 0.05 level of confidence.

[a] These analyses were performed with data from respondents living in thirteen nonfederally assisted new communities.

[b] Although 63 percent of all swimmers interviewed were completely satisfied with the swimming facilities they used, among swimmers who used those facilities for which facility characteristic data were collected, 60 percent reported complete satisfaction.

Table 7–8. Measures of Association between Respondents' Personal and Household Characteristics, Characteristics of Community Recreational Facilities and Participation in Tennis[a]

Variables	Measures of Association		Direction
	Chi-square Significance Level	Gamma	Respondents were more likely to participate in tennis if: (percent who participated)
Personal and Household Characteristics			all respondents (21%)
Race	.02	–.15	white (21%); black (11%)
Sex	NS	–.01	—
Age	.001	–.50	younger (under age 25, 39%; 55+, 3%)
Education	.001	.39	graduate school (30%)
Marital status	NS	.04	—
Employment of respondent	.001	–.17	part time (26%)
Family income	.001	.16	higher ($25,000+, 27%)
Number of children in household	NS	.06	—
Children under six years old	.001	.25	one or more (28%)
Children age six to eleven years old	.04	.11	one or more (27%)
Type of dwelling unit	NS	.12	apartment (25%)
Tenure	.001	.26	rent (29%)
Length of residence in community	.001	–.30	three years or less (26%)

Community Characteristics		
Tennis courts available in neighborhood[b]	.001	yes (28%)
Distance to nearest available tennis court	.001	under one-eighth mile (40%)
Supervised tennis program offered by community recreation agency	.001	no program (25%)
Climate	NS	—
Sample size	2574	

NS = Not significant at 0.05 level of confidence.

[a]These analyses were performed with data from respondents who lived in thirteen nonfederally assisted new communities.

[b]Residents' neighborhoods were defined as the area within a half-mile radius of their homes, or a smaller area if bordered on one or more sides by a major thoroughfare, body of water, undeveloped land or the community boundary.

Table 7–9. Measures of Association between Participants' Personal and Household Characteristics, Characteristics of Tennis Facilities Used and Frequent Participation in Tennis[a]

Characteristics of Tennis Facilities Used	*Measures of Association*		*Direction*
	Chi-square Significance Level	*Gamma*	*Participants were more likely to be frequent participants (50+ times) in tennis if: (percent frequent participants)*
			all participants (22%)
Personal and Household Characteristics			
Favorite out-of-home activity is tennis	.001	−.78	yes (57%)
Race	NS	−.06	—
Sex	NS	.009	—
Age	NS	.16	45 to 54 years old (36%)
Education	NS	.04	—
Marital status	NS	.04	—
Employment of respondent	.05	.18	not employed (29%)
Family income	.04	.20	$25,000+ (32%)
Number of children	NS	−.06	—
Children under six years old	NS	−.11	none (23%)
Children age six to eleven years old	NS	.07	one or more (24%)
Type of dwelling unit	NS	.01	—
Tenure	NS	−.04	—
Length of residence in community	NS	−.002	—
Characteristics of Tennis Facility Used			
Location within or outside of community	.001	−.29	within community (28%)

Distance to tennis facility used	NS	-.15	under one-eighth mile (35%)
Use fee	NS	.25	yes (39%)
Operating season	NS	-.06	—
Operating hours	NS	.15	12+ hours per day (29%)
Lighted courts	.001	.36	yes (34%)
Tennis instruction available	NS	-.002	—
Organized tennis activities	NS	.05	—
Organized social activities	.001	-.48	yes (41%)
Facilities at site:			
Pro shop	.005	-.39	yes (39%)
Locker room	.001	-.56	yes (44%)
Club house	.001	-.50	yes (40%)
Snack bar	.001	-.59	yes (48%)
Wet bar	.001	-.56	yes (50%)
Swimming pool	.009	-.29	yes (36%)
Golf course	NS	-.18	yes (31%)
Landscaping of site	.02	-.28	generous (34%)
Maintenance of site	NS	-.20	well-maintained (24%)
Satisfaction with Tennis Facility Used			
Satisfaction with facility	.02	-.19	completely satisfied (54%)
Climate			
Hours of sunshine	.001	.27	more hours of sunshine (3000+, 29%)
Sample size	547		

NS = Not significant at the 0.05 level of confidence.
[a]These analyses were performed with data from respondents living in thirteen nonfederally assisted new communities.

their stage of life, tennis players who participated frequently tended to have no children under six years old living in their households, but to have one or more children between the ages of six and eleven. Frequent participation in tennis was also proportionately greater among tennis players who were not employed and who had family incomes of $25,000 or more per year.

As with golf and swimming, frequent participation was associated with characteristics of the facilities tennis players most often used. Higher proportions of tennis players who used a tennis court within their own community (28 percent) and a court within one-eighth mile of their homes (35 percent) were frequent participants than tennis players who had to travel farther to the courts they most often used. The proportion of frequent participants in tennis dropped steadily with distance traveled up to five miles or more. The proportion of players who participated frequently by distance traveled was: under one-eighth mile, 35 percent; one-eighth mile to one-quarter mile, 26 percent; one-quarter to one mile, 24 percent; one to two miles, 23 percent; two to five miles, 20 percent; and over five miles, 15 percent.

Tennis players were more likely to be frequent participants if the courts they most often used were open twelve or more hours per day. The proportion of frequent participants was also greater among tennis players who used facilities that required payment of a use fee and that had correspondingly more elaborate facilities, including lighted courts, a pro shop, locker room, club house, snack bar, wet bar, swimming pool and golf course. The frequency of participation was not associated with the provision of tennis instruction or organized tennis activities, but was associated with the provision of social activities at the facility used.

These data suggest two patterns of frequent participation in tennis. For some players the availability of readily accessible tennis courts in their neighborhoods appears to induce greater participation; while for others the availability of tennis courts with a full array of supporting and complimentary facilities also resulted in high rates of participation, but at a greater monetary cost to their users.

As with frequent participation in golf and swimming, tennis players who were more satisfied with the facilities they most often used tended to participate in tennis more frequently. Fifty-four percent of those who expressed complete satisfaction with the facilities used, versus only 22 percent of all tennis players, participated frequently. Also as with golf and swimming, frequent participation was moderately associated with the climate. Twenty-nine percent of the tennis players who lived in communities with 3000 or more hours of sunshine played tennis frequently.

Satisfaction with Tennis Facilities Used

Table 7–10 summarizes relationships between the characteristics of the facilities tennis players most often used and their reported level of satisfaction with those facilities. Overall, 43 percent of the tennis players were completely satisfied with the facilities they used. Those who most often played tennis at a facility within their own community were only slightly more likely to be completely satisfied (45 percent) than those who played outside of their community. Satisfaction varied with the type of ownership of tennis facilities. The highest proportion of players were completely satisfied with commercial tennis courts (97 percent), followed by private tennis clubs (47 percent), quasi-public homes association and multi-unit project courts (46 percent), and public courts (36 percent). Satisfaction was also associated with a facility's operating season and operating hours. In both cases players were more satisfied with facilities that were available for use for longer periods of time. Tennis facilities that provided tennis instruction, organized tennis activities, and organized social activities contributed to the satisfaction of their users. As with golf and swimming facilities, the availability of organized social activities had the strongest effect on satisfaction. Fifty-seven percent of the tennis players who used facilities that sponsored social activities reported complete satisfaction with them.

Tennis facilities that provided a more complete array of facilities were associated with higher levels of satisfaction among their users. For example, tennis players who used a facility that provided a wet bar, snack bar, pro shop, club house, golf course, locker room, swimming pool or lighted courts were more likely to be completely satisfied.

A multiple regression analysis was performed to determine which of these variables had the strongest influence on tennis players' satisfaction with the facilities they most often used. Tennis players' personal and household characteristics explained only 2 percent of the variance in satisfaction. Characteristics of the facilities used explained 21 percent of the variance in satisfaction. After controlling for players' personal and household characteristics, the six facility characteristics with the strongest influence on satisfaction, as gauged by their beta coefficients in the regression equation, were: club house (available); organized social activities (available); wet bar (available); distance to the court used (closer); golf course available

Table 7–10. Measures of Association between Characteristics of Tennis Facilities Used and Satisfaction With Facilities[a]

Characteristics of Tennis Facilities Used	Chi-square Significance Level	Gamma	Direction — *Participants were more likely to be completely satisfied with the tennis facility used if:* (percent completely satisfied)
All participants			43% completely satisfied
Location within or outside of community	NS	.13	within community (45%)
Type of ownership	.002	−.23	commercial (96%); public (36%)
Distance to facility	NS	−.02	—
Operating season	NS	−.25	7+ months per year (44%)
Operating hours	.02	−.16	12+ hours per day (53%)
Tennis instruction	NS	.15	yes (47%)
Organized tennis activities	NS	.16	yes (47%)
Organized social activities	.01	.31	yes (57%)
Facilities at site:			
Pro shop	.01	.38	yes (60%)
Locker room	.01	.30	yes (54%)
Club house	.006	.32	yes (55%)
Snack bar	.001	.50	yes (67%)
Wet bar	.001	.54	yes (69%)
Swimming pool	NS	.18	yes (50%)
Golf course	NS	.26	yes (55%)
Landscaping of site	NS	.11	generous (49%)
Climate			
Hours of sunshine	.05	−.15	more hours of sunshine (3000+, 49%)
Sample size	561		

NS = Not significant at 0.05 level of confidence.
[a]These analyses were performed with data from respondents living in thirteen nonfederally assisted new communities.

at the site (available); and location within or outside of community (within community). Thus, tennis players were most satisfied with courts that were an integral part of a larger facility which, while providing opportunities to play tennis, also provided a number of amenities and opportunities for social interaction.

FACTORS INFLUENCING RESIDENTS'
OVERALL EVALUATIONS OF COMMUNITY
RECREATIONAL FACILITIES

The preceding sections of this chapter examined residents' participation in four recreational activities and their satisfaction with the facilities they used. This information is useful in estimating the potential demand for recreational facilities and planning facilities to accommodate demand, but it does not provide planners with insights into those aspects of the recreational system that are most strongly associated with residents' overall evaluations of community recreational facilities. This topic is addressed in this section through an analysis of the associations of four sets of variables—residents' personal and household characteristics, recreation participation rates and satisfaction with facilities used, accessibility of facilities, and variety of community recreational facilities and programs—with residents' overall evaluations of community recreational facilities.

Personal and Household Characteristics and
Overall Recreational Facility Ratings
The associations between residents' personal and household characteristics and their overall ratings of new community recreational facilities are summarized in Table 7—11. In a sense, these associations indicate the types of households whose needs were being met best by new community recreational service systems. Respondents who were most likely to rate community recreational facilities highly included those in the fifty-five to sixty-four age bracket; respondents who had some graduate school education; respondents whose annual family income was $25,000 or more and respondents who had no children living in their households. Thus, new community recreational systems performed best from the perspectives of persons who were in late middle age, affluent and whose children had left home. It should be noted, however, that even though new community recreational systems received higher ratings from these persons, differences in evaluations were not large. Also, recreational facilities were evaluated equally highly by both male and female residents, residents with different marital and employment statuses, living in different types of

Table 7–11. Measures of Association between Respondents' Personal and Household Characteristics, Characteristics of Community Recreational Facilities and Overall Evaluations of Community Recreational Facilities[a]

Variables	Measures of Association		Direction
	Chi-square Significance Level	Gamma	Respondents were more likely to rate community recreational facilities as excellent if: (percent rating facilities excellent)
Personal and Household Characteristics			
Race	.001	.25	all respondents (38%) white (38%); black (32%)
Sex	NS	.06	—
Age	.001	-.15	55 to 64 years old (48%)
Education	.02	-.10	graduate school (42%)
Marital status	NS	-.004	—
Employment of respondent	NS	-.01	—
Family income	.001	-.13	$25,000+ (46%)
Number of children in household	.001	.10	none (41%)
Children under six years old	.008	.11	none (40%)
Children age six to eleven years old	NS	.06	—
Type of dwelling unit	NS	-.04	—
Tenure	NS	.04	—
Length of residence in community	NS	-.02	—
Participation in Selected Activities during Previous Year			
Favorite out-of-home activity	.001	-.13	participated 50 or more times (44%)
Golf	.001	-.17	participated in golf (45%)
Swimming	.001	-.18	participated in swimming (42%)

Tennis	−.10	.04	participated in tennis (41%)
Bicycling	−.07	NS	—
Walking and hiking	−.15	.001	participated in walking (41%)
Number of five different activities in which respondent participated during previous year	−.14	.001	participated in three or more (44%)
Distance to Facility Most Often Used			
Golf course	.24	.001	under two miles (56%)
Swimming facility	.22	.001	under one-fourth mile (54%)
Tennis court	.16	.02	under one-fourth mile (49%)
Bicycling facility	−.10	NS	—
Walking facility	.06	NS	—
Park or playground	−.006	.06	under one-eighth mile (47%)
Satisfaction with Facility Most Often Used			
Facility used for favorite out-of-home activity	.31	.001	completely satisfied (50%)
Golf course	.41	.001	completely satisfied (63%)
Swimming facility	.31	.001	completely satisfied (50%)
Tennis facility	.35	.001	completely satisfied (55%)
Bicycling facility	.37	.001	completely satisfied (50%)
Walking facility	.37	.001	completely satisfied (50%)
Accessibility of Recreational Facilities			
Nearest park or playground	.008	.001	under one-eighth mile (41%)
Nearest golf course	.11	.001	under one mile (45%)
Nearest swimming facility	.15	.001	under one mile (43%)
Nearest tennis facility	.07	.001	under one-fourth mile (41%)
Nearest walking/bicycling facility	.18	.001	under one-fourth mile (46%)

Table 7–11 continued overleaf . . .

Table 7–11. continued

Variables	Measures of Association		Direction
	Chi-square Significance Level	Gamma	*Respondents were more likely to rate community recreational facilities as excellent if: (per-cent rating facilities excellent)*
Availability of Facilities in Neighborhood			
Park or playground	NS	.04	—
Neighborhood center	.001	.32	available (52%)
Library	NS	.01	—
Interior path system	.001	.28	available (48%)
Swimming facility	.001	.23	available (44%)
Tennis courts	.005	.12	available (42%)
Picnic area	.001	.17	available (43%)
Teen center	NS	.34	available (52%)
Characteristics of Community Recreational System			
Per capita operating expenditures	.001	−.10	$40 or more (49%)
Open space and recreational acreage per 10,000 population	.001	−.14	400 acres or more (42%)
Variety of recreational programs for children	.008	.02	—
Variety of recreational programs for young adults	.001	−.003	—
Variety of recreational programs for adults	NS	−.05	—
Variety of outdoor recreational facilities	.001	−.21	12 or more (47%)
Variety of indoor recreational facilities	.001	.05	—

Variety of entertainment facilities	.001	.04	—
Climate			
Hours of sunshine	.001	−.15	more hours of sunshine (3000+, 43%)
Sample size		2548	

NS = Not significant at 0.05 level of confidence.

[a]These analyses were performed with data from respondents living in thirteen nonfederally assisted new communities.

housing and by both those who owned their own homes and those who rented.

Participation and Overall Recreational Facility Ratings

New community residents who participated in a variety of leisure and recreational activities were somewhat more likely than non-participants to rate community recreational facilities as excellent. Respondents who had participated in golf were the most likely to rate recreational facilities as excellent, followed by those who had participated 50 or more times in their favorite out-of-home activity and those who participated one or more times during the previous year in swimming, tennis, walking for pleasure and hiking and bicycling. There was also some association between the variety of activities in which respondents had participated and their overall ratings of community recreational facilities. Forty-four percent of the respondents who participated in three or more of these five outdoor activities rated community recreational facilities as excellent.

Among new community residents who participated in various recreational activities, both the distances they traveled to participate and their satisfaction with the facilities they used were associated with their overall ratings of community recreational facilities. In the case of distances traveled, golfers who used a course within two miles of their home were much more likely to rate community recreational facilities as excellent than those who went further. Similarly, proportionately more swimmers and tennis players who most often used a facility within one-quarter mile of their homes rated community recreational facilities as excellent than did those who traveled further to the facilities they most often used. Parents whose children played at a park or playground within one-eighth mile of their homes also gave higher ratings to facilities. On the other hand, distances to the bicycling and walking facilities respondents used, which were overwhelmingly within one-eighth mile of their homes, were not associated with overall ratings.

Participants' satisfaction with the recreational facilities they most often used was strongly associated with their overall evaluations of the quality of community recreational facilities. The strongest of these associations was between satisfaction with the golf course used most often and overall ratings. Sixty-three percent of the golfers who were completely satisfied with the golf course they used rated community recreational facilities as excellent. The proportion of participants who were completely satisfied with other types of facilities who gave excellent ratings to community recreational facilities included: tennis facilities (55 percent); swimming facilities (50 percent); bicycling facilities (50 percent); walking and hiking facilities (50 percent); and facilities used for favorite out-of-home activities (50 percent).

Accessibility and Overall Recreational Facility Ratings

In general, road distances from respondents homes to the nearest available facilities for golf, swimming and tennis had less influence on overall ratings than the distances respondents actually traveled to participate. The proportion of respondents who rated community recreational facilities as excellent was highest for persons who lived within one mile of the nearest golf course, one mile of the nearest swimming facility, and one-fourth mile of a tennis facility. Although distance to the walking and bicycling facilities respondents used most often did not influence their overall ratings of community recreational facilities, distance to the nearest available facility did. Forty-six percent of the respondents who lived within one-fourth mile of the nearest walking facility (other than sidewalks or streets) versus only 29 percent of those who lived over two miles from the nearest facility rated community recreational facilities as excellent. Forty-one percent of the respondents who lived within one-eighth mile of the nearest park or playground rated community recreational facilities as excellent versus 35 percent of those who lived over two miles away.

The availability of several other facilities in respondents' neighborhoods was also associated with their overall ratings of recreational facilities. In particular, a higher proportion of respondents with a neighborhood recreational center (52 percent), neighborhood teen center (52 percent) and internal path system (48 percent) gave recreational facilities excellent ratings. Somewhat higher proportions of excellent ratings were also given by respondents if a swimming facility, tennis court or a picnic area was located in their neighborhood.

Community Recreational System Characteristics and Overall Recreational Facility Ratings

The final series of variables evaluated in terms of overall ratings of community recreational facilities was selected characteristics of the entire recreational system. As shown in Table 7—11, the three characteristics of the overall recreational system that were most strongly associated with respondents' ratings were the variety of different types of outdoor recreational facilities provided, per capita recreational operating expenditures, and the amount of open space and recreational acreage per 10,000 population. For example, in those new communities which spent $40 per capita or more on operating their recreational systems, 49 percent of the respondents rated recreational facilities as excellent. In the case of recreational systems that provided more than twelve of fifteen selected types of active outdoor facilities, 47 percent of the respondents rated facilities as excellent. In communities with 400 or more acres of recreational and open space land per 10,000 population, 42 percent of the respondents gave excellent ratings.

Key Factors Influencing Overall Evaluations

A multiple regression analysis was performed to evaluate the relative contributions of each set of variables to respondents' overall evaluations of new community recreational facilities. Together these variables explained 26 percent of the variance in respondents' evaluations. See Table 7–12. The regression analysis was performed in a step-wise manner so that with respondents' personal and household characteristics controlled, the relative influence of recreational participation, satisfaction with facilities used and characteristics of community recreational resources could be identified.

The most important set of variables influencing respondents' overall evaluations of community recreational facilities was the distances respondents' traveled to participate and their satisfaction with the facilities they used for various activities. Together, these variables explained 19 percent of the variance in respondents' overall evaluations. Personal and household characteristics explained 4 percent of the variance and selected characteristics of community recreational resources explained 3 percent. As shown in earlier sections of this chapter, the frequency with which people participate in various outdoor activities and their satisfaction with facilities used is, in part, a function of both the accessibility of facilities and their design. New community residents who lived closer to the recreational facilities they used most often and who used higher quality facilities that provided both recreational opportunities and social activities tended to be most satisfied with them.

The regression analysis also highlights the relative contribution of particular variables to residents' overall evaluation of new community recreational facilities. For example, among respondents' personal and household characteristics, the three most important variables are race, children in the household and education. White respondents with more formal education and fewer children living in their households gave higher overall ratings to community recreational facilities.

Seven variables associated with various aspects of respondents' participation in recreational activities and use of facilities were strongly related to their overall evaluations of recreational facilities. Higher overall ratings were given by respondents who traveled shorter distances to and were more satisfied with the golf courses they used; who traveled shorter distances to and were more satisfied with the tennis facilities they used; who were more satisfied with swimming and bicycling facilities used; and who had participated more times in their favorite out-of-home activities during the previous year.

Among the characteristics of community recreational resources, the variety of recreational programs offered for young adults, variety of outdoor recreational facilities, variety of entertainment facilities, availability of neighborhood centers in respondents' neighborhoods, and accessibility of the nearest golf course and walking path had the strongest influence on overall ratings of new community recreational resources.

The multivariate beta coefficients summarized in Table 7–12 indicate how much change in respondents' overall ratings of new community recreational facilities was produced by a standardized change in each of the independent variables when the other independent variables were controlled. Because of this characteristic of beta coefficients, they can be used to establish priorities among potential actions aimed at increasing the proportion of new community residents who evaluate community recreational facilities highly. For example, for all new communities, the multivariate analysis indicates that the following ten actions, in descending order of their effects, would have the greatest probability of producing higher ratings: (1) provide a greater variety of recreational programs for young adults; (2) provide greater access to golf courses; (3) increase user satisfaction with bicycling facilities; (4) increase user satisfaction with tennis facilities; (5) increase the accessibility of tennis facilities; (6) provide a greater variety of outdoor recreational facilities; (7) improve black residents' satisfaction with community recreational facilities; (8) increase user satisfaction with golf facilities; (9) increase user satisfaction with swimming facilities. and (10) provide neighborhood recreational centers within one-half mile or less of all residents. Characteristics of facilities that were related to greater user satisfaction were discussed in earlier sections of this chapter. Although the list of priorities would probably vary somewhat for each new community in the sample, it illustrates the value of this type of analysis. It

Table 7–12.   Factors Influencing Residents' Overall Evaluations of New Community Recreational Facilities: Multivariate Analysis[a]

Variable	Simple Correlation Coefficient	Multivariate Beta Coefficient	F-value[b]
Personal and Household Characteristics			
Race	.07	.11	35.82
Number of children in household	.07	.11	14.62
Education	-.05	-.05	6.84
Family income	-.10	-.04	3.22
Sex	.02	.03	2.62
Age	-.12	.03	1.02
Marital status	.01	.03	1.87
Length of residence	-.01	-.02	1.26
Children age six to eleven years old in household	.03	-.02	1.03
Children under six years old in household	.07	.02	0.72
Housing type	-.03	.02	0.36
Employment of respondent	-.01	-.01	0.13
Tenure	.02	.01	0.10
Participation in Selected Activities, Distance Traveled to and Satisfaction with Facilities Used			
Distance to golf course used	.23	.22	127.39
Satisfaction with bicycling facility used	.28	.19	82.12
Satisfaction with tennis facility used	.26	.19	80.96
Distance to tennis facility used	.08	.13	32.96
Satisfaction with golf course used	.20	.10	18.32
Satisfaction with swimming facility used	.17	.07	13.14
Frequency of participation in favorite out-of-home activity	-.01	.04	5.41
Frequency of participation in golf	-.08	-.04	3.75
Distance to walking path used	.06	-.03	2.81

Distance to swimming facility used	.19	.03	2.54
Satisfaction with walking facility used	.20	−.03	2.41
Frequency of participation in walking	−.08	−.03	2.26
Frequency of participation in swimming	−.12	−.02	0.85
Distance to bicyling facility used	−.02	−.02	0.74
Frequency of participation in tennis	−.08	.01	0.38
Satisfaction with facility used for favorite activity	.18	.01	0.03

Characteristics of Community Recreational Resources

Variety of recreational programs for young adults	−.03	−.31	46.48
Variety of recreational programs for children	.10	.28	46.24
Variety of outdoor recreational facilities	−.08	−.12	17.64
Recreational acreage per 10,000 population	−.07	.08	9.75
Neighborhood center available	.14	.05	4.92
Distance to nearest golf course	.08	−.05	4.74
Distance to nearest walking path	.07	−.05	4.70
Variety of entertainment facilities	.08	−.05	3.90
Park or playground in neighborhood	.03	−.03	2.01
Internal path system in neighborhood	.16	.04	1.78
Variety of recreational programs for adults	.08	.04	1.60
Teen center in neighborhood	.04	.02	0.60
Library in neighborhood	−.01	.01	0.57
Community per capita recreational operating expenditures	−.08	−.02	0.40

R^2 .26
F-value for equation 19.87
Sample size 2549

[a]This analysis was performed with data from respondents living in thirteen nonfederally assisted new communities.
[b]F-value of 3.9 or greater is significant at the 0.05 level of confidence.

also provides a useful list of factors recreational planners should be concerned with in the initial design of community recreational systems.

CONCLUSIONS AND PLANNING IMPLICATIONS

New community residents' participation in recreational activities, satisfaction with individual recreational facilities and evaluations of the overall quality of community recreational facilities are associated with their personal and household characteristics and the characteristics of recreational resources. Data presented in this chapter on the nature of these relationships have several implications for recreational planning in new communities.

One set of relationships that must be considered in recreational planning is the association of residents' personal and household characteristics with the frequency of their participation in outdoor activities. The analyses presented in this chapter confirm earlier findings (see, for example, Robert W. Marans 1971) that participation in different recreational activities is sensitive to different sets of personal and household characteristics. The frequency of children's play at parks and playgrounds increased with the number of children in the six to eleven age bracket living in a household and with residence in townhouses and rental dwelling units. Participation in golf was most sensitive to residents' racial, sex and socioeconomic characteristics; participation in swimming was most sensitive to residents' racial and age characteristics and to the number of children between the ages of six and eleven living in households; and participation in tennis was most sensitive to residents' age, race and socioeconomic characteristics. For each of the latter three activities, participation versus nonparticipation was more strongly associated with residents' personal and household characteristics than with the availability or accessibility of recreational facilities. Knowledge of these associations can be used by new community recreational planners to gauge the extent of participation likely to be generated from communities with various population characteristics and, hence, the likely demand for recreational facilities to accommodate this participation.

A second set of relationships that have important implications for recreational planning are those between characteristics of recreational facilities and the frequency of participation and level of satisfaction with facilities used. Although residents' characteristics had the most influence on participation rather than nonparticipation in recreational activities, once the participation threshold was passed the characteristics of recreational facilities had an important independent influence on the frequency with which participants engaged in various activities. Facility characteristics considered in the analyses reported in this chapter included the distances persons traveled to participate, the ownership of facilities, facility operating characteristics, including the number of months and daily hours they were open and types of programs they offered, the supporting facilities and amenities that were available and site landscaping and maintenance.

Distances respondents traveled to participate in recreational activities had a strong effect on the frequency they participated. In the case of children's use of parks and playgrounds, for example, participation was very high by children who lived within one-eighth mile of the park or playground they most often used. The proportion of children who frequently played at a park or playground then dropped sharply among children who lived between one-eighth and one-half mile of the facility used, and again dropped sharply for children who traveled over one-half mile to play at a park or playground. Frequent participation in golf (50 or more times during the previous year) was highest among golfers who lived within one mile of the golf course they used most often. The proportion of golfers who were frequent participants dropped among those who lived more than one mile from the course used, but did not decrease any further with greater distances from the course used. In the case of frequent participation in swimming, the highest proportion of frequent participants lived within one-eighth mile of the swimming facility they most often used. The proportion of frequent participants then dropped to an intermediate level among those who lived between one-eighth mile and one-half mile of the facility used, and then dropped steadily with increasing distances for those who lived over one-half mile from the swimming facility used. Finally, in the case of frequent participation in tennis, the highest proportion of frequent participants lived within one-eighth mile of the facility used most often. Frequent participation then steadily decreased with increasing distance to the tennis facility that was used. In sum, findings for the influence of accessibility on frequent participation suggest that new community recreational planners should decentralize facilities as much as possible in order to maximize their use.

In addition to accessibility, the characteristics of recreational facilities, themselves, also influenced frequent participation. The proportion of frequent participants tended to be great for facilities that were not operated by public agencies, that operated for longer seasons and for more hours per day and that provided a greater variety of supporting facilities and amenities. For golf courses these included locker rooms, club houses, wet bars, driving ranges and night lighting. In the case of swimming, frequent participation was greater among swimmers who used facilities with heated pools and club houses. Frequent participation in tennis was greater among tennis players who used facilities with pro shops, locker rooms, club houses and bars. For each of these activities, participants tended to engage in them more frequently if the facilities they used most often sponsored social activities. This is an indication that recreational participation is valued for the opportunities it provides participants to interact with other persons. Finally, frequent participation tended to be greater among participants who used recreational complexes that included facilities for a variety of outdoor activities at the same site.

Associations between the characteristics of facilities and frequent participation have opposite implications from those of accessibility. Rather than decentralizing facilities, which would result in the provision of more spartan facilities geared to small supporting populations, they suggest that frequent participation will be increased through the development of large recreational complexes that provide a variety of amenities in addition to recreational facilities. In fact, both centralized and decentralized approaches to the provision of recreational facilities should be included in community recreational plans, since it seems likely that each type of facility meets the needs of a different clientele. The best approach to planning new community recreational systems would appear to be one that combines one or two large recreational complexes, complete with golf courses, swimming facilities, tennis courts and a club house facility, with highly decentralized neighborhood and even sub-neighborhood swimming pools and tennis courts.

Respondents' satisfaction with the recreational facilities they used was more a function of the characteristics of these facilities than their personal and household characteristics. The distances traveled to facilities influenced participants' satisfaction with them. In the case of swimming and tennis facilities, users who traveled shorter distances were more satisfied. However, the opposite was true for golf. A higher proportion of golfers who traveled farther to the courses they used reported that they were satisfied than golfers who traveled shorter distances. In addition to accessibility, several other facility characteristics had strong influences on satisfaction. Golfers were most satisfied with longer golf courses that were generously landscaped and that included a bar among club house facilities. Swimmers were most satisfied with indoor pools with heated water that were run by commercial operators. Finally, tennis players were most satisfied with courts that included a club house and bar on the site and that offered organized social activities. Knowledge of these associations, and others reported in this chapter that had somewhat less influence on satisfaction, can help planners design facilities that are responsive to new community residents' needs and desires.

The final topic analyzed in this chapter was new community residents' overall evaluations of community recreational facilities. A multiple regression analysis was used to isolate those factors that had the strongest influences on residents' evaluations and to suggest those aspects of the recreational system that should be given priority in recreational planning. Results of this analysis suggested a number of actions (see above) that would produce higher ratings of community recreational facilities by residents.

※ *Chapter 8*

Recreation, Community
Marketing and the Quality
of Community Life

Although a primary function of open space and recreational facilities is to accommodate people's needs for
places to engage in outdoor activities, their importance to
a new community may be much broader. In particular, open space
and recreational facilities are often viewed as key elements in attracting people to move to new communities, in people's satisfaction with
a community after they are in residence and in residents' overall
quality of life. If open space and recreational systems do serve these
broader functions, developer and public attention to them may be
justified on broader grounds than their intrinsic value for recreational
pursuits and environmental preservation. They may represent important policy levers to influence the marketability of a new community, and thus its economic success, and to increase residents'
satisfaction with their lives in a community, and thus its social success.

This concluding chapter begins by first examining households'
reasons for moving to particular communities. How do nearness to
the outdoors and the availability of recreational facilities compare
with other reasons for moving to new communities? Are they more
important reasons for moving to new communities than to less
planned suburban communities? Are they more important in some
new communities than others? Are they more important to different
types of households than others or to households moving to different types of housing or to housing built at different densities? By
answering these questions a much better grasp of the potential role
of open space and recreation in community marketing should be

obtained. In addition, to the extent that open space and recreational facilities are more important in the moving decisions of some types of households than others, answers to these questions should indicate whether open space and recreational facilities affect the composition of the population likely to settle in a new community. This has important implications for new community policy, since it will indicate how goals for population heterogeneity in new communities are likely to be effected by community planning and marketing that emphasize open space and recreation.

Following the discussion of household moving decisions, the chapter then proceeds to consider the influence of the recreational system on residents' overall evaluations of their communities as places to live. Is residents' satisfaction with the recreational system a more important determinant of overall community satisfaction than their satisfaction with other service systems? Does the relative influence of the recreational system vary between new community residents and residents of less planned suburbs? Does it vary for different types of residents or for residents of different types of housing? Answers to the first question provide one basis for establishing priorities among community service systems. Answers to the succeeding questions indicate which community residents benefit most, at least in terms of their overall evaluation of new community livability, from policies aimed at increasing satisfaction with recreational service systems.

Finally, the chapter examines whether residents' perceptions of improvements in the quality of recreational facilities achieved by moving to new communities make a difference in their perceptions of improvements in their quality of life and whether recreational facilities and leisure satisfaction contribute to satisfaction with life as a whole.

OPEN SPACE AND RECREATIONAL FACILITIES AS REASONS FOR HAVING MOVED TO A NEW COMMUNITY

Households' decisions to move to new communities usually represent the end result of two interrelated decision processes. The first involves decisions to move from their existing residences; the second involves their choices of new homes. Previous research has established that relatively few households move from their existing residences because of the attraction of the homes to which they eventually move (Peter H. Rossi 1955; Nelson Foote, Janet Abu-Lughod, Mary M. Foley and Louis Winnick 1960). Instead, these two decisions tend to be sequential. Households are "pushed" out of their existing homes for various reasons, and they then decide where to move. If new communities are to succeed in the marketplace, they must attract a sufficient number of residents from the streams of already mobile households in the market. Their success depends in large part on the package of home and community that is offered and how this package is differentiated in consumers' eyes from the alternatives that are available. The provision of open space and recreational facilities is one means which new community developers can use to differentiate their product from competing housing products available to the consumer (see, for example, Carl Norcross 1966; Francine F. Rabinovitz and James Lamare 1970; and Carl Werthman, Jerry S. Mandel and Ted Dienstfrey 1965).

To discover which community attributes attracted households to new communities, respondents in each of the sample new and conventional communities were given a list of nineteen factors that might have influenced their decisions to move to a community. Respondents were then asked: "Thinking of what attracted you to this place, could you tell me which *three* of these factors were *most* important in your (family's) decision to move to this community (originally)?" The proportion of respondents who cited various reasons for moving to the new and conventional communities is shown in Table 8–1.[a]

Nearness to the outdoors and natural environment was cited by 26 percent of the respondents from thirteen nonfederally assisted new communities as one of the reasons they moved to those communities. Among the nineteen attributes respondents were able to select from, nearness to the outdoors ranked fourth in terms of the proportion of the respondents who cited it as a reason for having moved to a new community. Mentioned more often were the community as a good place to raise children, convenience to work and the layout and space of the dwelling and lot. Nearness to the outdoors was even more important in respondents' decisions to move to the two federally assisted new communities in the sample. Among Jonathan respondents, it was cited most often as a reason for moving to the community and among Park Forest South respondents it ranked third behind layout and space of the dwelling and the cost of buying or renting.

[a]Although moving to a new house is a major event in most people's lives, and thus can be recalled for some time afterward, the responses summarized in Table 8–1 should be viewed with some caution. They represent reports of past rather than current behavior and may have been influenced to some extent by people's experiences between the time they moved and the time they were interviewed. For an in-depth analysis of residential mobility in new communities, see Edward J. Kaiser (1976).

Table 8–1.   Reasons for Moving to New and Conventional Communities[a] *(percentage distribution of respondents)*

	Nonfederally Assisted		Federally Assisted			
Reason for Moving to Community	*Thirteen New Communities*	*Thirteen Conventional Communities*	*Jonathan*	*Chanhassen*	*Park Forest South*	*Richton Park*
Good place to raise children	31	33	49	39	35	23
Convenience to work	30	29	27	45[b]	29	35
Layout and space of dwelling and lot	28	37[b]	16	27[b]	42	30
Nearness to outdoors/natural environment	26	29	56	49	36[b]	14
Appearance of the immediate neighborhood	26	26	14	26[b]	22	15
Cost of buying (and financing) the dwelling or renting	24	28[b]	29	25	38	47
Overall planning that went into community	23[b]	7	34[b]	3	21[b]	6
Climate	21	22	1	1	0	2
Public schools	15	15	3	10	8	22[b]
Recreational facilities	12[b]	6	22[b]	3	9	11
Type of people living in the neighborhood	12	14	11	16	16	18
Shopping facilities	9	7	2	6	2	10[b]
Construction of dwelling	7	10[b]	2	7	5	7
Ease of getting around the community	7	7	6	4	4	7
Safety from crime	6	7	5	2	8	10
Opportunity for participation in community life	5	3	8	7	9[b]	1
Ease of finding a job in the community	4	4	6	12	5	8
Cost of living in the community	2	3	7	3	3	4
Health and medical services	2	1	1	0	0	0
Sample size	2838	1321	207	100	200	101

[a] *Question:* Thinking of what attracted you to this place, could you tell me which *three* of these factors were *most* important in your (family's) decision to move to this community (originally)?
[b] Statistically significant difference between new and conventional communities at the 0.05 level of confidence.

While nearness to the outdoors was an important aspect of the appeal of new communities, respondents appeared to be reacting more to the location of these communities than to characteristics of their design or to their reservations of community open space. For example, nearness to the outdoors was cited as a reason for having moved to their communities by a somewhat larger proportion (29 percent) of conventional community respondents. This suggests that proximity to nature may be useful in marketing new communities (since it forms the basis for the appeal of new communities to a sizable proportion of in-movers), but not in differentiating new community housing products from those offered by nearby competitors.

On the other hand, while community recreational facilities were cited much less frequently as one of the reasons respondents moved to new communities, they tended to differentiate the appeal of new communities from that of the nearby less planned conventional communities. The availability of community recreational facilities ranked tenth among the reasons cited for moving to new communities, but ranked sixteenth among the reasons cited by conventional community respondents. The proportion of new community respondents who moved to their community because of available recreational facilities was twice that of the conventional communities (12 percent versus 6 percent).

Among the federally assisted new communities, the availability of recreational facilities was mentioned by 22 percent of the Jonathan respondents (versus only 3 percent of the respondents in its paired conventional community), but by a much lower proportion of Park Forest South respondents (9 percent versus 11 percent for its paired conventional community). The marked difference in the role of recreational facilities in the appeal of Jonathan and Park Forest South was probably a result of the organization of the recreational systems in each community and the visibility of recreational facilities to consumers. Facilities provided in Park Forest South were less visible to prospective home buyers and renters and were operated by a number of organizations, including several automatic membership homes and recreation associations and the Village of Park Forest South. In contrast, Jonathan's recreational facilities were more visible to prospective residents and were operated by a community-wide homes association, so that facilities were equally available to all residents of the community.

Community Comparisons

Additional insights into the influence of the outdoors and recreational facilities on households' decisions to move to new communities are provided by the individual community comparisons summarized in Table 8—2. These data confirm earlier reports by Rabinovitz and Lemare (1970) about Westlake Village and Lansing, Marans and Zehner (1970) about Reston, that nearness to the outdoors and natural environment was a key factor in residents' decisions to move to these communities. In addition, nearness to the outdoors was cited by a quarter or more of the respondents from five other non-federally assisted new communities: Lake Havasu City (58 percent), Laguna Niguel (57 percent), Westlake Village (51 percent), Irvine (34 percent), Valencia (28 percent) and Columbia (26 percent). These communities, together with Jonathan and Park Forest South, had two features in common. First, they were located on the outer fringes of their metropolitan areas, or, in the case of Lake Havasu City, in the desert, and were surrounded by large expanses of undeveloped land. Second, in each case residential sales were begun after 1960 and none of the communities had reached more than 28 percent of its target population at the time of the household survey. Thus, the natural environment was close at hand and was an important factor in attracting residents.

Five of the six new communities where nearness to the outdoor was not an important aspect of their appeal to prospective residents—Elk Grove Village, Forest Park, North Palm Beach, Park Forest and Sharpstown—began residential development before 1960 and at the time of the 1973 household survey had achieved 39 percent or more of their target populations.[b] In addition, during their longer periods of development the areas surrounding these communities had developed more fully and had achieved an urban character that did not characterize the areas surrounding the new communities in earlier stages of the development process.

To further illuminate the effect of stage of development on the contribution of nearness to the outdoors to residents' moving decisions, the relationship between households' length of residence in the sample communities and moving because of nearness to the outdoors was analyzed. If stage of development was as important as the above data indicate, residents who moved to a community at an earlier stage in the development process should have been more concerned with the outdoors than residents who moved in at a later time. In fact, this hypothesis is supported. Among the five new communities where development began prior to 1960, 23 percent of the respondents who moved to them prior to 1960 gave nearness to the outdoors

[b]Foster City was the one exception. As noted in Appendix B, however, Foster City was developed on bay fill in a portion of San Mateo County that had become heavily urbanized during the 1950s.

Table 8-2. Nearness to the Outdoors/Natural Environment and Recreational Facilities as Reasons for Moving to a New Community (percentage distribution of respondents)

New Communities/Paired Conventional Communities	Moved to Community Because of:			
	Nearness to Outdoors and Natural Environment		Recreational Facilities	
	New Community	Conventional Community	New Community	Conventional Community
Nonfederally Assisted New Communities/ Paired Conventional Communities				
Thirteen new communities/thirteen conventional communities	26	29	12[a]	6
Lake Havasu City/Kingman	58[a]	37	30[a]	8
Laguna Niguel/Dana Point	57	51	17	14
Westlake Village/Agoura-Malibu Junction	51	60	17[a]	1
Reston/West Springfield	47[a]	17	19[a]	7
Irvine/Fountain Valley	34[a]	16	21[a]	11
Valencia/Bouquet Canyon	28	42[a]	11[a]	2
Columbia/Norbeck-Wheaton	26[a]	12	14[a]	3
North Palm Beach/Tequesta	16	34[a]	15	19
Elk Grove Village/Schaumburg	13	16	4	3
Forest Park/Sharonville	12	20	5	4
Park Forest/Lansing	12	7	2	0
Foster City/West San Mateo	11	15	9	5
Sharpstown/Southwest Houston	1	8[a]	5	4
Federally Assisted New Communities/ Paired Conventional Communities				
Jonathan/Chanhassen	56	49	22[a]	3
Park Forest South/Richton Park	36[a]	14	9	11

[a]Statistically significant difference between new community and paired conventional community at 0.05 level of confidence.

as one of the reasons for their selection of these communities as a place to live. This was the case for only 12 percent of the households who moved to the five communities in 1960 or later. A similar finding was obtained for the eight nonfederally assisted new communities that began residential development from 1960 onwards. In these communities 58 percent of the respondents who moved to their homes prior to 1965 did so in part because of nearness to the outdoors versus 37 percent of the households who moved to the communities between 1965 and 1973. Since residents most concerned with proximity to the outdoors were probably more likely than others to have moved away from the sample new communities as they became more urbanized, and were thus less likely to fall into the household survey sample, these findings provide very strong support for the conclusion that the influence of the outdoors and natural environment on households' moving decisions in transitory. As communities become more fully developed, the proximity of the outdoors should become less and less a part of their appeal to prospective residents.

The findings for the role of community recreational facilities in households' moving decisions generally parallel those for the role of nearness to the outdoors. As with nearness to the outdoors, recreational facilities tended to be cited most often as a reason for moving to the new communities that began development after 1960. This reflects developers recent attention to recreation as an important element in community design and marketing. In communities where development began prior to 1960, developers gave more attention to housing value and relatively less attention to the community environment (see Chapter 2).

There are two exceptions to this generalization. North Palm Beach, where residential development began in the mid-1950s, is an oceanfront community located between Lake Worth and the North Palm Beach Waterway in Palm Beach County, Florida. The community has a strong orientation to water recreation, and 15 percent of the household survey respondents reported moving there because of available recreational facilities. On the other hand, recreational facilities were somewhat important in households' decisions to move to Foster City, even though residential development began after 1960 and the community is oriented toward a lagoon system connected to San Francisco Bay. Werthman, Mandell and Dienstfrey (1965) noted that Foster City's lagoons changed the social ecology of San Mateo County, California by transforming a socially undesirable bay-front area to an acceptable place to live and were not valued for their intrinsic worth in outdoor recreational uses. The present data appear to confirm their earlier findings, although findings reported later in this chapter indicate that they cannot be generalized to other new communities. Interviews with marketing personnel from Centex Homes, which is now building a large proportion of the homes in Foster City, indicated that Foster City's appeal to prospective residents stemmed from the exceptional housing values offered in the community rather than the community environment. Foster City is the only developing community in the mid-peninsula area of San Mateo County that offers new homes in intermediate price ranges.

The availability of community recreational facilities was a key factor in residents' decisions to move to Lake Havasu City (cited by 30 percent of the respondents), and was cited by a significantly higher than average proportion of respondents from five other new communities: Jonathan (22 percent), Irvine (21 percent), Reston (19 percent), Laguna Niguel (17 percent) and Westlake Village (17 percent). Freestanding Lake Havasu City relied on its natural desert setting and recreational facilities (particularly Lake Havasu) to attract residents to relocate from its primary market areas in the Midwest and California. The other five communities in which recreational facilities stood out as part of their appeal to prospective residents were not freestanding but were located on the fringe of their metropolitan areas. Developers used recreational facilities, in conjunction with these communities' natural settings, to induce residents to settle further from more developed portions of metropolitan areas than they might otherwise have been willing to do in the absence of significant environmental amenities.

Comparisons by Housing and Household Characteristics

The importance of nearness to the outdoors and community recreational facilities in households' moving decisions varied with the characteristics of the housing to which households were moving and the characteristics of the households themselves. Table 8−3 summarizes measures of association between these factors and nearness to the outdoors as a reason for having moved to a new community. Nearness to the outdoors was a more important consideration in the moving decisions of households that moved to townhouses, rather than to single family units or apartments, and to households that moved to smaller homes, homes that were more expensive or that rented for more per month, homes located in very low and very high density sections of a new community, and to homes that bordered on amenities, such as water bodies, golf courses and other types of open space.

Table 8–3.   Measures of Association between Housing Characteristics, Household Characteristics and Moving to New Communities Because of Nearness to the Outdoors/Natural Environment[a]

Variables	Measures of Association		Direction
	Chi-square Significance Level	Gamma	Households were more likely to move to community because of nearness to outdoors if:
Housing Characteristics			all respondents (26%)
Housing type	.02	-.002	townhouse (32%)
Size of dwelling unit	.03	.01	four or fewer rooms (31%)
Tenure	NS	-.003	—
Present value of dwelling unit	.001	-.22	higher ($60,000+, 36%)
Monthly rent	.005	-.16	higher ($250+, 30%)
Density—immediate neighborhood[b]	.001	.08	less than 2.5 d.u./acre (55%)
Density—extended neighborhood[c]	.001	.08	less than 1.0 d.u./acre (53%); more than 8.5 d.u./acre (38%)
Dwelling unit borders on:			
water	NS	.08	yes (29%)
golf course	NS	.34	yes (41%)
other open space[d]	.001	.22	yes (33%)
Household Characteristics			
Race of household head	.03	.33	white (26%); black (15%)
Sex of household head	NS	-.05	—
Age of household head	.001	-.13	older (65+, 37%)
Education of household head	.001	-.07	graduate training (29%)
Employment of household head	.006	-.17	retired (36%)
Size of household	.001	.11	two persons (31%)

Family income	NS	.05	—
Status concern of respondent[e]	.001	.14	lower (35%)
Sample size	2838		

NS = Not significant at 0.05 level of confidence.

[a] Data for this table are from respondents living in thirteen nonfederally assisted new communities.

[b] The immediate neighborhood was defined as the area encompassed by the five to seven dwelling units immediately surrounding each respondent's home. In the case of multi-unit projects, immediate neighborhood density refers to the density of the entire project.

[c] The extended neighborhood was defined as the area within a half-mile radius of each respondent's home, or a smaller area if bounded on one or more sides by a major thoroughfare, body of water, undeveloped land or the community boundary.

[d] Open space of five or more acres.

[e] Scale constructed from three agree-disagree items.

Because the data refer to households' characteristics at the time of the interview rather than at the time households decided to move to their communities, associations between households' characteristics and reasons for having moved to a new community must be interpreted with caution. Nevertheless, the relationships between households' characteristics and moving decisions summarized in Table 8–3 are consistent with relationships found for housing characteristics, which should have remained relatively constant over time. For example, nearness to the outdoors was more important in the moving decisions of households with high socioeconomic status characteristics (education and income) who, as noted above, moved to more expensive homes. Nearness to the outdoors was also more important to households whose heads were older, retired, and to smaller households who, as noted above, moved to smaller housing units (fewer rooms). Nearness to the outdoors was more likely to have been cited as a reason for having moved to a new community by white households than by black households. Only 15 percent of the black households in the sample, versus 26 percent of the white households, selected a home in a new community because of proximity to the outdoors and natural environment. Finally, contrary to Werthman, Mandell and Dienstfrey's (1965) contention that environmental amenities are valued because of their social status connotations, the opposite appears to be true. Households who were less, rather than more, concerned with social status aspects of their living environment were more likely to move to new communities because of perceived nearness to the outdoors and natural environment.

In order to determine the relative importance of housing, household, and community characteristics in households' decisions to move to new communities because of nearness to the outdoors, a multivariate analysis was performed. In addition to the variables discussed above, the analysis included several measures of overall community characteristics, including two measures of the extent of community-wide open space and recreational facilities, the distance of a community from the metropolitan central business district, median family income of the community as a whole and the age of the community. This analysis revealed that community and housing characteristics explained more of the variance in households' decisions to move to a new community than did household characteristics. The five variables that contributed most to explaining households' decisions to move to a new community because of the nearness to the outdoors were, in order of importance: (1) stage of community development (earlier); (2) total open space and recreational acreage in the community (more); (3) distance to the nearest swimming facility (closer); (4) total number of developed recreational sites in the community (fewer); and (5) age of the respondent (older).

The appeal of new communities that stemmed from recreational facilities also varied among households with different characteristics who moved to different types of housing. See Table 8−4. Households were more likely to have viewed recreational facilities as an important consideration in their decision to move to a new community if they were moving to an apartment, a smaller dwelling unit, a rental unit, a more expensive ownership unit or to a dwelling unit in a very low density (1.0 dwelling unit per acre or less) or high density (8.5 dwelling units per acre or more) neighborhood.

In addition, households who cited recreational facilities as an important factor in their decision to move to a new community were more likely to have moved to a dwelling unit that was located adjacent to a water body, a golf course, and closer to the nearest swimming facility and tennis court. These households were also more likely to participate in outdoor activities after they were in residence than households who moved to new communities for reasons other than the availability of recreational facilities. Differences in recreational participation between the two groups included golf, 39 percent versus 23 percent participated; swimming, 67 percent versus 57 percent participated; and tennis, 32 percent versus 20 percent participated. These data further refute Werthman, Mandell and Dienstfrey's (1965) claim that recreational facilities are valued more for their social status connotations than their use value, at least for those households who were attracted to new communities by the availability of such facilities.

In a number of respects households who reported that the availability of recreational facilities was an important factor in their decision to move to a new community were similar to those who were concerned with the natural environment. These households tended to be smaller (one or two persons) and to be moving to apartments and smaller dwelling units. Households with retired household heads were more concerned with recreational facilities, but so were households whose heads were under age 25. Income and housing prices were also associated with the attention given to recreational facilities—higher income families who moved into more expensive dwelling units tended to be more concerned with recreational facilities in their moving decisions. Blacks were not likely to move to new communities because of community recreational facilities. Also, the effect of housing density was bifurcated. Households who moved to very low density housing (1.0 dwelling unit per acre or less) and

Table 8–4.   Measures of Association between Housing Characteristics, Household Characteristics and Moving to New Communities Because of the Availability of Recreational Facilities[a]

Variables	Measures of Association		Direction
	Chi-Square Significance Level	Gamma	Households were more likely to move to community because of recreational facilities if:
			all respondents (12%)
Housing Characteristics			
Housing type	.001	-.35	apartment (19%)
Size of dwelling	.001	.36	four or fewer rooms (20%)
Tenure	.001	-.28	rent (17%)
Present value of dwelling unit	.02	-.13	higher ($60,000+, 18%)
Monthly rent	NS	-.03	—
Density—immediate neighborhood[b]	.001	-.06	1.0 d.u./acre or less (30%); 8.5 d.u./acre or more (17%)
Density—extended neighborhood[c]	.001	-.04	1.0 d.u./acre or less (27%); 8.5 d.u./acre or more (27%)
Unit borders on:			
water	.01	.28	yes (18%)
golf course	NS	.30	yes (21%)
other open space[d]	NS	.07	—
Distance to nearest:			
golf course	NS	.13	under one-half mile (19%)
swimming facility	.001	.17	under one-eighth mile (19%)
tennis court	.001	.11	under one-eighth mile (23%)
walking path	.01	.06	one-fourth to one-half mile (15%)
Household Characteristics			
Race of household head	NS	.12	white (12%); black (7%)
Sex of household head	NS	-.04	—

Age of household head	.001	−.03	under 25 (24%); 65 or older (15%)
Education of household head	NS	−.07	—
Employment of household head	.004	−.18	retired (19%)
Size of household	.001	.26	one person (18%); two persons (16%)
Family income	.02	−.04	$25,000 or more (15%)
Status concern of respondent	NS	−.02	—
Sample size	2838		

NS = Not significant at 0.05 level of confidence.

[a] Data for this table are from respondents living in thirteen nonfederally assisted new communities.

[b] The immediate neighborhood was defined as the area encompassed by the five to seven dwelling units immediately surrounding each respondent's home. In the case of multi-unit projects, immediate neighborhood density refers to the density of the entire project.

[c] The extended neighborhood was defined as the area within a half-mile radius of each respondent's home, or a smaller area if bounded on one or more sides by a major thoroughfare, body of water, undeveloped land or the community boundary.

[d] Open space of five or more acres.

[e] Scale constructed from three agree-disagree items.

higher density housing (8.5 dwelling units per acre or more) were the most likely to have cited recreational facilities as a reason for their move to a new community. Finally, the availability and accessibility of various recreational facilities were associated with household moving decisions. Households were more likely to have cited recreational facilities as a reason for having moved to a new community if the home to which they moved bordered on a body of water or golf course and if the home was located within one-eighth mile of a swimming facility or tennis court or within one-half mile of a golf course.

OPEN SPACE, RECREATIONAL FACILITIES AND COMMUNITY LIVABILITY

New community respondents indicated that they were highly satisfied with the overall livability of their communities. In the case of the thirteen nonfederally assisted new communities, 90 percent of the respondents rated their communities as excellent or good places in which to live. Eighty-six percent of the conventional community respondents rated community livability that highly. To explore the reasons underlying residents' evaluations of new and conventional community livability, the respondents were asked to elaborate on their ratings. The most frequently given reasons for positive evaluations of community livability are summarized in Table 8-5.

The quality of the environment, including the perceived lack of crowding, nearness to nature and the outdoors and the attractiveness of the community, was mentioned most often as a reason for respondents' satisfaction with the livability of their communities. Among individual nonfederally assisted new communities, nearness to nature and the outdoors was mentioned by 23 percent or more of the respondents from five new communities: Irvine (31 percent); Laguna Niguel (29 percent); Reston (24 percent); Valencia (23 percent); and Westlake Village (23 percent). On the other hand, natural features of the environment were mentioned by 11 percent or fewer of the respondents who lived in Columbia, Elk Grove Village, Forest Park, Foster City, North Palm Beach and Sharpstown. These findings generally parallel those for nearness to the outdoors as a reason for having moved to a new community. That is, open space and other natural features of the environment were more important factors in households' moving decisions and satisfaction with community livability in communities that had been under development for a shorter period of time and where the area surrounding the community was relatively undeveloped.

Six percent of the new community respondents mentioned the

Table 8-5.   Reasons Most Frequently Given for Rating Community as an Excellent or Good Place to Live[a] (percentage distribution of respondents)

Reasons for Positive Ratings	Thirteen Nonfederally Assisted New Communities[b]	Thirteen Conventional Communities[b]
Quality of the Environment		
Lack of crowding	16	23[d]
Nearness to nature and the outdoors[c]	*15*	*16*
Attractiveness	15[d]	11
Convenience of Facilities		
Shopping	11	9
Recreation	*6*	*6*
Schools	5	3
Health care	1	1
Other (church, cultural, entertainment, etc.)	16	15
Quality of Facilities		
Schools	8	9
Recreation	*5*	*3*
Shopping	4	6
Health care	1	0
Other (church, cultural, entertainment, etc.)	2	2
Type of People Living in Community		
Friendliness	10	10
High social status	8	9
Planning of Community	12[d]	4
Sample size	2838	1321

[a]*Question:* From your own personal point of view, would you rate this area as an excellent place to live, good, average, below average or poor? Why do you say that?

[b]Responses add to more than 100 percent because some respondents mentioned more than one reason for rating their communities as excellent or good places to live.

[c]Includes respondents who mentioned open space, greenbelts, trees, hills, rivers and other natural features.

[d]Difference between new communities and conventional communities is statistically significant at the 0.05 level of confidence.

convenience of community recreational facilities as a reason for rating community livability highly, while 5 percent of the respondents cited the quality of community recreational facilities. The quality and/or convenience of community recreational facilities were mentioned by 13 percent or more of the respondents living in Elk Grove Village, Foster City, Irvine, Laguna Niguel, North Palm Beach and

Valencia. Recreational facilities received the fewest mentions as a reason for positive evaluations of community livability among the respondents who were living in Forest Park (6 percent) and Columbia (5 percent).

In order to provide additional insights into the contributions of recreational facilities to residents' evaluations of community livability, a multivariate analysis was performed using respondents' ratings of overall community livability as the dependent variable and their evaluations of various community attributes as the independent variables. To control for respondents' personal and household characteristics, the analysis was performed in a step-wise mode with respondents' characteristics entering the regression equations before their evaluations of community attributes. The results for nonfederally assisted new and conventional communities are summarized in Table 8−6. The first and third data columns indicate the relationship between each independent variable and respondents' evaluations of overall community livability, with the effects of the other variables not controlled. The multivariate beta coefficients in the second and fourth data columns indicate how much change in community livability ratings was produced by a standardized change in each of the independent variables, controlling for the effects of all of the other independent variables.

The results presented in Table 8−6 show that on the basis of the simple correlation coefficients, respondents' evaluations of recreational facilities ranked third among community attributes in explaining the variance in community livability evaluations. When other variables were controlled in the multivariate analysis, the influence of recreational facilities increased to second among personal characteristics and ratings of community attributes in its influence on livability evaluations. Satisfaction with the immediate neighborhood had more influence on evaluations of community livability; satisfaction with the dwelling unit had an equivalent effect; and respondents' ratings of schools, health care facilities and services, their homes association, transportation, shopping facilities and religious facilities were less important. In comparison with its effect in new communities, respondents' evaluation of recreational facilities had much less influence on conventional community respondents' overall evaluations of the livability of their communities.

To ascertain whether the influence of recreational facilities on respondents' overall evaluations of community livability varied for different types of persons, a series of multivariate analyses were performed for various population groups. Table 8−7 shows the multivariate beta coefficient (and its rank in each equation) that was obtained for respondents' evaluations of community recreational facilities when this variable was included in each multivariate equation. The format for these analyses paralleled the analysis summarized in Table 8—5, with respondents' personal and household characteristics entered into the equations in a step-wise manner before respondents' ratings of community attributes were entered.

The influence of respondents' evaluations of community recreational facilities on their overall evaluations of new communities as places to live was fairly stable across different segments of the population. Nevertheless, evaluations of community recreational facilities had somewhat more influence on the overall community livability evaluations of some population groups than others, including those of women, younger and older persons, persons with annual family incomes under $10,000 and persons who were living in condominium (ownership) apartments.

OPEN SPACE, RECREATIONAL FACILITIES
AND THE QUALITY OF LIFE

It has long been assumed that proximity to the natural environment and the availability of community recreational facilities and programs contribute to residents' overall quality of life (see Hjelte and Shivers 1972, p. 27). To test this assumption, two approaches to measuring the quality of life were used. The first approach is based on questions that asked respondents what they felt were the key determinants of their quality of life and whether, in these terms, moving to the community where they were living at the time of the interview had improved the quality of their lives, made it worse or hadn't made much difference. Respondents were also asked whether various attributes of their communities were better, about the same or not as good as in the communities from which they had moved. The analyses of these data were designed to determine what proportion of respondents perceived community environmental characteristics and recreational facilities as important determinants of their quality of life and whether perceived improvements in these community attributes after moving to a new community were associated with respondents' perceptions of improvements in the overall quality of life.

The second approach that was used focused on a global assessment of respondents' personal well-being at the time they were interviewed. This was based on a question which asked, "We have talked about various parts of your life; now I want to ask you about your life as a whole. How satisfied are you with your life as a whole these

Table 8–6. The Influence of Recreational Facility Evaluations on Evaluations of Overall Community Livability: Multivariate Analyses[a]

Independent Variables	Thirteen Nonfederally Assisted New Communities		Thirteen Conventional Communities	
	Simple Correlation Coefficient	Multivariate Beta Coefficient	Simple Correlation Coefficient	Multivariate Beta Coefficient
Personal and Household Characteristics				
Sex of respondent	.01	.03	.02	.03
Age of respondent	-.10	-.01	-.09	.004
Marital status	.04	-.01	.02	-.02
Education of respondent	-.03	-.03	.03	.006
Length of residence in community	-.02	-.03	.04	.03
Housing cost	-.21	-.03	-.15	-.07
Family income	-.15	-.07	-.03	.02
Tenure	.14	.04	.12	-.0003
Number of children	.01	-.01	.002	-.001
Evaluations of Community Attributes[b]				
Immediate neighborhood[c]	.44	.30	.38	.25
Recreational Facilities	.24	.12	.16	.07
Dwelling unit	.33	.12	.30	.15
Schools	.14	.08	.14	.09
Health care facilities and services	.16	.08	.05	-.03
Homes association	.23	.06	.14	.03
Transportation	.08	.05	.11	.09
Shopping facilities	.03	-.04	.09	.02
Religious facilities	.07	.02	.02	-.01

R^2	.26	.18
Sample size	2590	1296

[a] Community livability evaluations were measured with a five-point scale running from excellent (1) to poor (5).

[b] Community attribute evaluation measures are based on several different scales. Ratings of health care, recreational facilities, schools and shopping are five-point scales (excellent to poor); ratings of the dwelling unit and homes association are based on seven-point scales (completely satisfied to completely dissatisfied). Satisfaction with religious facilities is a two-point scale (availability-unavailability of facilities desired); transportation ratings are based on a six-point scale constructed from ratings of convenience to work and ease of getting around the community (better, same, or not as good as previous community); and satisfaction with the immediate neighborhood is a fifteen-point scale constructed from three five-point semantic differential items (very good place to live/very poor place to live, pleasant/unpleasant and attractive/unattractive).

[c] The immediate neighborhood was defined for respondents as "the area near here which you can see from your front door—that is, the five or six homes nearest to yours around here."

Table 8–7.   Influence of Evaluation of Recreational Facilities on Evaluations of Overall Community Livability: Comparisons among Population Groups

Population Group[a]	Influence of Community Recreational Facility Evaluations in Multivariate Equation		Number of Cases in Equation[b]
	Beta	Rank in Equation	
All respondents	.12	2	2590
Sex			
Male	.10	4	1140
Female	.13	2	1450
Age			
Under 35	.17	2	1013
35 to 55	.07	6	1131
55 or over	.19	3	424
Education			
High school or less	.14	2	892
Some college or college graduate	.10	5	1227
Graduate or professional training	.12	3	423
Income			
Under $10,000	.19	2	283
$10,000–$14,999	.09	4	534
$15,000–$24,999	.14	2	1140
$25,000 and over	.06	5	472
Number of children			
None	.11	3	1012
One or more	.11	3	1584
Housing Type/Tenure			
Single-family detached/own	.10	4	1735

Townhouse/own	.09	11	187
Townhouse/rent	.06	11	118
Apartment/own	.29	1	97
Apartment/rent	.08	6	357

[a]The dependent variable in these equations was respondents' overall evaluation of their communities as places to live. The independent variables, in addition to respondents' ratings of community recreational facilities, included their sex, age, marital status, education, length of residence in the community, housing cost, family income, tenure, number of children and ratings of their dwelling unit, immediate neighborhood and homes association, and ratings of community schools, health care facilities and services, transportation, shopping facilities and religious facilities.

[b]All analyses were performed with data from respondents who were living in thirteen nonfederally assisted new communities.

days?" Responses were measured on a seven-point scale, from completely satisfied to completely dissatisfied. In addition to this overall measure, respondents were asked about their satisfaction with a series of life domains and about their evaluations of various attributes of their communities. The objective of the analyses was to identify the relative contributions of satisfaction with the use of leisure time and evaluations of community recreational facilities to respondents' overall satisfaction with their life as a whole.

Improvement in the Quality of Life
After Moving

In defining what their own quality of life depended upon, eleven factors were mentioned by 10 percent or more of the new and conventional community respondents. Factors associated with the quality of the physical environment were mentioned by 18 percent of the new community respondents and 16 percent of the conventional community respondents. In each setting environmental factors ranked fifth behind respondents' mentions of economic security, good/happy family life, personal strengths and values and rewarding interpersonal relationships. Enjoyment of leisure and recreational activities ranked eighth in the new communities (mentioned by 16 percent of the respondents) and ninth in the conventional communities (mentioned by 13 percent of the respondents). The quality and accessibility of community recreational facilities were mentioned by fewer than 10 percent of the respondents in each setting as factors that determined the quality of their lives.

Two-thirds of the respondents in the thirteen nonfederally assisted new communities and thirteen conventional communities reported that the quality of their lives had improved after moving to their present communities. Among the federally assisted new communities, 75 percent of the Jonathan respondents reported that their quality of life had improved while a somewhat lower proportion of Park Forest South respondents (64 percent) reported the same result. The relationships between reported improvements in various aspects of the community and reported improvements in respondents' quality of life are summarized in Table 8–8. As in the analysis of community satisfaction, both univariate (uncontrolled) correlation coefficients and multivariate (controlled for other variables) beta coefficients were used to assess the relative importance of nearness to the outdoors and community recreational facilities. Respondents personal and household characteristics were used in the multivariate analyses to control for their effect on perceptions of improvement in life quality.

As shown in Table 8-8, respondents' perceptions of improvements in a number of attributes of their communities in relation to their previous communities were associated with perceptions of improvements in their quality of life. When other variables were controlled in the multivariate equation, perceived improvements in recreational facilities ranked second behind perceived improvements in the type of people in the community. Perceived improvements in proximity to the outdoors and natural environment after moving to the community were also positively associated with perceived improvements in the quality of life of both new and conventional community residents, but had less of an effect than perceived improvements in recreational facilities when other variables were controlled in the multivariate equations.

The analyses summarized in Table 8-8 were repeated for a number of population groups to determine whether improvements in recreational facilities attained by moving to a new community were equally important in each group's perception of improvements in the quality of life. The results obtained indicated that perceptions of improvements in recreational facilities had the most influence on perceived improvements in the quality of life of older (fifty-five and over) persons and of persons whose family income was less than $10,000 per year. Also, recreational facilities had more of an effect on perceived improvements in townhouse (both ownership and rental) residents' quality of life, the quality of life of persons with low (rather than moderate or high) concern for social status, and the quality of life of persons with no children living in their households. Recreational facilities were equally likely to contribute to perceived improvements in the quality of life of white and black respondents.

Satisfaction with Life as a Whole

The second approach used to gauge respondents' quality of life was based on their reported satisfaction with their "life as a whole" at the time they were interviewed in the spring of 1973. Eighty-eight percent of the new community respondents and 87 percent of the conventional community respondents reported that they were satisfied with their lives. A slightly lower proportion of respondents from the federally assisted new communities in the sample were satisfied with their lives: Jonathan (85 percent) and Park Forest South (85 percent).

Information was also obtained about respondents' satisfaction with a number of aspects or "domains" of their lives, including satisfaction with the use of their leisure time. In comparison with their satisfaction with life as a whole, a much lower proportion of re-

Table 8–8.   The Influence of Respondents' Perceptions of Improvements in Nearness to the Outdoors and Community Recreational Facilities on Perceptions of Improvement in Their Quality of Life

Variables	Thirteen Nonfederally Assisted New Communities		Thirteen Conventional Communities	
	Simple Correlation Coefficient	*Multivariate Beta Coefficient*	*Simple Correlation Coefficient*	*Multivariate Beta Coefficient*
Personal and Household Characteristics				
Sex of respondent	.05	.02	.09	.07
Age of respondent	.08	.03	.12	.04
Marital status	.11	.06	.11	.05
Education of respondent	-.01	-.001	.03	-.03
Length of residence in community	.04	-.01	.004	.01
Housing cost	-.07	-.04	-.01	.01
Family income	-.03	.02	.03	.02
Tenure	.10	-.01	.12	.04
Number of children	-.06	-.02	-.06	.009
Evaluation of Community Attributes in Relation to Previous Community[a]				
Type of people in neighborhood	.37	.20	.36	.20
Recreational facilities	.28	.13	.20	.06
Neighborhood appearance	.33	.11	.35	.10
Layout and space of dwelling	.27	.06	.33	.11
Opportunity for participation in community life	.30	.07	.31	.09
Proximity to natural environment	.28	.08	.29	.08
Convenience to work	.10	.05	.06	.02

Quality of house construction	.22	.05	.25	.03
Public schools	.22	.04	.20	.01
Ease of getting around community	.17	.04	.16	.05
Health and medical services	.11	.04	.06	−.007
Cost of living	.07	.02	.10	.03
Safety from crime	.23	.02	.26	.05
Shopping facilities	.06	.02	.02	.002
R^2	.26		.26	
Sample size	2590		1296	

[a] Respondents were asked: "Now, I'd like you to compare this community to the one you lived in just before you moved here. For each item . . . please tell me if where you're living now is better, not as good or about the same as where you lived before."

spondents were satisfied with the ways in which they spent their leisure. Only 72 percent of the respondents in the thirteen nonfederally assisted new communities and 66 percent of the respondents in the paired conventional communities were satisfied with this aspect of their lives. Jonathan (70 percent satisfied) and Park Forest South (68 percent satisfied) respondents fared no better. Among individual nonfederally assisted new communities, respondents' satisfaction with the use of their leisure time was highest in communities in warmer climates that were freestanding or located near natural amenities, such as water bodies or large amounts of undeveloped land. These communities included Foster City, Laguna Niguel, North Palm Beach, Valencia and Westlake Village (see Table 5–14). There was little relationship between variation in respondents' personal and household characteristics and variation in their leisure satisfaction. In general, older respondents ($r = -.13$) with no children living in the household ($r = .10$) who had lived in a new community a longer period of time ($r = .08$) tended to be more satisfied. Respondents' sex, education, income and tenure had no significant influence on leisure satisfaction.

Although new community residents were less satisfied with the use of their leisure time than with a number of other aspects of their lives, leisure satisfaction was strongly associated with overall life satisfaction.[c] As shown in Table 8–9, satisfaction with the use of leisure time ranked just behind satisfaction with the standard of living in its influence on respondents' satisfaction with their lives as a whole, and ahead of satisfaction with marriage, job, family life, and health. On the other hand, respondents' evaluations of community recreational facilities had almost no effect on their overall satisfaction with life. Curiously, respondents' evaluations of community recreational facilities were also only weakly ($r = .09$) associated with satisfaction with the use of their leisure time. The lack of association between evaluations of community recreational facilities and satisfaction with the use of leisure time confirms an observation made by Herbert J. Gans (1967) in his analysis of the master plan developed for Levittown, New Jersey. Noting that the first of the plan's objectives called for an environment that provided for leisure activities, Gans commented:

[c]The proportion of new community respondents who were satisfied with other life domains included: marriage (93 percent); community livability (90 percent); neighborhood livability (89 percent); personal health (88 percent); family life (87 percent); dwelling unit (86 percent); standard of living (86 percent); job (85 percent); and housework (71 percent). For further discussion of life satisfaction in new communities, see Raymond J. Burby, III, Shirley F. Weiss *et al.* 1976, Chapter 17 and Robert B. Zehner 1976.

> Leisure needs are to be met by township parks, playgrounds, playfields, tot-lots, walking areas, a marina, and a golf course. However desirable, these offer only athletic outdoor recreation, principally for children (especially boys), for men, and for families affluent enough to own a boat. No provision is made for nonathletic forms of leisure, such as commercial entertainment, and nothing is said about facilitating sociability and reducing social isolation. . . . (Gans 1967, p. 388).

Thus, while leisure is important to new community residents' quality of life and recreational facilities influenced perceived improvements in the quality of life upon moving to a new community (see above), developers' overwhelming attention to outdoor recreational facilities that improved the appearance and marketability of their communities had only a minimal direct and indirect (through leisure satisfaction) effect on residents' overall satisfaction with their lives.

SUMMARY

This chapter has shown that open space and recreational facilities can be important aspects of the appeal of new communities to prospective residents; that open space and community recreational facilities contributed to residents' satisfaction with their communities as places to live; and that residents' satisfaction with the use of their leisure time influenced their perceived quality of life.

Although more residents moved to new communities because of perceived nearness to the outdoors than because of the availability of recreational facilities, nearness to the outdoors did not differentiate the appeal of new communities from competitive housing in nearby less planned communities. Nearness to the outdoors as an aspect of a new community's appeal to prospective residents also appeared to be as much or more a product of the location of a new community in a sparsely settled area on the outskirts of a metropolitan region as it was of planned open spaces within a community. As new communities grew over time, the contribution of nearness to the outdoors in attracting prospective residents declined. Available recreational facilities were cited by less than half the proportion of residents who cited nearness to the outdoors as a reason for having moved to a new community. However, unlike nearness to the outdoors, the availability of recreational facilities differentiated the appeal of new communities from competitive housing in nearby conventional communities.

Open space and recreational facilities were not equally important in the moving decisions of all households. As a result, their emphasis

Table 8–9. The Influence of Leisure Satisfaction and Community Recreational Facilities on Satisfaction with Life as a Whole

Independent Variables	Thirteen Nonfederally Assisted New Communities		Thirteen Conventional Communities	
	Simple Correlation Coefficient	Multivariate Beta Coefficient	Simple Correlation Coefficient	Multivariate Beta Coefficient
Personal and Household Characteristics				
Sex of respondent	−.03	.01	−.02	.002
Age of respondent	−.05	.08	.01	.13
Marital status	.14	.04	.26	.08
Education of respondent	.02	.002	.06	.06
Length of residence in community	.02	−.006	.03	−.003
Housing cost	−.13	−.01	−.08	.04
Family income	.15	−.05	−.09	−.05
Tenure	.09	−.01	.12	−.01
Number of children	.03	.01	.01	−.007
Satisfaction with Life Domains[a]				
Standard of living[a]	.44	.21	.44	.20
Use of leisure time[a]	.42	.19	.43	.18
Marriage	.36	.16	.39	.15
Job[a]	.35	.15	.29	.13
Family life[b]	.42	.15	.45	.16
Personal health[a]	.28	.11	.28	.10
Sex role (housework)[c]	.14	.05	.16	.04

Evaluation of Community Attributes[d]				
Dwelling unit	.32	.10	.36	.16
Homes association	.21	.10	.09	.09
Transportation	.02	-.04	.006	-.03
Recreational facilities	*.08*	*-.03*	*.14*	*.01*
Schools	.09	.01	.17	.11
Health care facilities and services	.09	.01	.03	-.04
Immediate neighborhood[e]	.23	.01	-.02	-.04
R^2		.45		.47
Sample size		2590		1296

[a]Satisfaction with the standard of living, use of leisure time, marriage, job, and personal health were measured by seven-point scales running from completely satisfied (1) to completely dissatisfied (7).

[b]Satisfaction with family life was measured by a four-point scale indicating whether respondents agreed strongly, agreed somewhat, disagreed somewhat, or disagreed strongly to the statement, "All things considered, I am very satisfied with my family life—the time I spend and the things I do with members of my family."

[c]Satisfaction with housework was measured by a four-point scale indicating whether respondents agreed strongly, agreed somewhat, disagreed somewhat, or disagreed strongly to the statement, "As often as not, I actually enjoy cooking, cleaning and doing other chores around the house."

[d]See footnote b, Table 8–6.

[e]See footnote c, Table 8–6.

in community design and marketing has implications for the composition of the population attracted to new communities. Open space and recreational facilities were more important to the moving decisions of white rather than black households; households moving to smaller dwelling units; dwelling units in both high density (8.5 dwelling units per acre or more) and very low density (1.0 dwelling units per acre or less) sections of new communities; smaller households; households with older household heads (age fifty-five or older); and households with very high family incomes. In addition, recreational facilities were cited as a reason for their move to a new community by a higher than average proportion of households whose heads were under twenty-five years old and by households who moved to apartment dwelling units, rental units and dwelling units that were located closer to recreational facilities. Contrary to Werthman, Mandell and Dienstfrey's (1965) conclusion that recreational facilities are important in new communities because of their social status connotations, persons who moved to new communities because of available recreational facilities had lower rather than higher orientations to social status. In addition, they tended to participate more frequently in a variety of outdoor recreational activities than households who did not cite available recreational facilities as a reason for having moved to a new community.

Data presented in this chapter indicate that investments in improving the quality of community recreational facilities will produce greater increases in residents' satisfaction with their communities as places to live than will investments in most other community attributes. The contribution of community recreational facilities to residents' evaluations of overall community livability varied among residents with different characteristics. Recreational facilities had more influence on the overall community livability evaluations of women than men, of younger (under age twenty-five) and older (over age fifty-five) persons than middle-aged persons, on persons with annual family incomes which were under $10,000, and on persons who lived in condominium apartments. Efforts to improve residents' satisfaction with their communities as places to live through investments in recreational facilities will have more influence on the community satisfaction of these residents than on others living in new communities.

Residents' perceptions of improvements in recreational facilities achieved by moving to new communities were associated with perceptions of improvements in their overall quality of life. However, residents' satisfaction with their lives as a whole was more strongly associated with satisfaction with the use of leisure time, rather than satisfaction with community recreational facilities. In fact, there was very little relationship between satisfaction with community recreational facilities and satisfaction with the use of leisure time. This may have been due to developers' and local governments' tendencies to concentrate recreational expenditures on open space and outdoor recreational facilities and generally to neglect facilities for nonathletic leisure pursuits. In order to have a more positive influence on residents' quality of life, the concept of recreation in new communities should be expanded to encompass a broad definition of leisure that includes entertainment and social activities as well as outdoor sports, and greater attention should be given to recreational programing and personalized advice to residents on the use of their leisure time.

Appendixes

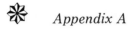 *Appendix A*

Sampling and Data Collection Procedures

The data reported in this study were collected in a sample of thirty-six new and conventional communities in the United States. Three data collection procedures were used. These included a household survey, surveys of developers and professional personnel who were involved in the provision of recreational facilities and services and field inventories and map measurements. This appendix describes the methods used in selecting new and conventional communities for the study and in conducting the various surveys and field measurements.

SELECTION OF SAMPLE COMMUNITIES

The thirty-six communities studied included fifteen new communities, fifteen paired conventional communities, two retirement new communities, two conventional suburban communities with predominantly black residential areas and two conventional suburban communities with subsidized housing for low- and moderate-income residents.

Selection of the New Communities
The sample of new communities was selected in stages. First, 63 new communities and large-scale developments were identified from a list prepared by the New Communities Division of the Department of Housing and Urban Development (1969). The communities on the HUD list were screened against two sets of criteria. First, the

communities were evaluated in terms of their conformance to five criteria which are basic to the new community concept:

1. *Unified ownership*—community development under the direction of a single entrepreneur or development company to assure unified and coordinated management of the development process.
2. *Planning*—development programmed in accordance with an overall master plan.
3. *Size*—2000 or more acres planned for an eventual population of 20,000 or more people to allow for social diversity and to support a variety of urban functions.
4. *Self-sufficiency*—provision for a variety of urban functions through the reservation of land for residential, commercial, industrial, public and institutional uses.
5. *Housing choice*—provision of a variety of housing choices, including, at a minimum, opportunities for owning and renting and for single-family and apartment life styles.

The application of these criteria to the communities on the HUD list significantly narrowed the number of projects that were eligible for inclusion in the study. Large-scale land development projects that were excluded from the study at this stage included special purpose communities, such as resort and retirement projects; suburban planned unit developments, which could not meet the size and self-sufficiency criteria; and new towns-in-town, which could not meet the size criterion.

Three additional criteria were applied to meet the specific needs of the overall new communities study. These included:

6. *Location*—communities located outside of the contiguous 48 states were eliminated in order to limit data collection costs.
7. *Age*—communities that ceased all active development prior to 1960 were eliminated in order to simplify recall problems in case studies of development decisions.
8. *Population*—communities with fewer than 5000 residents on January 1, 1972 were eliminated to assure that communities had enough homes, facilities and services in place to provide an adequate basis for evaluation.

The two screening processes eliminated 36 of the 63 communities on the HUD list.

From the 27 remaining new communities, thirteen privately developed communities were selected for intensive study. Five new communities were selected because they contained unique features of particular interest to the research team:

1. Columbia, Md.—100 percent sample of stratum: communities with 10 percent or more nonwhite population on January 1, 1972.
2. Irvine, Calif.—100 percent sample of stratum: regional cities with projected populations over 150,000.
3. Lake Havasu City, Ariz.—100 percent sample of stratum: free-standing new communities.
4. Park Forest, Ill.—100 percent sample of stratum: recognized outstanding completed post World War II new community.
5. Reston, Va.—100 percent sample of stratum: recognized outstanding design.

A simple random sample of eight additional communities was then selected from the 22 communities remaining in the sample frame. These included:[a]

6. Elk Grove Village, Ill.
7. Forest Park, Oh.
8. Foster City, Calif.
9. Laguna Niguel, Calif.
10. North Palm Beach, Fla.
11. Sharpstown, Tex.
12. Valencia, Calif.
13. Westlake Village, Calif.

The privately developed new communities selected for study allow adequate coverage of the range of variation in the characteristics of nonfederally assisted new communities now under development in the United States. There is no evidence that the inclusion of a greater number of new communities would have yielded greater variation in community characteristics.

Finally, although both Jonathan, Minn. and Park Forest South, Ill. had fewer than 5000 residents as of January 1, 1972, these two communities were selected to assure the inclusion in the study of new

[a]After these eight communities were selected, the fourteen communities remaining in the new community sampling frame were: (1) Clear Lake City, Tex.; (2) Coral Springs, Fla.; (3) Diamond Bar, Calif.; (4) Janss/Conejo (Thousand Oaks), Calif.; (5) Lehigh Acres, Fla.; (6) Litchfield Park, Ariz.; (7) Miami Lakes, Fla.; (8) Mission Viejo, Calif.; (9) Montbello, Col.; (10) Montgomery Village, Md.; (11) Northglenn, Col.; (12) Palm Beach Gardens, Fla.; (13) Pikes Peak Park, Col.; and (14) Rancho Bernardo, Calif.

communities that were participating in the federal new communities program. At the time the sample was drawn, the universe of federally assisted new communities included: Flower Mound, Tex.; Jonathan, Minn.; Maumelle, Ark.; Park Forest South, Ill.; Riverton, N.Y.; and St. Charles Communities, Md. Most of these were in the very initial stages of development. Only Jonathan and Park Forest South had enough occupied housing for a baseline evaluation. Because at least two federally assisted new communities were required to avoid the problem of generalizing from a unique case, both were included in the sample.

Selection of the Paired
Conventional Communities

For each of the sample new communities, a less planned conventionally developed area was delineated to serve as a control and basis of comparison. The new communities and paired conventional communities were otherwise matched in terms of the age of housing, range of housing costs and location within the metropolitan area. In some cases it was necessary to delineate a set of contiguous subdivisions as a comparison area in order to match more nearly the range of housing costs in the paired new community. An effort was also made to match on the mix of housing types; however, this could not be done consistently because the range of housing types available in new communities was not found regularly in other suburban settings. Where older, established communities were listed as comparison communities, only the tracts or neighborhoods within these communities that matched the new community as to age and price range of housing were included in the universe from which the household sample was selected. However, respondents in such areas were asked about the whole community rather than only the subselected tracts in which they lived in household survey questions that referred to the community as a whole.

The paired conventional communities were chosen on the basis of information gathered during site visits to the market areas of the sample new communities and from consultations with county and municipal planning agencies and local real estate firms, analyses of census tract data and visual inspection of all areas that met the matching criteria. The sample new communities and their paired conventional communities include:

New Community	*Paired Conventional Community*
(1) Columbia, Md.	Norbeck-Wheaton, Md.
(2) Elk Grove Village, Ill.	Schaumburg, Ill

(3) Forest Park, Oh.	Sharonville, Oh.
(4) Foster City, Calif.	West San Mateo, Calif.
(5) Irvine, Calif.	Fountain Valley, Calif.
(6) Jonathan, Minn.	Chanhassen, Minn.
(7) Laguna Niguel, Calif.	Dana Point/Capistrano Valley, Calif.
(8) Lake Havasu City, Ariz.	Kingman, Ariz.
(9) North Palm Beach, Fla.	Tequesta, Fla.
(10) Park Forest, Ill.	Lansing, Ill.
(11) Park Forest South, Ill.	Richton Park, Ill.
(12) Reston, Va.	West Springfield, Va.
(13) Sharpstown, Tex.	Southwest Houston, Tex.
(14) Valencia, Calif.	Bouquet Canyon, Calif.
(15) Westlake Village, Calif.	Agoura/Malibu Junction, Calif.

Table A-1 summarizes information as to the location, population, and acreage of the sample new communities at the start of the study, together with comparable data on the location and population of the paired conventional communities. Population estimates for the paired conventional communities are based on the whole community as defined for the respondents rather than for subselected tracts or neighborhoods from which the household sample was drawn. Vignettes describing the characteristics of the sample new communities and paired conventional communities are provided in Appendix B.

Selection of Retirement New Communities, Conventional Black Suburban Areas and Subsidized Housing Projects in Conventional Communities

Six additional communities were selected to serve as controls and as another base of comparison with the responses of new community elderly residents, black residents, and low- and moderate-income residents of subsidized housing. Two of the communities, as described in Chapter 6, were retirement new communities designed specifically for the elderly. Rossmoor Leisure World is located in the Laguna Hills section of Orange County, Calif. Sun City Center is located in Hillsborough County, south of the city of Tampa, Fla. Two conventional communities, the Seat Pleasant area, Md. and Markham, Ill., contained predominantly black single-family detached subdivisions that provided housing similar to that available to black families in new communities. In two other communities, Laurel, Md. and Chicago Heights, Ill., federally subsidized housing projects were utilized as sampling frames to select low- and moderate-income households

Table A—1.   Distance from Central Business District, Estimated Population, and Target Acreage for Sample New Communities and Their Paired Conventional Communities at Beginning of Study

New Communities/Paired Conventional Communities	New Communities and Conventional Communities	
	Number of Miles from Metropolitan Central Business District[a]	
	New Community	Conventional Community
Nonfederally Assisted New Communities/Paired Conventional Communities		
Average for thirteen nonfederally assisted new communities/thirteen conventional communities	21.5	22.5
Columbia/Norbeck-Wheaton, Md.	19	15
Elk Grove Village/Schaumburg, Ill.	26	30
Forest Park/Sharonville, Oh.	15	15
Foster City/San Mateo, Calif.	25	30
Irvine/Fountain Valley, Calif.	8	11
Laguna Niguel/Dana Point, Calif.	23	27
Lake Havasu City/Kingman, Ariz.	b	b
North Palm Beach/Tequesta, Fla.	7	17
Park Forest/Lansing, Ill.	29	27
Reston/Springfield, Va.	18	13
Sharpstown/Southwest Houston, Tex.	10	12
Valencia/Bouquet Canyon, Calif.	32	38
Westlake Village/Agoura/Malibu Junction, Calif.	40	35
Federally Assisted New Communities/Paired Conventional Communities		
Jonathan/Chanhassen, Minn.	25	20
Park Forest South/Richton Park, Ill.	32	30

[a]Road distance from central business district of central city of Standard Metropolitan Statistical Area (as defined for the 1970 United States Census) in which community is located.

[b]Freestanding community (i.e., not in a Standard Metropolitan Statistical Area).

[c]Data from 1970 United States Census.

that could be compared to similar groups living in new communities.

The primary criterion used in the selection of these special comparison communities was that they be located in the vicinity of the

Table A−1. continued

New Communities and
Conventional Communities

Estimated Population		New Communities Only		
New Community	Conventional Community	Percent of Target Population	Target Population	Target Acreage
17,900	21,800	38.5	71,346	11,646
24,000	20,000	22	110,000	18,000
23,000	25,200	39	58,500	5,760
17,000	11,000[c]	49	35,000	3,725
15,000	79,000[c]	42	36,000	2,600
20,000	49,900	6	338,000	64,000
8,500	6,600	21	40,000	7,936
8,500	7,300[c]	14	60,000	16,630
12,500	2,600[c]	42	30,000	2,362
30,600	25,800[c]	87	35,000	3,182
20,000	35,000	27	75,000	7,400
34,000	10,000	97	35,000	4,100
7,000	6,000	28	25,000	4,000
13,000	5,000	26	50,000	11,709
1,500	5,100	3	50,000	8,194
3,200	4,800	3	110,000	8,291

sample new communities. This was done in order to limit regional variation and to facilitate comparisons among the communities. The special comparison communities are comparable to the other sample communities in terms of the age and price range of housing available. They were selected in much the same manner as the paired conventional communities—on the basis of site visits and consultations with local planning agencies and realtors.

THE HOUSEHOLD SURVEY

Residents living in the 36 new and conventional communities were interviewed during the period from February through May 1973. Portions of the interview schedule that were used for the analyses in this book are reproduced in Appendix C. The number of households interviewed in each community is shown in Table A−2.

Selection of Sample Households and Respondents

The universe sampled for the household survey included family heads and their spouses living in the 36 sample communities. The sample was selected in such a manner that every head or spouse who had moved into his or her dwelling before January 1, 1973 had a known probability of selection. The method of selecting the household sample was as follows.

Visits were made to all 36 sample communities between mid-October 1972, and mid-January 1973 to identify all occupied dwellings on large-scale maps showing lot lines for each community. These maps, with the location and number of occupied dwellings delineated, were used to outline clusters of from five to seven dwelling units. The number of units to be included in a cluster was chosen on the basis of projected field costs, expected response rate and the number of clusters needed to generate a household sample representative of the sample communities. The eventual analysis of housing clusters was considered in delineating sample clusters. Accordingly, the clusters were outlined so as to include dwellings that faced one another across a street or common court. Dwellings strung out in a row were rarely defined as clusters.

For apartment buildings where the location of individual dwellings was unknown, the total number of units in the building was divided into a designated number of five-, six- or seven-dwelling clusters. For buildings containing fewer than ten apartments, two or three neighboring buildings were grouped together and clusters were designated for all units in the group. Where the location of apartments within a building was known, it was possible to cluster these units directly as in the procedure described above.

After clusters were defined for a community, a probability sample of clusters was selected. The samples in paired conventional communities that had more than one type of dwelling unit available were stratified by dwelling unit type (single-family detached houses, townhouses or apartments) so that the proportion of selected clusters of each dwelling type approximated the proportions of dwelling unit types found in the paired new community. Overall, the selection of sample clusters was designed to obtain 200 interviews in each of the thirteen nonfederally assisted new communities and two federally assisted new communities, and 100 interviews in each of the paired conventional communities, retirement new communities and conventional communities used to obtain interviews with subsidized housing and black residents.

Subsample of new community households occupying subsidized housing. Five of the sample new communities (Columbia, Forest Park, Jonathan, Lake Havasu City and Reston) had FHA Sections 235 (owner) and/or 221(d)3 or 236 (rental) subsidized housing occupied at the time of the sampling process. In each of these communities the sampling frame was divided into two strata, one of subsidized housing units and one of nonsubsidized housing units. Separate random probability cluster samples were drawn from each stratum in the manner described above. Selection of clusters was designed to produce 50 interviews with households occupying subsidized housing and 200 interviews with households occupying nonsubsidized housing in each of the five communities.

Subsample of new community black households. In each of the five sample new communities known to have more than 100 resident black households (Columbia, Forest Park, Park Forest, Park Forest South and Reston) a special subsample of black households was selected to supplement those falling into the regular cluster samples. Lists suitable for use as sampling frames were not available in all five of the communities. Therefore, sampling frames were constructed by referrals from the random sample respondents. Addresses generated by the referral procedure were listed and duplications were eliminated. The five resulting lists were used as the sample frames from which simple random samples of addresses were drawn, aimed at producing 50 additional interviews with black households in each of the five communities.

It should be noted that because it is a referral sample this subsample of black households does not constitute a random sample representative of the population of black family heads and their spouses in these communities. However, comparison of black subsample respondent characteristics and attitudes with those of black respondents from the random sample in the five communities indicated that the two groups were very similar. See Table A−3. Therefore, responses from the black subsample were included with those of random sample blacks in the analysis presented in Chapter 6 to

Table A-2. Number of Household Interviews

Communities	Total	Basic Sample	Number of Interviews		
			Subsidized Housing Residents	Black Residents (Subsamples)	Young Adults
Total	6,485	5,087	274	150	974
Thirteen Nonfederally Assisted New Communities	3,546	2,619	219	131	577
Thirteen Paired Conventional Communities	1,585	1,321	NA	NA	264
Federally Assisted New Communities and Paired Conventional Communities					
Jonathan, Minn. (NC)	219	152	55	NA	12
Chanhassen, Minn. (CC)	118	100	NA	NA	18
Park Forest South, Ill. (NC)	247	200	NA	19	28
Richton Park, Ill. (CC)	104	101	NA	NA	4
Two Retirement New Communities (NC)	204	204	NA	NA	NA
Two Subsidized Housing Conventional Communities (CC)	215	187	NA	NA	28
Two Black Conventional Communities (CC)	246	203	NA	NA	43

Nonfederally Assisted New Communities and Paired Conventional Communities

Columbia, Md. (NC)	341	213	61	37	30
Norbeck-Wheaton, Md. (CC)	151	123	NA	NA	28
Elk Grove Village, Ill. (NC)	258	199	NA	NA	59
Schaumburg, Ill. (CC)	116	102	NA	NA	14
Forest Park, Oh. (NC)	374	202	53	51	68
Sharonville, Oh. (CC)	145	115	NA	NA	30
Foster City, Calif. (NC)	202	176	NA	NA	26
West San Mateo, Calif. (CC)	112	93	NA	NA	19
Irvine, Calif. (NC)	239	202	NA	NA	37
Fountain Valley, Calif. (CC)	117	102	NA	NA	15
Laguna Niguel, Calif. (NC)	245	208	NA	NA	37
Dana Point, Calif. (CC)	139	105	NA	NA	34
Lake Havasu City, Ariz. (NC)	324	209	47	NA	68
Kingman, Ariz. (CC)	108	93	NA	NA	15
North Palm Beach, Fla. (NC)	245	202	NA	NA	43
Tequesta, Fla. (CC)	126	111	NA	NA	15
Park Forest, Ill. (NC)	253	200	NA	16	37
Lansing, Ill. (CC)	78	64	NA	NA	14
Reston, Va. (NC)	331	197	58	27	49
West Springfield, Va. (CC)	114	95	NA	NA	19
Sharpstown, Tex. (NC)	248	203	NA	NA	45
Southwest Houston, Tex. (CC)	134	108	NA	NA	26

Table A–2. continued overleaf . . . .

Table A-2. continued

Communities	Number of Interviews		Subsamples		
	Total	Basic Sample	Subsidized Housing Residents	Black Residents	Young Adults
Valencia, Calif. (NC)	235	202	NA	NA	33
Bouquet Canyon, Calif. (CC)	124	103	NA	NA	21
Westlake Village, Calif. (NC)	251	206	NA	NA	45
Agoura/Malibu Junction, Calif. (CC)	121	107	NA	NA	14

NC = New Community
CC = Conventional Community
NA = Not Applicable

Table A–3.   Comparison of Responses from Random Sample Blacks and the Nonrandom Black Subsample in Five Sample Communities

	Percent of Black Respondents from[a]	
Characteristic or Attitude	*Random Sample*	*Nonrandom Black Subsample*
Number of Persons in Respondent's Household		
One	2.2	2.7
Two	23.7	10.0
Three to five	62.6	70.7
Six or more	11.5	16.7
Number of Children in Respondent's Household		
None	23.5	12.7
One	28.2	24.0
Two	28.3	30.0
Three or more	20.0	33.3
Age of Family Head		
Under 35	50.4	45.0
35–44	32.1	37.6
45–54	14.1	16.1
55 or older	3.5	1.3
Marital Status of Household Head		
Married	89.9	86.7
Widowed	0.1	2.0
Divorced or separated	9.0	6.0
Never married	1.0	5.3
Education of Household Head		
High school graduate or less	39.7	33.6
Some college to college graduate	34.5	33.6
Graduate or professional training	25.9	32.9
Employment Status of Household Head		
Employed	95.8	97.3
Retired	1.3	0.0
Not employed (not retired)	2.8	2.7
Family's Total Income in 1972 (before taxes)		
Under $10,000	13.2	15.6
$10,000–$14,999	23.9	13.6
$15,000–$24,999	42.1	44.9
$25,000 or more	20.8	25.9

Table A–3 continued overleaf . . .

Table A—3. continued

Characteristic or Attitude	Percent of Black Respondents from[a]	
	Random Sample	Nonrandom Black Subsample
Tenure		
Owns or buying	67.3	85.8
Rents	32.1	13.5
Other	0.6	0.7
Length of Residence in the Community		
One year or less	47.2	32.4
Two or three years	31.8	30.4
Four or five years	17.2	27.0
Six or more years	3.9	10.1
Rating of Recreational Facilities		
Excellent	35.9	26.8
Good	32.9	36.9
Average	16.6	20.1
Below average or poor	14.5	16.1
Rating of the Community Overal		
Excellent	38.0	31.5
Good	44.6	58.4
Average	15.2	10.1
Below average or poor	2.2	0.0

[a]The responses of blacks falling into the random cluster sample in five sample communities known to have more than 100 resident black households at the time the sample was drawn are shown in the first column; the percentages are based on 95 interviews. Responses from blacks in the nonrandom referral subsamples in the same five communities are shown in the second column; the percentages are based on 150 interviews. The five communities are: Columbia, Md.; Forest Park, Oh.; Park Forest, Ill.; Park Forest South, Ill.; and Reston, Va. To be statistically significant, differences between percents in the table that are around 50 percent need to be at least 14.8 percent; differences between percents around 30 percent or 70 percent need to be at least 13.6 percent; and differences between percents around 10 percent or 90 percent need to be at least 8.9 percent.

increase the reliability of estimates for new community blacks without introducing substantial sampling error. Interviews obtained from the black subsample are not included in community totals presented in other chapters.

Subsample of new community and conventional community young adults. The universe for the young adult subsample included all persons fourteen through twenty years old (other than family heads and their spouses) who were found to be living in sample dwellings. If one such young adult was found at a sample dwelling, this person was selected for the young adult sample. If two or more were found, the interviewer selected one of these at random using a random selection table stamped on the young adult questionnaire. Thus, choice of young adult respondents was specified for interviewers rather than left to their discretion.

Designation of the household survey respondent. The prospective respondent was randomly designated as either the head of the family residing at the address or the spouse of the family head for each address in the regular cluster sample, the subsidized housing subsample, and the black subsample prior to assignment of addresses to interviewers. The head was designated as the respondent for half of the addresses sampled in each community; the spouse was designated as the respondent for the remaining half. Interviews were allowed only with the designated respondent except where the spouse was designated and there was no spouse of family head living in the household. In such situations the interview was to be taken with the family head. If a household was occupied by more than one family unit, the head or spouse of the head of each family unit was to be interviewed.

These procedures left no freedom to interviewers in the choice of respondents. The dwellings at which interviews were to be taken and the individuals to be interviewed within the dwellings were specified.

Interviewing Methods

Interviewers were instructed to ask questions using the exact wording appearing in the questionnaire. When probing was necessary to obtain full answers to open-end questions, interviewers were to use nondirective probes (such as, "How do you mean?" or "Could you tell me more about that?") to avoid influencing the responses.

When recording responses to open-end questions, interviewers were to write the actual words spoken as nearly as possible and to indicate when they had probed for additional information. Recording of responses to closed-end questions simply required checking the appropriate precoded response in most cases.

In situations where the respondent could not be contacted on the first call at a sample household, interviewers were required to call back at the household up to six times in order to obtain the interview. These callbacks were to be made at different times of day and on different days of the week to maximize the chance of a contact. Addresses at which the designated individuals refused to be interviewed were generally reassigned to a second interviewer who contacted the individuals and attempted to persuade them to be interviewed.

No substitutions for sample households or sample respondents were allowed. The addresses of sample households (including apartment designations) were listed for each cluster, and the proper respondent (head or spouse of head) was designated for each address listed prior to assignment of clusters to interviewers. Interviewers were required to interview the designated individuals at the addresses listed.

Reliability of the Data

Sample surveys, even though properly conducted, are liable to several kinds of errors. These include response errors which arise in the reporting and processing of the data; nonresponse errors, which arise from failure to interview some individuals who were selected in the sample; and sampling errors, which arise from the choice by chance of individuals for the sample who may make the sample unrepresentative of the population from which it was drawn. Some evaluation of each of these types of error is necessary for the proper interpretation of any estimates from survey data.

Response errors. Such errors include inaccuracies in asking and answering questions in the interview, recording responses, coding the recorded responses and processing the coded data. They can be reduced by thoroughly pretesting field procedures and instruments, training interviewers and coders and exercising quality controls throughout the data collection, coding and editing phases of the research process.

The questionnaires and field procedures used in the household survey were pretested in the autumn of 1972.[b] Pretesting was carried out in a planned community, Crofton, Md. in the Washington, D.C. metropolitan area, with respondents similar to the populations in the sample. Analysis of pretest interviews resulted in some revisions, such as the rewording of questions to make their meaning more clear to respondents and interviewers.

Interviewer training included a question-by-question review of the household interview instrument, the taking of a practice interview, and discussion of this interview with the interviewer's supervisor. Supervisors reviewed interviewers' work with them throughout the field period.

The coding operation involved two procedures. Responses to closed-end questions were scored directly on the household inter-

---

[b]The field and coding operations for the household survey were conducted by The Research Triangle Institute, Research Triangle Park, N.C. Members of the research team monitored all phases of these operations.

view and young adult questionnaire forms which had been printed so that the scored responses could be machine read directly from the forms onto computer tape. Responses to open-end questions were hand coded onto coding forms and keypunched from these forms. Coders were trained as to the codes and coding conventions used prior to the beginning of this work. Hand coding was checked by coding 10 percent of the interviews and questionnaires twice and comparing the two codings for discrepancies. Errors found were corrected.

Data tapes were checked for inconsistencies and incorrect codes and indicated corrections were made.

Nonresponse errors. Some proportion of the sample in any survey fails to respond, usually because of refusals or the failure of the interviewers to contact potential respondents despite repeated attempts. In the random sample for the thirty-six communities there were a total of 7626 addresses at which there was an eligible respondent after elimination of those addresses whose occupants had moved in on January 1, 1973 or later, as well as addresses that were vacant, commercial establishments and others at which no one lived permanently. Interviews were obtained with the selected respondent at 5361 of these addresses—an overall response rate of 70.3 percent. Response rates varied somewhat from community to community.

Because response rates were lower than anticipated (80 to 85 percent overall), a study was conducted to assess the extent to which nonrespondents differed systematically from respondents. First, response rates were computed by dwelling unit type and found to differ. Households living in higher density housing were somewhat underrepresented. Since residents in higher density areas tended to have fewer children, for example, and were thought likely to view the community and its facilities from a different perspective than residents of single-family detached homes, interviews in each of the sample communities were weighted to give responses from residents of each of the three dwelling unit types a weight proportional to that of the dwelling unit type in the community's original sample.

In addition, a survey of nonrespondents was conducted to gather basic demographic and attitude data.[c] Analyses of these data in comparison with household survey data revealed no significant differences between respondent and nonrespondent households for eight of thirteen demographic items (including race, income, marital status

[c]The nonrespondent follow-up survey, involving telephone interviews and mailback questionnaires, was carried out during February and March of 1974 by Chilton Research Services, Radnor, Pa.

and employment status). For five of seven community and quality of life rating items there were no significant differences between respondents and nonrespondents (including their overall rating of community livability, ratings of schools and recreational facilities and satisfaction with life as a whole). The major differences which occurred between respondent and nonrespondent households included age of household, length of residence and ratings of health care and shopping facilities. Since most differences which occurred could be explained by the length of time which elapsed between the original survey and the nonrespondent follow-up survey, it is estimated that the lower than expected response rates obtained for the original household survey do not bias the study findings.

Sampling errors. If all family heads or their spouses living (as of January 1, 1973) in new communities and conventional communities fitting the inclusion criteria noted earlier had been interviewed, the percentages and other values reported in the text would be population values. Because a sample of persons was interviewed in a sample of communities, the reported statistics are estimates of the population values. Any distribution of individuals selected for a sample will differ by chance somewhat from the population from which it was drawn. If more than one sample were used under the same survey conditions, the estimates from one sample might be larger than the population value for a given variable while the estimates from another sample were smaller. The magnitude of random variability of sample statistics from population values (sampling error) can be calculated for any sample providing it is known exactly how and with what probability the sample was selected.

Sampling errors associated with observed differences in percentages between subgroups (e.g., between individual new communities and their paired conventional communities) indicate the minimum size of a percentage difference required for the difference to be considered statistically significant—i.e., for it to reflect a true difference between the subgroups in the population rather than chance variation because of sampling. Statistically significant differences between subgroups are noted in most tables and in the text of this book. Estimates of average sampling errors based on experiences with other studies in urban areas were adjusted for the clustering in the sample to estimate the statistical significance of percentage differences. Conservative estimates of the sampling error in the sample have been used.

DATA WEIGHTS

Before combining the nonfederally assisted new community and paired conventional community samples to produce estimates presented in this book, cases were weighted by factors that include adjustments for each community's probability of selection and expected number of interviews in the community (200 for new communities, 100 for less planned suburban conventional communities, and 50 for subsidized housing subsample). Cases in the five communities having subsidized housing subsamples (Columbia, Forest Park, Jonathan, Lake Havasu City and Reston) have also been weighted to adjust for oversampling of households in subsidized housing in the community. In addition, each case is weighted by the proportion of its dwelling unit type (single-family detached, townhouse/rowhouse or apartment) in the original sample for its community to adjust for differential response rates among the three dwelling unit types.

Data presented for combined nonfederally assisted new communities and combined paired conventional communities are weighted to make all the adjustments listed above: each community's probability of selection, dwelling unit type, disproportionate selection of subsidized housing and expected number of interviews. Data presented for individual communities exclude the weight for the community's probability of selection. Weights for subsidized housing have been applied only for the five new communities with a subsidized housing subsample and only when data for this sample are presented in combination with those from the basic random sample.

THE SURVEYS OF PROFESSIONALS
AND DEVELOPERS

Information about the organization and management of recreational service systems and objective data on recreational resources were collected during the spring of 1973 from interviews with professional recreation personnel, officials of automatic homes associations and school principals who were working in or serving the new and conventional communities. Additional data about recreational service systems were collected during the summer of 1974 through interviews with new community developers and their staffs. A different interview schedule was developed for each type of professional to be interviewed. These questionnaires were pretested in Forest Park and Sharonville in February 1973 and were revised on the basis of the pretest. The number of professional personnel and developer interviews obtained in each new and conventional community are summarized in Table A−4. Interviews were hand coded by coders on the project staff. One-tenth of the coding for each survey was completely checked. Consistent errors involving a misunderstanding of the code were corrected in all interviews before the coded data were keypunched. In addition, all responses to open-end questions were recorded on index cards for use in the analysis.

Recreation Professional Survey

Interviews were sought with recreation directors (or persons in equivalent positions) of every major organization providing recreational facilities or services in each of the 36 sample communities. So as to assure that a significant provider of such facilities and services was not omitted, each respondent was asked the following question as part of the interview:

(Q. 46) Before we conclude, could you help us to identify any other persons or organizations involved in providing recreational services for the people of (NAME OF COMMUNITY)? Whom esle would you recommend that we interview?

The breakdown of interviews by affiliation of respondent is as follows:

Municipal Recreation Departments	20
County Recreation Departments	19
Park and Recreation Districts	17
Community (Homes) Associations[d]	7
Voluntary Recreation Associations	5
Other County Agencies	3
Other Municipal Agencies	2
School Districts	2
State Recreation Agencies	2
New Community Developer Staff	1
Total	78

The recreation professional interview schedule is reproduced in Appendix D. The interviews were structured and generally required about an hour for administration, which was done by appointment

[d]Although most homes associations provide some recreational facilities and services, only those with full-time, paid recreation staff participated in the recreation survey. In addition, the homes association survey described below included several sections focusing on association recreational facilities and programs.

with the respondents. Interviewers were instructed to ask the questions exactly as worded and in the order presented in the questionnaire. Interviewing was carried out primarily by members of the study team. Each interview was taken with specific reference to a particular new community or conventional community. Some professionals (e.g., county recreation officials) had responsibility for facilities or services in more than one sample community. In such cases separate questionnaires were filled out for each community involved.

Homes (Community) Association Survey

Automatic community or homes associations (i.e., those to which residents automatically belong when they purchase a home or sign a lease) have responsibility for public services and amenities in many new communities in the United States. Such associations exist at various levels in new communities. Associations may draw membership from and provide services to an entire new community, a village or neighborhood within the community or a single townhouse cluster within a neighborhood. Interviews were sought with the presidents and executive directors of all community and neighborhood or village level automatic associations in the ten sample new communities where such associations were in existence. These communities included: Columbia, Elk Grove Village, Foster City, Irvine, Jonathan, Laguna Niguel, Park Forest South, Reston, Valencia and Westlake Village. In addition, homes association interviews were conducted in the two retirement new communities, Rossmoor Leisure World (Laguna Hills) and Sun City Center. The questionnaires used in these interviews, which are on file at the Center for Urban and Regional Studies, The University of North Carolina at Chapel Hill, were designed to gather information about the organization, management, operating policies and facilities and services of the homes associations in each community.

School Principals Survey

Interviews were sought with the principal of every public school attended by children in the new and conventional communities. The school principal questionnaire, which is on file at the Center for Urban and Regional Studies, The University of North Carolina at Chapel Hill, was used to gather information about the availability of recreational facilities at school sites, policies regarding their use by community residents and the existence of community school programs. Interviews were completed with 240 principals of public schools serving the new and conventional communities.

Table A–4. Professional Personnel and Developer Interviews

Community	Total	Recreation Personnel	Homes and Community Associations	School Principals	Developers
Total	390	78	60	240	12[a]
Thirteen Nonfederally Assisted New Communities	196	34	48	114	10[a]
Thirteen Paired Conventional Communities	115	29	NA	86	NA
Federally Assisted New and Paired Conventional Communities					
Jonathan, Minn. (NC)	8	2	1	4	1
Chanhassen, Minn. (CC)	4	1	NA	3	NA
Park Forest South, Ill. (NC)	8	1	3	3	1
Richton Park, Ill. (CC)	7	1	NA	6	NA
Two Retirement New Communities (NC)	11	3	8	NA	NA
Two Subsidized Housing Conventional Communities (CC)	22	4	NA	18	NA
Two Black Conventional Communities (CC)	9	3	NA	6	NA
Nonfederally Assisted New Communities and Paired Conventional Communities					
Columbia, Md. (NC)	27	3	8	15	1
Norbeck-Wheaton, Md. (CC)	14	2	NA	12	NA
Elk Grove Village, Ill. (NC)	20	2	3	15	[a]
Schaumburg, Ill. (CC)	15	2	NA	13	NA

Forest Park, Oh. (NC)	10	2	NA	8	a
Sharonville, Oh. (CC)	9	4	NA	5	NA
Foster City, Calif. (NC)	11	3	2	5	1
West San Mateo, Calif. (CC)	7	3	NA	4	NA
Irvine, Calif. (NC)	22	3	11	6	2
Fountain Valley, Calif. (CC)	15	2	NA	13	NA
Laguna Niguel, Calif. (NC)	13	2	5	5	1
Dana Point, Calif. (CC)	6	2	NA	4	NA
Lake Havasu City, Ariz. (NC)	8	3	NA	7	1
Kingman, Ariz. (CC)	6	3	NA	3	NA
North Palm Beach, Fla. (NC)	9	3	NA	6	a
Tequesta, Fla. (CC)	3	1	NA	2	NA
Park Forest, Ill. (NC)	25	1	NA	24	a
Lansing, Ill. (CC)	7	2	NA	5	NA
Reston, Va. (NC)	16	4	5	6	1
West Springfield, Va. (CC)	7	2	NA	5	NA
Sharpstown, Tex. (NC)	9	2	NA	7	a
Southwest Houston, Tex. (CC)	9	2	NA	7	NA
Valencia, Calif. (NC)	13	2	4	6	1
Bouquet Canyon, Calif. (CC)	7	2	NA	5	NA
Westlake Village, Calif. (NC)	23	4	10	7	2
Agoura/Malibu Junction, Calif. (CC)	10	2	NA	8	NA

NC = New Community   CC = Conventional Community   NA = Not Applicable
[a] Developer interviews were not conducted with the developers of communities that began development prior to 1960.

New Community Developer Survey

In July and August of 1974 a series of informal interviews were conducted by members of the study team with the developers of the ten sample new communities where active development began after 1960. The purpose of these interviews was to determine what actions developers had taken in providing community recreational services, especially those that seemed particularly successful or problematic in their own communities on the basis of preliminary analysis of the household survey data. Additional objectives were to obtain developers' interpretations of their residents' responses to the household survey and to learn what changes had occurred in the communities after completion of the household survey and other data collection procedures in the spring of 1973.

The developer interviews were limited to the sample communities that began active residential development after 1960 in order to reduce or eliminate problems of recall and staff turnover. The ten communities included in the survey were: Columbia, Foster City, Irvine, Jonathan, Laguna Niguel, Lake Havasu City, Park Forest South, Reston, Valencia and Westlake Village. Although the developers of the five sample new communities begun in the 1940s and 1950s (Elk Grove Village, Forest Park, North Palm Beach, Park Forest and Sharpstown) were not included in the developer interviews, letters soliciting reactions to the findings of the household survey were sent to them as well as to various institutional officials, such as mayors, city councilmen, city managers, planning directors and leaders of homes associations in their communities.

Developer interviews were based on a series of community profiles that summarized residents' evaluations of various aspects of the community. Prior to the interview the developer was sent copies of the profile for his community, which showed the new community residents' responses in comparison with the responses from residents of the paired conventional community and with the combined responses of residents of the thirteen nonfederally assisted new communities in the sample. In addition, a document summarizing the strengths and weaknesses of each community, as revealed by the household survey, was prepared for discussion during the interview.

The interviews themselves were informal and unstructured. Respondents were the developer (i.e., president of the development corporation) and those members of his staff whom he asked to participate. The interviews were arranged by prior appointment and conducted in the developers' offices. They took from 90 to 120 minutes to complete. Each interview was taped.

THE COMMUNITY INVENTORIES
AND MAP MEASUREMENTS

The Community Inventories

Community-level data were collected in the community inventories. The inventory in each sample community was made concurrently with the field work for the professional personnel surveys in that community. The inventory served both as a listing of facilities and services available in the community upon which selection of professional respondents could be based and as an independent data set. Among other data, information collected in each inventory included: (1) location and population data for the sample community and for the county and SMSA in which it was located; (2) a listing of all automatic homes (community) associations in the community; (3) a listing of school districts and the public schools serving the community together with inventories of selected characteristics of the schools; (4) characteristics of community, county and special district governments; (5) housing mix available in the community and selected recreational facilities available at townhouse and apartment complexes in which sample clusters had yielded interviews; (6) a listing of recreation organizations and recreational facilities serving the community together with selected characteristics of the listed facilities; and (7) availability within the community of selected commercial, cultural, entertainment and recreational facilities. This information was gathered from public records, questioning of knowledgeable persons and observation at the identified recreational facilities and sites. Because of the complexity of the data on recreational facilities and services, a summary form was prepared using data taken from the professional surveys and from the community inventory.

All recreational facilities that existed within a sample community and also those outside the community that were viewed by professional respondents as serving the community (including schools) or were mentioned by household survey respondents as those they usually used for a given recreational activity were inventoried and located on maps. Recreational facilities that were located outside each community that were mentioned by household survey respondents as those they used were obtained from listings of responses to appropriate questions from approximately half of the household interviews taken in each community. Facilities or sites mentioned by two or more respondents that were located outside a sample community but within the same SMSA as the community were located on maps and were usually inventoried.[e]

[e]To help the study team locate these facilities, respondents were asked for the name of the facility, the names of the streets of the intersection nearest the

Map locations of the various facilities and sites were transferred to plat maps of the sample communities so that map measurements could be made.

Map Measurements and Computations

Two phases of map measurements were carried out. The first was designed to measure accessibility of facilities and services for household survey respondents and to provide data descriptive of their neighborhoods. The second was to measure accessibility of these respondents to facilities they used most frequently. The procedures used were the same for both phases.

Preparation of maps. Two maps were used for each community: a plat map of the community showing property lines and a regional map of the area within which the community was found. The locations of all household survey sample clusters that had yielded interviews for the community were shown on the community plat map.[f] The locations of facilities found in the community inventory were marked on the map. Inventoried facilities lying outside the community were located and marked on the regional map. For the phase two measurements, any facilities mentioned by household survey respondents that had not already been located on a map were added to the appropriate map. Virtually all such additions involved facilities outside the community and therefore additions to the regional map.

Facility location markers were placed on the maps at the location of the building containing or associated with the facility if such a building existed and its location was known. Otherwise they were placed at the center of the parcel containing the facility with two exceptions: (1) markers locating path or trail systems were placed at all publicly available entrances to the system; and (2) markers locating golf courses were placed at the street entrance to the course if the location of the clubhouse was not known. On community plat maps

---

facility and of the community in which it was located. Since respondents could not always remember precise names and intersection locations, not all facilities they mentioned could be found. However, the fact that a number of respondents in a community often used a given facility and some could give the name and location precisely helped in determining which facilities were used by those who could remember only the name or only the location. Thus, a high proportion of the facilities used by the respondents were located.

[f]The community plat maps used were the same as those used in selecting the household survey sample. Therefore, they showed the location of all housing in the community that had been occupied as of the fall of 1972, as well as the location of clusters sampled for the survey.

color-coded boundaries for areas served by different school districts and automatic homes associations were shown.

Distance measurement procedures. The initial procedures for phase one, and the only procedures for phase two, were those associated with measuring distances from sample clusters to particular facilities.

For phase one, road distances were measured from the center of each sample cluster to the center of the marker locating the nearest available facility for each of fifteen given types. Distances were measured in inches (to the nearest fraction of an inch shown on the map-measuring wheel used), and converted to feet in accordance with the scale of the map. All distances measured in phase one were road distances, and were measured along the shortest street route from the sample cluster to the marker locating the facility. When two or more available facilities were equidistant from a cluster, the facility accessible by the route that could accommodate the largest amount of traffic (i.e., arterial streets rather than residential and local streets) took precedence. Where a cluster was adjacent to a facility, the straight-line distance from the center of the cluster to the center of the marker was used.

In considering which facility of a given type was closest to the cluster, only facilities available to the cluster were considered. Facilities operated by homes (community) associations (including community, village, neighborhood, townhouse complex and apartment complex associations) were considered available only to clusters located within the association boundaries shown on the maps. Public facilities were considered available to all clusters, as were facilities where residents could pay for use if they wished. The latter included commercial facilities and those operated by private membership groups other than community associations (e.g., country clubs).

For phase two (distances to facilities used by household respondents) the same procedures were used as for phase one with one exception. It was necessary to locate the facility of a given type each respondent said he or she used most often rather than the facility nearest the housing cluster. Distances were measured for the following types of facilities about which respondents had been asked in the household interview: park or playground usually used by a child under twelve years old in the household; golf course, swimming facility, tennis court, bicycle path and walking or hiking path. Road distance was measured from the center of a respondent's sample cluster to the facility usually used.

Other computations (phase one only). A number of characteristics of household respondents' neighborhoods were computed or otherwise determined from the maps. In this study neighborhood was conceptualized in two ways, as the extended neighborhood and the immediate neighborhood (housing cluster). Characteristics related to each concept were measured for each sample cluster which had yielded household interviews.

The extended neighborhood was defined as the area within a half-mile radius of a given sample cluster and within distinct boundaries such as major highways, freeways, undeveloped land, bodies of water or the community boundary as defined by the sample frame. To determine the extended neighborhood of any given cluster on a map, a transparent, circular overlay with a radius of one-half mile by the scale of the map was placed on the map with its center on the center of the cluster. Then a number of measurements were made. First, the existence of certain facilities located on the map, including some types other than those to which distances had been measured, within the extended neighborhood was recorded.[g] Next, the number of sides on which the extended neighborhood had distinct boundaries such as those noted in the definition of the concept was recorded. Finally the housing density was computed (number of units per acre). The plat maps had been marked to show all housing occupied as of the fall of 1972 as part of the sampling procedures, so determination of the number of units in the neighborhood was a straightforward matter of counting. The number of square inches in the area was determined through use of a gridded transparent overlay. This number was converted to acreage according to the scale of the map, and density was computed.

The immediate neighborhood was defined as the sample cluster itself for clusters of single-family detached housing. For sample clusters from apartment or townhouse complexes, the entire complex was defined as the immediate neighborhood; its perimeter was the external lot lines of the complex. Housing density of the immediate neighborhood was computed using procedures similar to those involved in the computation of extended neighborhood density. In addition, the following were recorded for the immediate neighborhood: (1) whether it bordered on water, a golf course or other open space of five acres or more; (2) design of the intersecting or immediately adjacent street; (3) for townhouse and apartment complexes

[g]These included: elementary school; park or playground; neighborhood or community center; library; internal path system; swimming facilities; tennis courts; bar or tavern; billiard parlor; bowling alley; movie theater; picnic area with tables; restaurant; roller skating rink; ice skating rink; and teen center.

only, the land use immediately in front of and behind the units in the cluster; and (4) the automatic community association(s) and school district(s) serving the cluster.

One worker did the measurements for all sample clusters in a community for at least one phase of the work on that community. Measurements were independently checked for at least 10 percent of the clusters in each community. Where consistent errors were found, all such measurements for all clusters in the community were checked and corrected.

Appendix B

The New Communities
and Their Paired
Conventional Communities

The sampling procedures described in Appendix A resulted in the selection of a cross section of new communities that are now under development in the United States. The new communities chosen for the study all meet basic criteria for new community status. They are large. Their development has been guided by comprehensive master plans and directed by unified development organizations. Each community contains a variety of housing types and land uses. At the same time, the communities selected differ in a number of important ways. The diversity among the new communities studied is highlighted by the following vignettes, which describe the development status and selected characteristics of each community.

COLUMBIA, MARYLAND

Columbia is being developed on 18,000 acres in rural Howard County, Md. midway between the beltways surrounding Washington, D.C. and Baltimore. The idea for this new community was conceived by Baltimore mortgage banker and shopping center developer, James Rouse, in mid-1962, when he began secretly acquiring more than 140 parcels assembled for Columbia's development. On October 29, 1963 Rouse announced that he had acquired a tenth of the land in Howard County and proposed the building of an entirely new city. In mid-1965 the plans for Columbia were approved by Howard County and the development site was rezoned in accordance with a recently completed new-town section of the county zoning ordinance. Construction began in June 1966, and the first homes in Columbia were occupied the following year.

Columbia's land use plan starts with a neighborhood of 2000 to 5000 people built around a neighborhood center consisting of an elementary school, park and playground, swimming pool, community center building and, in some cases, a convenience store. Two to four neighborhoods are then combined to form a village of from 10,000 to 15,000 people. Village centers provide supermarkets and other convenience shopping facilities, community meeting facilities, land for middle and high schools and major community recreational facilities. Nine villages surround a town center complex that will include a regional mall, office buildings, a hotel-motel, restaurants, theaters and a 40-acre town center park and music pavilion. More than 20 percent of Columbia's development acreage will be set aside for open space, with another 20 percent reserved for business and industry.

When study of Columbia began in 1972, the population had grown to 24,000 of a projected 110,000 residents at full development. As shown in Table B−1, Columbia provided a relatively high proportion of rental housing (43 percent) and a variety of housing types, with over a third of the housing stock composed of apartments and townhouses. Twenty percent of the population was nonwhite, but Columbia residents, both white and nonwhite, tended to be middle class and affluent.

By 1972 Columbia's residents had access to a wide variety of community facilities and services. These included an assortment of recreational facilities—an indoor ice rink, two lakes for boating, an indoor swimming pool and eight outdoor neighborhood pools, two golf courses, an indoor tennis club and numerous outdoor courts, an athletic club, miniature golf, a professional dinner theater, an outdoor concert pavilion, several restaurants and lounges and hundreds of acres of parks and open spaces. Shopping facilities included the Columbia Mall, a regional center with two department stores, and three village centers with supermarkets, banks, drug stores, gas stations and assorted specialty shops. The Howard County Public Library operated a branch in Columbia, and four college-level institutions were present in the community. These included the two-year Howard Community College, the new four-year Dag Hammarskjold College, a branch of Antioch College and Loyola College of Baltimore. Over 65 firms had located in the Columbia industrial parks. Total employment in the community was more than 15,000.

Columbia's growth and development had also been marked by a number of institutional innovations. Recreational facilities, early childhood educational programs and a community transit system were operated by the Columbia Park and Recreation Association, a unique automatic membership homes association that was incorporated in 1965. The Protestant Columbia Cooperative Ministry was formed in 1966 to seek out new opportunities for mission and service. Catholics, Jews and Protestants shared common religious facilities in The Interfaith Center, located in Wilde Lake Village. The Columbia Medical Plan, a prepaid group practice health care program provided by the Columbia Hospital and Clinics Foundation in affiliation with The Johns Hopkins Medical Institutions, was formed to meet community health care needs. Innovation in the schools, including operation of a model high school in Wilde Lake Village, had drawn national attention.

Norbeck-Wheaton, Maryland

Columbia was paired with the conventional community of Norbeck-Wheaton, located on the urban fringe of Montgomery County 15 miles northwest of downtown Washington. Major facilities serving the community's 20,000 residents included the Aspen Hill and Rock Creek Village neighborhood shopping centers, Manor Country Club, four neighborhood parks, sections of the North Branch and Rock Creek (regional stream valley) parks, ten schools and a public library. There were no hospital or medical facilities in Norbeck-Wheaton and only one major employment facility, Vitro Laboratories, which employed about 3600 persons. Although Norbeck-Wheaton did not have as large a minority population as Columbia, other characteristics of the population, including education, occupation and income were similar (see Table B—1).

ELK GROVE VILLAGE, ILLINOIS

Elk Grove Village is being developed by the Centex Construction Company on a 5760-acre site located 26 miles northwest of Chicago's Loop. The original plan for Elk Grove Village, prepared by the Dallas firm of Phillips, Proctor, Bowers and Associates, envisioned a community of neighborhood schools and parks surrounded by single-family subdivisions and apartments. Shopping needs were to be accommodated by a series of small community shopping centers within easy access of residential neighborhoods. With room for over 450 establishments, the Centex Industrial Park in Elk Grove Village was designed to provide a major source of employment opportunities for community residents, as well as to assure an adequate tax base.

In order to free itself of Cook County zoning and subdivision con-

Table B–1.   Housing and Population Characteristics, Spring 1973

| Communities | Tenure (%) | | Housing Characteristics[a] | | | Median Home Value |
	Own	Rent	Single Family	Townhouse	Apartment	
Columbia, Md. (NC)	57	43	57	14	29	$44,100
Norbeck-Wheaton, Md. (CC)	53	47	69	7	24	52,200
Elk Grove Village, Ill. (NC)	83	17	79	2	19	38,400
Schaumburg, Ill. (CC)	83	17	72	9	19	36,300
Forest Park, Oh. (NC)	88	12	85	6	9	27,300 →
Sharonville, Oh. (CC)	85	15	84	4	13	26,100
Foster City, Calif. (NC)	71	29	53	16	31	46,100
West San Mateo, Calif. (CC)	74	26	69	0	31	61,400
Irvine, Calif. (NC)	80	20	56	28	16	42,800
Fountain Valley, Calif. (CC)	84	16	59	24	17	36,200
Jonathan, Minn. (NC)	52	48	45	16	39	33,500
Chanhassen, Minn. (CC)	59	41	59	0	41	40,600
Laguna Niguel, Calif. (NC)	96	4	80	0	20	40,300 →
Dana Point, Calif. (CC)	95	5	100	0	0	36,100
Lake Havasu City, Ariz. (NC)	68	32	65	0	35	31,800
Kingman, Ariz. (CC)	74	26	70	0	30	20,900
North Palm Beach, Fla. (NC)	88	12	50	0	50	35,500
Tequesta, Fla. (CC)	98	2	50	0	50	40,300

continued below

Table B–1. continued

Communities	Population Characteristics			
	Race[b]	Education[c]	Occupation[c]	Median
	White (%)	Some College + (%)	White Collar (%)	Income
Columbia, Md. (NC)	80	83	89	$17,300
Norbeck-Wheaton, Md. (CC)	98	79	87	17,800
Elk Grove Village, Ill. (NC)	99	56	65	17,600
Schaumburg, Ill. (CC)	99	55	68	15,400
Forest Park, Oh. (NC)	91	60	58	16,400
Sharonville, Oh. (CC)	100	41	61	15,100
Foster City, Calif. (NC)	93	76	81	20,200
West San Mateo, Calif. (CC)	92	71	89	20,300
Irvine, Calif. (NC)	95	80	87	19,000
Fountain Valley, Calif. (CC)	97	75	76	17,500
Jonathan, Minn. (NC)	97	62	75	11,800
Chanhassen, Minn. (CC)	100	69	81	15,000
Laguna Niguel, Calif. (NC)	99	79	77	17,500
Dana Point, Calif. (CC)	99	73	70	15,300
Lake Havasu City, Ariz. (NC)	100	42	48	12,100
Kingman, Ariz. (CC)	98	40	46	12,800
North Palm Beach, Fla. (NC)	99	65	82	16,900
Tequesta, Fla. (CC)	99	61	83	17,500

Table B–1. continued

Communities	Tenure (%)		Housing Characteristics[a] Housing Type (%)			Median Home Value
	Own	Rent	Single Family	Townhouse	Apartment	
Park Forest, Ill. (NC)	78	22	63	35	2	24,800
Lansing, Ill. (CC)	80	20	79	0	21	30,300
Park Forest South, Ill. (NC)	68	32	48	12	40	30,600 ↑
Richton Park, Ill. (CC)	66	34	47	16	37	25,300
Reston, Va. (NC)	52	48	25	25	50	58,000
West Springfield, Va. (CC)	37	63	30	31	39	50,800
Sharpstown, Tex. (NC)	62	38	52	11	37	31,200
Southwest Houston, Tex. (CC)	74	26	56	4	40	30,800
Valencia, Calif. (NC)	82	18	80	0	20	37,500
Bouquet Canyon, Calif. (CC)	95	5	100	0	0	30,400
Westlake Village, Calif. (NC)	81	19	56	13	31	47,500
Agoura/Malibu Junction, Calif. (CC)	99	1	80	0	20	35,400

continued below ↑

NC = New Community
CC = Conventional Community

[a]Housing characteristic data are based on household surveys in each of the study communities. Because respondents in the conventional communities were sampled to match the housing distribution in the paired new communities, housing characteristic data do not necessarily reflect housing characteristics of an entire conventional community.

[b]Refers to race of household survey respondents.

[c]Data refer to characteristics of household heads.

Table B–1. continued

| | Population Characteristics | | | | |
| | Race[b] | Education[c] | Occupation[c] | | Median Income |
Communities	White (%)	Some College + (%)	White Collar (%)		
Park Forest, Ill. (NC)	91	67	75		16,100
Lansing, Ill. (CC)	100	50	63		12,800
Park Forest South, Ill. (NC)	90	74	73		16,800
Richton Park, Ill. (CC)	99	54	57		12,700
Reston, Va. (NC)	95	85	90		19,900
West Springfield, Va. (CC)	97	82	87		20,100
Sharpstown, Tex. (NC)	95	85	85		15,900
Southwest Houston, Tex. (CC)	100	79	90		17,600
Valencia, Calif. (NC)	97	79	81		19,000
Bouquet Canyon, Calif. (CC)	96	71	68		15,300
Westlake Village, Calif. (NC)	97	81	87		21,600
Agoura/Malibu Junction, Calif. (CC)	95	69	85		17,500

trols and also to meet the need for municipal services, Centex incorporated Elk Grove Village in 1956, fully thirteen months before the first homes in the community were occupied. By 1972 the population stood at 22,900, and over 27,000 persons were employed in the industrial park. A relatively high proportion (41 percent) of Elk Grove Village's residents had migrated from Chicago. They were predominantly middle class and overwhelmingly white.

Major facilities in Elk Grove Village included the Alexian Brothers Hospital, a community high school and ten elementary and junior high schools, four neighborhood and community shopping centers and a municipal center. The Elk Grove Village Park District, formed in 1966, operated recreational programs at nineteen park sites, including a large community recreational center and swimming pool complex. Village residents also had access to the adjacent 3800-acre Ned Brown Forest Preserve, which is owned and operated by the Cook County Forest Preserve District.

Schaumburg, Illinois

Paired with Elk Grove Village, the village of Schaumburg lies just to the west, some 30 miles from the Loop. Schaumburg also incorporated in 1956 and by 1970 had a population of 18,830 persons housed in a series of residential subdivisions, apartments and condominium complexes. Schaumburg is the location of one of the largest regional shopping centers in the nation, the Woodfield Mall, which opened in 1971 with three levels, 215 shops, three department stores and over two million square feet in its initial phase. Other facilities found in Schaumburg included a number of strip commercial shopping centers, five industrial parks, ten neighborhood and community parks and a commuter bus service. Schaumburg residents also benefited from Cook County Forest Preserve District lands which surrounded the community on three sides and provided some 10,000 acres for recreational use.

FOREST PARK, OHIO

Forest Park is located in Hamilton County, 15 miles northwest of the city of Cincinnati. The development site was once part of a 6000-acre parcel acquired by the federal government in the early 1930s for the Greenbelt Program. In addition to building the town of Greenhills, the federal government used part of the land for a flood control project and gave some 2000 acres to Hamilton County for a regional park. In 1952 the remaining acreage was declared surplus and the government began looking for a buyer.

In order to prevent the land from being developed in a piecemeal fashion, a group of Cincinnati leaders formed the Cincinnati Community Development Corporation to acquire 3400 acres from the federal government for a planned new community. In 1954 the Warner-Kanter Corporation acquired the site and retained the firm of Victor Gruen Associates to prepare a master plan, which according to the terms of its land sales agreement, the Community Development Corporation reviewed and approved. Gruen's plan featured a series of residential neighborhoods surrounding neighborhood elementary schools. Land was also reserved for industrial uses and for a community center.

The first residents moved to Forest Park in 1956. In 1961 the residents voted to incorporate, in part to ward off an annexation attempt by neighboring Greenhills. By 1972 the population of Forest Park had grown to 17,000, almost half of its target population of 35,000. Compared with most of the other new communities in the sample, Forest Park had attracted a larger black population (9 percent), and had a lower proportion of household heads who had attended college (60 percent) and who were employed in white collar occupations (58 percent). However, as is also shown in Table B–1, Forest Park was solidly middle class, with the median family income standing at $16,400. In addition, Forest Park had the highest proportion of residents (85 percent) among the study communities who were living in single-family detached homes.

The major facilities found in Forest Park included a growing industrial park, which in 1972 had attracted twelve manufacturing firms, the corporate headquarters and home office of the Union Central Life Insurance Company and a neighborhood shopping center. Educational needs were accommodated at a community high school located adjacent to a municipal center and central park and at three elementary schools and a junior high school. Recreational facilities included a nonprofit community swimming pool and the Winton Woods regional park, which was operated by the Hamilton County Park District.

Sharonville, Ohio

Forest Park was matched with the conventional town of Sharonville, located several miles to the east and 12 miles north of Cincinnati. Although the town was originally platted in 1818, it had barely 1000 residents in 1950 when it began a period of steady growth. Sharonville was in the path of major industrial growth out the Mill Creek Valley from Cincinnati. By the early 1970s over 30 manufacturing plants with over 7000 employees had located in the community. This strong industrial base enabled the city of Sharonville to establish a park and open space system that included two community swimming pools and adjacent recreational centers. An additional amenity is the Sharon Woods regional park operated by the Hamilton County Park District. Compared with the residents of Forest Park, those living in Sharonville had similar socioeconomic characteristics. Sharonville, however, had no black residents.

FOSTER CITY, CALIFORNIA

Foster City is being developed on the west shore of San Francisco Bay, 25 miles south of San Francisco. The 2600-acre development site was acquired by T. Jack Foster and his three sons in 1959. Known as Brewer's Island, the land had been used as pasture by a dairyman early in the century and was later partially converted to evaporating ponds by Leslie Salt Company. A unique feature of Foster City's development was the creation of the Estero Municipal Improvement District in 1960 to finance reclamation of the low-lying development site and to provide a vehicle for the provision of various urban services. During the first years of development the district was controlled by the Fosters and caused considerable controversy in Foster City because of its high bonded indebtedness ($63.86 million in 1970) over which the residents had no control.

Foster City's General Plan was prepared in 1961 by the firm of Wilsey, Ham and Blair. The plan laid out a series of nine residential neighborhoods, a town center, satellite shopping centers and an industrial park. Each neighborhood was to be served by small parks and schools. A key feature of the plan was a lagoon system that was designed to provide a major recreational amenity and to serve as the key to successful marketing of the project.

By 1972 Foster City had grown to a community of 15,000 people living in six of the projected nine residential neighborhoods. Three shopping centers were in operation and a professional theater made its home in the community. However, the location of a nearby regional shopping center had slowed growth of Foster City's town center, and school construction was far behind schedule. In order to gain more control over the development process, the residents of Foster City voted to incorporate in April 1971. With incorporation, the Estero Municipal Improvement District was made a subsidiary of the new city government.

The residents of Foster City tended to be affluent (the median income was $20,200) and high proportions of the residents had attended college (76 percent of the household heads) and were working in white collar occupations (81 percent of the employed household heads). The community was racially integrated (3 percent black) and had attracted a number of families of Asian descent (4 percent).

West San Mateo, California

Foster City was paired with two residential subdivisions and adjacent apartment complexes located 30 miles south of San Francisco, at the western edge of the city of San Mateo, which borders Foster City. San Mateo had experienced its most rapid growth during the 1950s. While Foster City was developing during the 1960s on bayfill to the east, much of the remaining undeveloped land in San Mateo developed in the hills to the west.

San Mateo is an established city of 79,000 persons. In 1972 it had a well-developed downtown, a major regional shopping center and an extensive municipal park system. Other amenities and facilities included the Bay Meadows Race Track, Peninsula Golf and Country Club, College of San Mateo and the San Mateo County Hospital. Most of these facilities, however, were as accessible to Foster City residents as to the conventional subdivisions in West San Mateo. Although median home values were considerably higher in West San Mateo than in Foster City ($61,400 versus $46,100), in most other respects the residents of these two communities were very similar (see Table B-1).

IRVINE, CALIFORNIA

The 88,000-acre Irvine Ranch is strategically located in the path of Southern California population growth, 40 miles south of Los Angeles in Orange County. Extending 22 miles inland from the Pacific Ocean, the Irvine Ranch will be the site of the nation's largest new community. A population of over 150,000 is expected by 1990.

Planning for a new community at Irvine began in 1959 when 1000 acres were donated to the University of California for a new university campus. William L. Pereira was retained by the University to plan the campus. Seeing the need for a supporting community, he was commissioned by The Irvine Company to prepare the plans for a 10,000-acre university-oriented community in the central portion of the Irvine Ranch. Pereira's plan was subsequently incorporated into the South Irvine Ranch General Plan, which was approved by the Orange County Board of Supervisors in February 1964. This plan was then superseded by the 1970 Irvine General Plan which proposed that a new city of 53,000 acres be developed in the central portion of the ranch. Incorporated in 1971 as the City of Irvine, this portion of the Irvine Ranch was selected for the study.

Originally encompassing 18,300 acres and a population of about 20,000 persons, the city of Irvine has since annexed over 7000 additional acres and has extended its long-range planning over an area of 64,000 acres comprising its approved sphere of influence. The city has adopted a plan that includes three growth options. Option 1 follows Irvine Company plans for a series of villages and environmental corridors, two large industrial complexes, and a new regional commercial center at the juncture of the Santa Ana and San Diego freeways. A midrange population of 337,800 is projected. Option 2 assumes maximum urbanization and projects a midrange population of 453,000. Option 3 is based on minimum urbanization assumptions, including reservation of a 10,000-acre section of coastal hills as open space, and projects a midrange population of 194,000.

When Irvine was selected for study in 1972, work was underway on five villages within the city limits: Walnut, Valleyview, New Culver, University Park and Turtle Rock. The villages were composed of individual neighborhoods with neighborhood recreational facilities operated by homes associations. A neighborhood shopping center was operating adjacent to University Park and another was ready for construction next to Walnut Village. The University of California at Irvine was in full operation, and a small town center building was open adjacent to the university. A public golf course had been constructed by The Irvine Company. Over 16,000 employees were working in the highly successful Irvine Industrial Complex, the first of the two industrial areas to be developed. As shown in Table B—1, Irvine residents were affluent (median income of $19,000), and overwhelmingly tended to be employed in white collar occupations. Eighty percent of the residents owned their own homes. The median home value was $42,800. Ninety-five percent of the residents were white.

Fountain Valley, California

Fountain Valley is located along the San Diego Freeway 4 miles north of Irvine. Although the community incorporated in 1957, residential tract development did not begin until January 1962 when the first 100 acres were approved for residential use. During the next ten years, approximately 2500 acres were zoned or developed for single-family homes and apartments. Population growth was equally spectacular, increasing from 597 persons when the community incorporated to 31,826 in 1970 and an estimated 49,000 in 1972. Fountain Valley contained a number of neighborhood shopping centers, a large industrial area, a county park with a golf course and a community civic center. Ninety-seven percent of the population was white, with three fourths of the sampled household heads having attended college and about the same proportion (see Table B–1) employed in white collar occupations. The median income of the Fountain Valley households included in the study was $17,500.

JONATHAN, MINNESOTA

Jonathan was the first new community to be approved for assistance under the provisions of Title IV of the 1968 Housing and Urban Development Act. It is located in rural Carver County, 25 miles southwest of downtown Minneapolis within the Twin Cities Metropolitan Area. The planning area for the community encompassed 8166 acres of rolling hills interspersed with wooded areas along a ravine system that runs through the property. Jonathan is located a short distance north of and has been annexed by the farm-center town of Chaska, which had over 5000 residents when the study began in 1972.

The development of Jonathan was initiated in 1966 when the Ace Development Corporation (subsequently to become the Jonathan Development Corporation) was formed to manage the development process and the Carver Company was organized to spearhead land acquisition for a new community envisioned by the late Henry T. McKnight, a former Minnesota State Senator with interests in downtown real estate, land development and cattle ranching. Between 1965 and 1970, when a project agreement with the Department of Housing and Urban Development was signed, the concept for Jonathan evolved through three distinct phases. As originally planned, the community was to be developed on about 3000 acres in two upper- and middle-income residential villages. However, on the basis of a financial analysis and development program prepared by the firm of Robert Gladstone and Associates in 1966, the scope of the project was expanded to encompass 4800 acres with a target population of 41,300 persons after a 20-year development period. Finally, the project was further expanded when Jonathan finalized its application for a federal loan guarantee under Title IV. The project area was expanded to 6000 acres (and subsequently to over 8000 acres); projected population was increased to approximately 50,000; industrial acreage was expanded from 500 to 1989 acres; and a commitment was made to provide over 6500 housing units for low- and moderate-income families.

The design concept for Jonathan is shaped by the existing road system and a 1700-acre open space grid (21 percent of the site) following the natural ravines and drainage courses through the property. Within the matrix of existing highways and proposed open space, five villages, each to house approximately 7000 residents in a variety of housing types, were proposed. Village centers were to provide basic facilities for daily living, including shopping, post offices, municipal services and elementary schools. A town center was to serve as a regional multifunctional center with major retail, medical, office and entertainment facilities.

In 1972, when Jonathan was selected for the study, the population of the community stood at 1500 persons housed in 420 dwelling units, 148 of which were constructed under the FHA Section 235 and 236 subsidized housing programs. The initial phase of the first village center was in operation and provided some convenience shopping facilities. A man-made lake had been constructed adjacent to the village center, with an accompanying recreational pavilion. Walking paths connected homes to the village center, the lake and a neighborhood park with a baseball diamond and tennis court. Although schools had yet to be constructed in Jonathan, the industrial park was growing, with 45 firms providing 1080 jobs by the end of 1973.

Reflecting the character of the Twin Cities area, Jonathan's population was predominantly (97 percent) white. However, because of the high proportion of subsidized housing, the median income of the Jonathan households, $11,800, was the lowest of any of the communities studied. Almost two-thirds of the household heads had attended college and three-fourths were employed in white collar jobs.

Chanhassen, Minnesota

Jonathan was paired with the nearby village of Chanhassen, which was located adjacent to Jonathan's northeast and eastern planning boundaries. Encompassing 24 square miles, Chanhassen's population was estimated at 5100 in 1972. The community had a small downtown with a nationally known dinner theater, 60-acre village park, elementary school and a high school. Housing included a series of scattered single-family detached subdivisions and a number of apartment houses located near the downtown. The residents sampled in Chanhassen .were somewhat more affluent than those in Jonathan (median income of $15,000 versus $11,800), but were similar in terms of educational attainment and occupation.

LAGUNA NIGUEL, CALIFORNIA

Laguna Niguel is being developed within and on the hills overlooking a valley extending seven miles from the Pacific Ocean to the San Diego Freeway in southern Orange County. The 7936-acre development site, once part of the Moulton Ranch, was acquired in 1960 by the Boston firm of Cabot, Cabot & Forbes. Victor Gruen and Associates prepared the community master plan, which included a parkway running from the Pacific Coast Highway to the San Diego Freeway to serve as the spine of the community, with a series of residential neighborhoods located on either side. Nineteen schools and six neighborhood shopping centers were envisioned for an ultimate population of 80,000. A major civic and town center was planned in the heart of the community. An industrial area was to be located adjacent to the freeway and a resort complex adjacent to the Pacific beaches.

Because of slow sales throughout the 1960s, Laguna Niguel was sold to the Avco Corporation in 1971, after some 2300 homes had been completed. Since that time, Avco has invested heavily to speed the pace of development. However, concern for the fragile environment of the Southern California coastal hills and the increasing cost of developing hillside land has led to a sharp reduction in the projected population—to 43,000 residents by 1983.

In 1972, when Laguna Niguel was selected for the study, the community had 8500 residents. Most of them, 96 percent, owned their own homes and 80 percent of the households occupied single-family detached dwellings. Like most of the other new communities studied, Laguna Niguel had attracted a middle class population. Median family income was $17,500, almost 80 percent of the household heads had attended college and 77 percent were employed in white collar occupations. Laguna Niguel had also attracted a higher than average proportion of retired households (21 percent).

In spite of its slow development pace, Laguna Niguel residents had a variety of community facilities available for their use. These included three shopping centers, a medical office building, a golf course, a tennis club and a beach club. Orange County had completed its South Coast Regional Civic Center in Laguna Niguel, located adjacent to the town center; Niguel Regional Park, which occupies a 167-acre site surrounding Niguel Lake; and a county beach park. Fifty-five firms had located in the Laguna Niguel Industrial Park, and North American Rockwell had completed construction of a 1,000,000-square foot building designed to house 7000 employees, which has since been acquired by the United States General Services Administration.

Dana Point/Capistrano Valley, California

This conventional community, located just to the south of Laguna Niguel, consists of several subdivisions of single-family detached homes and a small shopping area located next to the Pacific Coast Highway. Major amenities in the area include the Dana Point Harbor and Marina, Doheny State Park and Beach and a neighborhood park operated by the Capistrano Bay Park and Recreation District. The community, like Laguna Niguel, is in an unincorporated portion of Orange County. In 1972 its population was estimated to be 6600. The Dana Point residents were somewhat less affluent than those living in Laguna Niguel. Median home value was $36,100 (versus $40,300 in Laguna Niguel) and the median family income was $15,300 (versus $17,500 in Laguna Niguel). Both Dana Point and Laguna Niguel were overwhelmingly white (99 percent).

LAKE HAVASU CITY, ARIZONA

Located 150 air miles northwest of Phoenix and 235 miles east of Los Angeles, Lake Havasu City is the only freestanding new community selected for the study. The idea of building an entirely new city in the Arizona desert originated with Los Angeles oilman and manufacturer, Robert P. McCulloch. In 1959 McCulloch acquired 3500 acres adjacent to Lake Havasu for an outboard motor testing site. Two years later, when he was unable to expand his outboard motor plant in Los Angeles, McCulloch turned to the Lake Havasu site as the location for a new plant and a new city. With C.V. Wood, the former general manager of Disneyland, McCulloch went about acquiring an additional 12,990 acres of desert in a complex series of transactions that required release of the federally owned land to the state of Arizona and its subsequent sale at a public auction. McCulloch was the only bidder, paying approximately $73 an acre.

The general plan for Lake Havasu City was drawn up by Wood. Some 22 miles of lakefront were set aside for community use and are being developed as part of Lake Havasu State Park. The rest of the land was divided into some 40,000 residential, commercial and industrial building sites. In addition, thirty-six lots were set aside for neigborhood parks. Land sales have been conducted on a nationwide basis, with a private airline used to transport prospective lot purchasers to the community.

By 1972 Lake Havasu City had an estimated 8500 residents and most of the elements of a complete community. To bolster the economic base, McCulloch transferred his chain saw manufacturing operation (which has since been sold) to Lake Havasu City and brought the historic London Bridge and reassembled it in Lake Havasu City to bolster the tourist industry. Schools were provided by organizing an elementary school district from scratch (two elementary schools and a junior high school have been built) and by persuading the Mohave County Union High School District to build a community high school. Private investors have helped to build a thriving downtown, including a movie theater and a bowling alley which were originally built by McCulloch and later sold to private operators. Two developer-owned golf courses are in operation. Lake Havasu City is also served by a weekly newspaper and local radio station.

Lake Havasu City is the only one of the study new communities with less than a majority (42 percent) of the household heads with at least some college education and with less than a majority (48 percent) employed in white collar jobs. The median income of Lake Havasu City households was $12,100, well below the average ($17,500) of the thirteen nonfederally assisted new communities studied. Because it is a freestanding community, Lake Havasu City has had to provide housing for the workers employed in its manufacturing and service jobs. In addition, it has attracted a relatively high proportion of retired households (23 percent versus 10 percent for the entire sample of thirteen nonfederally assisted new communities).

Kingman, Arizona

Located 56 miles across the Arizona desert from Lake Havasu City, Kingman is the closest comparably sized community on the Arizona side of the Colorado River. Kingman was founded in the early 1880s, but was not incorporated as a city until 1952. With a population of 7312 in 1970, Kingman had a small downtown clustered near the Mohave County Courthouse, a long strip commercial section running along U.S. Highway 66 and a series of residential neighborhoods which follow a grid pattern of development. The economy centers on government, transportation and commercial services, with a small manufacturing sector. A golf course, three city parks and a municipal pool provided recreational amenities for Kingman's residents. As shown in Table B—1, the socioeconomic characteristics of the residents interviewed in Kingman were similar to those of the Lake Havasu City respondents, though the median home value in Kingman was much lower ($20,900 versus $31,800).

NORTH PALM BEACH, FLORIDA

North Palm Beach is a 2362-acre waterfront community located along the intercoastal waterway, seven and one-half miles north of West Palm Beach. The development site was acquired by North Palm Beach Properties in 1955. Early land development operations included the dredging of a series of canals and the bulkheading of all waterfront properties. The overall planning of the community was honored by the National Association of Home Builders for its design, layout, restrictions and facilities.

North Palm Beach Properties incorporated the community shortly after the development site was acquired and some months before the first homes were sold. The village government originally restricted its activities to public safety and housekeeping, but has gradually increased its functions. In addition to the North Palm Beach Country Club, which was purchased from the developer in 1961, the village operates a public marina, library, art center and a small park system.

In recent years Palm Beach County has been one of the best housing markets in the country, and the village of North Palm Beach has the highest growth rate in the county. During the past five years condominium apartment construction has soared. Commercial development is located in a series of shopping centers along U.S. Highway 1, the major north-south artery through the town. A small area is zoned for industrial use but has not been occupied.

In 1972, the population was estimated to be 12,500, 42 percent of the 30,000 population projected at full development. Approximately half of the residents lived in apartments, though a high proportion (88 percent) owned their own dwelling units. North Palm Beach households tended to be white and middle class. The median family income was $16,900. A relatively high proportion of the household heads (27 percent) were retired.

Tequesta, Florida

North Palm Beach was paired with the small incorporated village of Tequesta, located 9 miles to the north on the Loxahatchee River at Jupiter Inlet. This conventional community consisted of a patchwork of small subdivisions and condominiums. Community amenities include the Tequesta Country Club, the Community Public Library and a small art institution, the Lighthouse Gallery. In 1970 the population of Tequesta was 2576, with 4323 persons living in adjacent unincorporated areas. As shown in Table B–1, Tequesta's residents were similar to those living in North Palm Beach in terms of socioeconomic characteristics. However, a higher proportion of the household heads (53 percent) were retired.

PARK FOREST, ILLINOIS

Park Forest is the oldest new community included in the study. The community was begun in 1947 on some 2200 acres of Illinois prairie in southeast Cook County by American Community Builders, Inc., a partnership consisting of Nathan Manilow, Phillip M. Klutznick and Jerrold Loebl. Land planning was under the direction of Elbert Peets, who had earlier designed the town of Glendale for the United States Housing Authority.

Because of the vast housing market created by returning war veterans and the availability of financing for rental housing for veterans, initial residential building consisted of 3010 rental townhouses grouped in courts near the center of Park Forest. Several years later these courts received national publicity as the home of William Whyte's "organization man." Families who occupied the rental housing units and the single family subdivisions that were subsequently built provided customers for a large shopping center located at the geographical and population center of Park Forest. The shopping center was one of the first open malls in the country.

Park Forest incorporated as a village in 1949, and the village government assumed responsibility for various urban services in the community. The village established an aggressive park development program on land donated by the development company. In 1973 the village recreation and parks department maintained 275 acres of parks, operated a nine-hole golf course, and supervised and staffed some 80 recreational programs, ranging from preschool through adult activities. A nonprofit community swimming pool corporation built and operated an "aquatic center" open to all Park Forest residents.

Although industrial land was set aside in Park Forest, poor highway access limited its appeal to prospective firms. However, the community's location at the end of the Illinois Central's commuter rail line to the Loop meant that the developer did not have to rely on local employment as a source of housing demand. In fact, most of the community's early residents worked 29 miles away in downtown Chicago.

By 1960 Park Forest had a population of 30,000, just short of current numbers. American Community Builders, Inc. disbanded in 1959. Since that time development has been limited. Park Forest had the lowest median home value ($24,800) of any of the new communities studied. Nevertheless, two-thirds of the household heads had attended college and three-fourths were working in white collar occupations. The median family income of $16,100 was not too much lower than the median of $17,500 for all thirteen nonfederally assisted new communities studied. Nine percent of the households in Park Forest were nonwhite.

Lansing, Illinois

Park Forest was paired with the village of Lansing, located adjacent to the Indiana state line in southeastern Cook County, 26 miles from Chicago's Loop. Although Lansing was incorporated as a village in 1893 (with a population of 200), major residential growth did not occur until after World War II. In 1950 both Lansing and Park Forest had a population between 8000 and 9000 residents. Both communities more than doubled in population during the 1950s. Lansing, however, had somewhat greater success than Park Forest in attracting industrial development. In 1970 there were 30 manufacturing establishments and a total of 1000 manufacturing employees in the community. Major amenities in Lansing include a community park and swimming pool operated by the Lan-Oak Park District, a number of small neighborhood parks and a section of the Cook County Forest Preserve adjacent to the community's southwest boundary. The population of Lansing was 25,218 in 1970.

PARK FOREST SOUTH, ILLINOIS

Park Forest South, the second federally assisted new community selected for the study, is located in Will County, 32 miles south of the Chicago Loop and immediately south of Park Forest. The idea for the community originated with the late Nathan Manilow, who was one of the principal partners involved in the building of Park Forest. When Park Forest's development company, American Community Builders, Inc., disbanded in 1959, Manilow retained control of the Park Forest Plaza shopping center through his solely-owned company, Park Forest Properties. In the mid-1960s Nathan Manilow and his son Lewis saw the potential for the expansion of Park Forest to a community of some 60,000 residents and began to assemble the necessary acreage to the south in Will County.

In June 1967 the Manilows persuaded the residents of a small bankrupt subdivision surrounded by Manilow land holding to incorporate as the Village of Park Forest South. The Manilows then retained the firm of Carl L. Gardner and Associates to develop a comprehensive plan for the village and to prepare zoning and subdivision regulations. When these were completed, the Manilows requested annexation of 1200 acres of adjoining land, which had been pre-zoned for a large planned unit development. This was accom-

plished on January 26, 1968 in exchange for a promise by the Manilows to support village fire protection and police services.

In order to secure development capital and financing, the Manilows then proceeded on two fronts. First, additional equity participation in the venture was achieved in 1968 when Mid-America
Improvement Corporation (owned by Illinois Central Industries,
Inc.) became a partner in the new community and in 1969 when
United States Gypsum Urban Development Corporation (owned
by The United States Gypsum Company) was recruited. Each company took a 25 percent interest in the Park Forest South Development Company, with the Manilow Organization, Inc. acting as
managing partner. Second, to generate the long-term capital required
to develop a full-scale new community, assistance was sought from
the Department of Housing and Urban Development under Title IV
of the 1968 Housing and Urban Development Act. Park Forest
South's participation in the federal new communities program was
formally accomplished on March 17, 1971 when a project agreement
with HUD was signed.

The Park Forest South planning area encompassed 8291 acres,
which were to be developed over a fifteen-year period for a target
population of 110,000. Highlights of the development plan included
the 753-acre campus of Governors State University, Governors Gate-
way Industrial Park and a multifunctional town center. These three
elements were to be connected by the "Main Drag"—a three-mile
linear strip development containing major commercial, recreational
and municipal facilities served by a rapid transit system. Other commercial and institutional facilities were to be provided in a number of
neighborhood centers designed to serve day-to-day needs. Rapid
transit service to Chicago was to be initiated through an extension of
the Illinois Central Gulf commuter rail line when 3000 dwelling units
were occupied. A major hospital and medical complex with close
connections with the university were planned. Almost 900 acres of
major open space were to be provided, together with a more intimate
open space network and path system running through individual
neighborhoods. Finally, Park Forest South was expected to provide
an estimated 4500 housing units to be constructed with assistance
from federal low- and moderate-income housing subsidy programs
and an employment base of over 28,000 jobs.

When Park Forest South was selected for the study in 1972, the
community had a population of 3200 residents living in 1310 dwelling units. Recreational facilities were provided at two neighborhood
swimming and recreational centers, which were operated by private

automatic membership associations. An elementary school had been completed, as well as a small convenience shopping center and a commercial ice skating rink. Development was well underway in the industrial park which had thirty-four firms employing 925 persons by the end of 1973.

Because subsidized housing had yet to be occupied in Park Forest South at the time of the household survey in the spring of 1973, the median family income in the community ($16,800) was considerably higher than that of Jonathan ($11,800). However, Park Forest South had attracted a number of nonwhite families (10 percent of the population).

Richton Park, Illinois

Richton Park is located directly north of Park Forest South and adjacent to the western boundary of Park Forest. In 1972 the community had an estimated 4800 residents and was undergoing rapid residential growth. Recently developed projects included a large subdivison of single-family detached homes marketed under the FHA Section 235 subsidized home ownership program, as well as conventional single-family subdivisions, townhouses and apartments. Major community facilities included an elementary school and a high school, strip commercial shopping centers, a golf course and a neighborhood park and playground. Unlike Park Forest South, Richton Park's population was almost entirely white. However, the median income of residents was lower ($12,700), and lower proportions of the household heads had attended college (54 percent) and were working in white collar occupations (57 percent).

RESTON, VIRGINIA

Reston is being developed on 6750 acres located in Fairfax County, 18 miles northwest of Washington, D.C. The development site was acquired in March 1961 by Robert E. Simon, Jr. after he and his family had sold Carnegie Hall in New York City. The Reston master plan was prepared by the New York architectural firm of Whittlesey and Conklin and was approved by the Fairfax County Board of Supervisors in June 1962. The plan assigned about 23 percent of the site for recreational areas, provided for a 970-acre industrial park and for a variety of housing types and commercial areas. These land uses were organized in a series of seven villages, each with a projected population of 10,000 to 12,000 people. A town center was designated to serve Reston's projected 75,000 residents and some 50,000 people in the surrounding region.

Throughout its early years Reston was plagued by a slow development pace and financial difficulties. These problems came to a head in September 1967 when the Gulf Oil Corporation, which had made a major loan to Simon for Reston's development, took over full financial and operational responsibility and formed Gulf-Reston, Inc. to manage the development process. Gulf increased its investment in Reston and by 1972 was able to report a positive cash flow.

In 1972 Reston had an estimated 20,000 residents living in two villages, Lake Anne and Hunters Woods. Over fifty tenants occupied the Lake Anne Village Center, which had attracted national attention because of its urbane design and mixture of shops and apartments. Two golf courses were operating as well as a series of neighborhood swimming and tennis facilities and a riding stable. Medical and day care centers were functioning. Over 2000 persons were employed in Reston and construction was underway on a $54 million headquarters building for the United States Geological Survey.

Reston had one of the most educated and affluent populations of any of the new communities selected for the study. Eighty-five percent of the household heads had attended college, 90 percent were employed in white collar occupations and the median income was $19,900. The median home value was $58,000. Reston was racially integrated (5 percent of the population was nonwhite) and economically integrated (11 percent of the housing stock consisted of subsidized units).

West Springfield, Virginia

This conventional community in Fairfax County is located 18 miles southeast of Reston and 13 miles southwest of downtown Washington. With almost 35,000 residents in 1972, the West Springfield community was served by four neighborhood and community shopping centers but made no provision for industrial development. Recreational facilities were provided at Lake Accotink, Cardinal Forest and West Springfield Golf and Country Club and at facilities provided by individual tract and apartment developers. As shown in Table B–1, the socioeconomic characteristics of the West Springfield residents were very similar to those of the Reston residents, although a significantly higher proportion rented their homes (63 percent versus 48 percent).

SHARPSTOWN, TEXAS

Sharpstown, which began development in 1953 on a 4100-acre site, is located 10 miles southeast of downtown Houston. The community master plan followed traditional patterns, with single-family subdivisions surrounding neighborhood elementary schools and small parks. Although little emphasis was placed on architectural merit, homes were built and marketed within the means of a broad spectrum of consumers.

In 1972 Sharpstown had over 11,000 homes and apartments. The Sharpstown Center, a regional shopping center occupying a 77-acre site in the heart of the community, had opened in 1960. Other projects completed in the 1960s included a boy's preparatory school operated by the Society of Jesus, Houston Baptist College, which occupied a 196-acre campus in Sharpstown, a branch of the Houston Public Library, the Memorial Baptist Hospital's Southwest Branch and the Sharpstown General Hospital. Recreational and entertainment facilities included several neighborhood parks, the Sharpstown Country Club, a drive-in theater, 2100-seat movie theater, and 3000-seat professional theater. Employment opportunities were provided at the many commercial establishments in Sharpstown and by firms located in the 755-acre Sharpstown Industrial Park.

Sharpstown is a middle class community. Eighty-five percent of the household heads had attended college and 85 percent were employed in white collar occupations. The median family income was $15,900. Five percent of the population was nonwhite.

Southwest Houston, Texas

This conventional community consists of three large subdivisions located southwest of Sharpstown at the edge of the Houston city limits. The subdivisions were developed gradually over a period of years and were tied together by a major thoroughfare and series of strip-commercial shopping centers. Major amenities and recreational facilities included the Braeburn Country Club, Southwest Branch of the Houston YMCA and the City of Houston's Southwest Tennis Center. Although the median income of households was higher than in Sharpstown ($17,600 versus $15,900), educational and occupational characteristics of the household heads were similar, as was the median home value.

VALENCIA, CALIFORNIA

Valencia is located 32 miles northeast of downtown Los Angeles in an unincorporated section of Los Angeles County. The community is being developed by the Newhall Land and Farming Company on a 4000-acre section of the 44,000-acre Newhall Ranch. The land was originally purchased by Henry Mayo Newhall in the 1870s.

The stimulus for the development of a new community on the Newhall Ranch was provided by approaching urbanization in the San Fernando Valley, 7 miles to the south, and the Palmdale International Airport, which was proposed for nearby Antelope Valley. The general plan for Valencia was prepared by Thomas L. Sutton and Victor Gruen and Associates and was adopted by the Los Angeles County Regional Planning Commission in October 1965. The Valencia plan combines individual neighborhoods with schools and parks into a series of villages, each with its own shopping and recreational centers, high schools, library and church. Paseos (pathways) connect superblocks of homes with neighborhood schools and parks. An open space system separates the villages. A major regional shopping and civic center is planned in the heart of the community, with employment opportunities to be provided at the 1000-acre Valencia Industrial Center.

By 1972 Valencia had an estimated 7000 residents living in over 2000 homes and garden apartments. The first village shopping center was in operation. Two educational institutions, California Institute of the Arts, a four-year art and music school conceived by Walt Disney, and College of the Canyons, a community college, had begun operations. In order to attract potential residents to Valencia the Newhall Land and Farming Company had invested heavily in regional recreational and entertainment facilities. These included three golf courses, a $30 million family ride park called Magic Mountain, a public riding stable, a travel trailer park and a dune buggy/motorcycle park. Some fifteen companies had located in the Valencia Industrial Center, thus creating an employment base approaching 3000 jobs.

The median income of Valencia residents was $19,000. Seventy-nine percent of the household heads had attended college and 81 percent were employed in white collar occupations. Ninety-seven percent of the residents were white.

Bouquet Canyon, California

The hills and valleys northeast of Valencia began to develop several years before Valencia's master plan was approved. The Bouquet Canyon community consists of a series of single-family detached residential subdivisions on the canyon floor. Shopping facilities were available at two centers located near the mouth of Bouquet Canyon and its junction with San Francisquito Canyon. The community was also served by a small park operated by the Los Angeles County Park and Recreation Department. As shown in Table B−1, the Bouquet Canyon residents tended to be less affluent than those living in Valencia. The median family income was $15,300, $3700 less than in Valencia.

WESTLAKE VILLAGE, CALIFORNIA

Westlake Village is surrounded by mountains in the picturesque Conejo Valley, 40 miles northwest of the Los Angeles Civic Center. The community is being developed on the 11,709-acre Albertson Ranch, which was acquired by shipping magnate Daniel K. Ludwig in 1964 after one year of litigation over title to the property. During 1964 and 1965 the Bechtel Corporation conducted master plan studies for Ludwig's American-Hawaiian Steamship Company, which was to manage the development process. Earthmoving began in 1966 and the first homes were occupied in 1967.

The Westlake Village master plan is based on interrelating a series of neighborhood clusters composed of homes, schools, parks, recreational facilities and small neighborhood shopping centers. A major regional shopping center was planned along the Ventura Freeway, which bisects the community, and approximately 500 acres along the freeway were set aside for industrial use. Unique among American new communities, the Westlake Village plan also reserved a 170-acre parcel at the community's southern boundary for a cemetery. The theme for Westlake Village was established by a 150-acre artificial lake which cost $2 million to construct.

In 1972 Westlake Village had an estimated 13,000 residents. Major community facilities and amenities included a community shopping center and two satellite centers, a motel-restaurant complex, an eighteen-hole, night-lighted golf course and tennis club, individual neighborhood swimming pools and recreational centers, two riding stables, a marina at Lake Westlake and a community hospital. A number of nationally known firms had located in the industrial parks. Employment in Westlake Village was estimated to be 4500. Nevertheless, Westlake Village was in financial difficulty. In 1969 the Prudential Insurance Company converted a $30 million land loan into an equity investment in Westlake Village's development. By late in 1972 disagreements between Prudential and the American-Hawaiian Steamship Company led to dissolution of the partnership, with Prudential keeping the undeveloped acreage in the community and American-Hawaiian the income property. Prudential has completed a second golf course and is proceeding with development.

Westlake Village had the highest median family income of the new communities studied ($21,600) and the second highest median home value ($47,500). Eighty-one percent of the household heads had attended college and 87 percent were employed in white collar occupations. Ninety-seven percent of the residents were white.

Agoura/Malibu Junction, California

The Malibu hills and canyons between Westlake Village and the new community of Calabassas Park, several miles to the south along the Ventura Freeway, have been steadily developing since the late 1960s. This conventional community of some 5000 residents consisted of a series of unrelated and widely separated subdivisions located on either side of the freeway. Shopping facilities were provided at a small convenience center located just off of the freeway. A 12-acre park site is owned by the Simi Valley Recreation and Park District and several subdivisions had neighborhood recreational facilities operated by homes associations. The residents were affluent (median income of $17,500) and high proportions of the household heads had attended college (69 percent) and were employed in white collar occupations (85 percent). Ninety-five percent of the residents were white.

Appendix C

Household Survey Questionnaire

Face Sheet and Selected
Recreation Questions
Nos. 25–27, 53–57

I. D. NUMBER

(0)(0)(0)(0)(0)(0)
(1)(1)(1)(1)(1)(1)
(2)(2)(2)(2)(2)(2)
(3)(3)(3)(3)(3)(3)
(4)(4)(4)(4)(4)(4)
(5)(5)(5)(5)(5)(5)
(6)(6)(6)(6)(6)(6)
(7)(7)(7)(7)(7)(7)
(8)(8)(8)(8)(8)(8)
(9)(9)(9)(9)(9)(9)

A NATIONAL STUDY OF
ENVIRONMENTAL PREFERENCES
AND THE QUALITY OF LIFE
JANUARY – APRIL 1973

OFFICE USE ONLY

Supporting Agency	National Science Foundation Research Applied to National Needs Division of Social Systems and Human Resources Research Grant Number GI-34285

Research Organization	Center for Urban and Regional Studies, University of North Carolina at Chapel Hill	Field Work Subcontractor	Research Triangle Institute Research Triangle Park, North Carolina

A.   Sample Cluster Number: _____ - _____   B.   Sample Line Number: _____

C.   Street Address:_____

D.   City or Town: _____

E.   Respondent Designated on Cluster Listing Sheet: ○ Head   ○ Spouse

F.   Hello, I'm _____ representing the Research Triangle Institute, a not-for-profit national research organization and the University of North Carolina. We are conducting a survey about the attitudes, preferences, living conditions, and activities of people in a number of communities across the United States. Since your household falls into our sample in this community, I would like to ask you a few questions. All the answers you give will be strictly confidential and will be used only in statistical tables where your name can in no way be connected with your answers. Of course, no one is required to participate, but I hope very much that you will, and I think you'll find it interesting.

G.   Before we start, however, I need to know if you and your family have moved to this address since the first of the year (1973) or if you've been living here longer than that.
        ○ SINCE FIRST OF YEAR - - THANK RESPONDENT AND TERMINATE INTERVIEW
        ○ "LONGER THAN THAT" - - CONTINUE WITH HOUSEHOLD LISTING

H.   Time is now: _____

I.   Good. Now first, I need some information about the people who live here with you. I don't need the names, just the relationships of the people who live here. Let's start with the adults. What is the age of the head of household? (PAUSE. OBTAIN ALL INFORMATION ABOUT HEAD OF HOUSEHOLD AND CONTINUE WITH OTHER HOUSEHOLD MEMBERS.) Have we missed anyone -- a roomer, someone who lives here but who is away right now?

IF HEAD AND SPOUSE ARE LIVING IN A HOUSEHOLD, INTERVIEW PERSON INDICATED ON CLUSTER LISTING SHEET (AND TRANSFERRED TO ITEM E ABOVE). IF HEAD IS NOT NOW MARRIED, OR SPOUSE IS NOT LIVING IN HOUSEHOLD, INTERVIEW HEAD.

ADULTS

All Persons:
*   21 or Older
        or
*   Married, any Age
        or
*   Under 21 and
    Living Away From
    Parents

NCS Trans-Optic S388C-321

List All Adults By Relation to the Head	Sex	Age	Marital Status	Indicate R "X"
1. Head of Household				
2.				
3.				
4.				

25. How do you feel about the places <u>right near your home</u> for children under 12 to play out of doors -- would you say they are excellent, good, average, below average, or poor?

①　Excellent　　　　②　Good　　　　③　Average　　　　④　Below average　　　　⑤　Poor

   25a.　Why do you say that? _____

_____

_____

26. Is there a park or playground near here where young children can play?

①　Yes　　　　　　　　　　　　　　　　　⑤　No -- Go to Q. 27

   26a.　Where is that?

      NAME OF PARK OR PLAYGROUND: _____

      NEAREST INTERSECTION: _____
                         (Street)　　　　　　　　(Cross Street)

   26b.　About how many minutes would it take a child
      to walk there from your front door?　_____ MINUTES　　⓪①②③④⑤⑥⑦⑧⑨ / ⓪①②③④⑤⑥⑦⑧⑨

   26c.　And when the weather is good, do(es) your child(ren) -- those under 12 -- play there every day, several times a week, once a week, once or twice a month, or less often?

      ⑤　Every day　　④　Several times a week　　③　Once a week　　②　Once or twice a month　　①　Less often

27. When your child(ren) -- those under 12 -- play(s) outdoors where do(es) (they/he/she) usually play? (HAND CARD C)

①　Your yard/apartment or townhouse grounds　　②　Neighbor's yard　　③　Park or playground　　④　Street/parking areas
⑤　Vacant lots　　⑥　Woods or open space away from your yard/apartment grounds

⑦　Somewhere else (specify): _____

53. We are also interested in what people do in their spare time. What is your favorite type of leisure or recreational activity to do outside the house?　　　　　　　⓪　No favorite activity -- Go to Q. 54

FAVORITE ACTIVITY: _____

   53a.　About how often did you (ACTIVITY) last year, not counting when you were on vacation? (ACCEPT RANGES)

      _____ TIMES　　⓪①②③④⑤⑥⑦⑧⑨ / ⓪①②③④⑤⑥⑦⑧⑨

   53b.　Where do you go most often?
      NAME OF FACILITY: _____

      NEAREST INTERSECTION: _____　　TOWN: _____
                 STREET　　　　CROSS STREET

   53c.　The last time you went (ACTIVITY) there, did you go and (ACTIVITY) by yourself or with someone else? (PAUSE) Who (ACTIVITY) with you? (MARK ALL THAT APPLY)

Yes	No		Yes	No		Yes	No	
ⓐ	ⓐ Self only		ⓒ	ⓒ Child(ren)		ⓔ	ⓔ Friend(s)	
ⓑ	ⓑ Spouse		ⓓ	ⓓ Other relative		ⓕ	ⓕ Other	

   53d.　Overall, how satisfied are you with that place as a place to (ACTIVITY)? Which number comes closest to how you feel?

      CARD E　　Completely Satisfied　①　②　③　④　⑤　⑥　⑦　Completely Dissatisfied

54. Here is a list of recreational activities. (**HAND CARD H**) I'd like to know which of these you have taken part in within the last year, not counting when you were on vacation. (COMPLETE Q. 54a FOR ALL FIVE ACTIVITIES, <u>THEN</u> COMPLETE b FOR EACH ACTIVITY, <u>THEN</u> COMPLETE c-f FOR EACH ACTIVITY THAT IS NOT R'S FAVORITE.)

	GOLF	SWIMMING
a. Participate?	① Yes ⑤ No	① Yes ⑤ No
b. Interviewer: (CHECK ONE) If activity is · · · · · · · · ·	① Favorite, go to next activity ⑤ Not favorite, complete column	① Favorite, go to next activity ⑤ Not favorite, complete column
c. About how often did you (ACTIVITY) last year, not counting when you were on vacation?	TIMES: ⓪①②③④⑤⑥⑦⑧⑨ ⓪①②③④⑤⑥⑦⑧⑨	TIMES: ⓪①②③④⑤⑥⑦⑧⑨ ⓪①②③④⑤⑥⑦⑧⑨
d. Where did you go (most often)?	NAME OF PLACE: NEAREST INTERSECTION: STREET CROSS STREET TOWN: _____	NAME OF PLACE: NEAREST INTERSECTION: STREET CROSS STREET TOWN: _____
e. The last time you went (ACTIVITY) there did you go and (ACTIVITY) by yourself or with someone else? Who (ACTIVITY) with you? (MARK ALL THAT APPLY)	Yes No Yes No ①⑤ Self only ①⑤ Other relative ①⑤ Spouse ①⑤ Friend(s) ①⑤ Child(ren) ①⑤ Other	Yes No Yes No ①⑤ Self only ①⑤ Other relative ①⑤ Spouse ①⑤ Friend(s) ①⑤ Child(ren) ①⑤ Other
f. Overall, how satisfied are you with that place as a place to (ACTIVITY)? Which number comes closest to how you feel? HAND CARD E	Completely Satisfied ① ② ③ ④ ⑤ ⑥ ⑦ Completely Dissatisfied	Completely Satisfied ① ② ③ ④ ⑤ ⑥ ⑦ Completely Dissatisfied

TENNIS	BICYCLING	WALKING AND HIKING
① Yes ⑤ No	① Yes ⑤ No	① Yes ⑤ No
① Favorite, go to next activity ⑤ Not favorite, complete column	① Favorite, go to next activity ⑤ Not favorite, complete column	① Favorite, go to next activity ⑤ Not favorite, complete column
TIMES:	TIMES:	TIMES:
NAME OF PLACE:	NAME OF PLACE:	NAME OF PLACE:
NEAREST INTERSECTION:		NEAREST INTERSECTION:
STREET CROSS STREET		STREET CROSS STREET
TOWN: _____	TOWN: _____	TOWN: _____
Yes No Yes No ①⑤Self only ①⑤Other relative ①⑤Spouse ①⑤Friend(s) ①⑤Child(ren) ①⑤Other	Yes No Yes No ①⑤Self only ①⑤Other relative ①⑤Spouse ①⑤Friend(s) ①⑤Child(ren) ①⑤Other	Yes No Yes No ①⑤Self only ①⑤Other relative ①⑤Spouse ①⑤Friend(s) ①⑤Child(ren) ①⑤Other
Completely Satisfied ① ② ③ ④ ⑤ ⑥ ⑦ Completely Dissatisfied	Completely Satisfied ① ② ③ ④ ⑤ ⑥ ⑦ Completely Dissatisfied	Completely Satisfied ① ② ③ ④ ⑤ ⑥ ⑦ Completely Dissatisfied

55. All things considered, how good would you say the recreational facilities in this community and its immediate vicinity are for the people who live here -- excellent, good, average, below average, or poor?

① Excellent   ② Good   ③ Average   ④ Below average   ⑤ Poor

56. We'd like to ask you about other types of leisure activities too. For example, how many different days in the last week did you spend an hour or more:

DO NOT MARK

a. watching television?	_____ DAYS	⓪	①	②	③	④	⑤	⑥	⑦
b. reading a book in your spare time?	_____ DAYS	⓪	①	②	③	④	⑤	⑥	⑦
c. working at a hobby?	_____ DAYS	⓪	①	②	③	④	⑤	⑥	⑦
d. playing cards with friends?	_____ DAYS	⓪	①	②	③	④	⑤	⑥	⑦
e. reading newspapers and/or magazines?	_____ DAYS	⓪	①	②	③	④	⑤	⑥	⑦
f. doing community volunteer work?	_____ DAYS	⓪	①	②	③	④	⑤	⑥	⑦

57. Overall, how satisfied are you with the ways you spend your spare time? (HAND CARD E) Which number comes closest to how you feel?

Completely Satisfied   ①   ②   ③   ④   ⑤   ⑥   ⑦   Completely Dissatisfied

✻ *Appendix D*

Recreation Professional
Survey Questionnaire

Community:_____   Interview No. _____

PERFORMANCE CRITERIA FOR NEW COMMUNITY
DEVELOPMENT: EVALUATION AND PROGNOSIS
NSF RESEARCH GRANT GI-34285

Recreation Survey

Respondent's Name:_____   Interviewer's Name:_____

Address:_____   Date of Interview:_____

City:_____ State:_____   Place of Interview:_____

Telephone Number:_____   _____

Respondent's Position:_____   City:_____ State:_____

Name of Organization:_____

Address:_____

City:_____ State:_____

Telephone Number:_____

* * * * * * * * * * * *

Hello. I'm from the Center for Urban and Regional Studies at the
University of North Carolina. We are conducting a study of residential living conditions in communities across the United States.
One of the most important aspects of this study concerns the provision of recreation services. We are especially interested in the
experience of persons like yourself who hold positions of leadership in the community. As you answer the following questions,
please keep in mind that we will not use direct quotes of your
opinions on the matters we discuss without your permission. Of
course, you are not required to participate, but I hope very much
that you will and I think that you will find it interesting.

* * * * * * * * * * * *

Center for Urban and Regional Studies
University of North Carolina at Chapel Hill

February 1973

Organization of Recreation

First, I have some questions about the organization of recreation in (NAME OF COMMUNITY).

1. What are the principal organizations providing parks and recreation services for the people of (NAME OF COMMUNITY)? PAUSE Are there any others?

Yes	No	Organizations
1	5	a. State agency (SPECIFY:_____)
1	5	b. County recreation department or commission
1	5	c. Other county agency (SPECIFY:_____)
1	5	d. City recreation department or commission
1	5	e. Other city agency (SPECIFY:_____)
1	5	f. Park (and recreation) district (SPECIFY:_____)
1	5	g. School district(s) (SPECIFY:_____)
1	5	h. Community association(s) (SPECIFY:_____)
1	5	i. Voluntary associations
1	5	j. Commercial establishments
1	5	k. Community developer and/or builders
1	5	l. Other (SPECIFY:_____)

2. Does your organization provide recreation facilities and/or services for the entire population of (NAME OF COMMUNITY)?

5 NO   1 YES

2a. What part of (NAME OF COMMUNITY) do you serve?

_____

_____

3. Do you provide recreation facilities and/or services in any areas or communities besides (NAME OF COMMUNITY)?

1 YES   5 NO

3a. What other communities or areas do you serve?

_____

_____

4. What is the total population of your service area?

POPULATION:_____

5. Does your organization provide any services in addition to recreation?

[1] YES   [5] NO

5a. What are these services?

_____

_____

6. INTERVIEWER: CHECK ONE

[1] COMMUNITY ASSOCIATION -- GO TO Q. 8

[2] OTHER ORGANIZATION -- ASK Q. 7

7. Does (NAME OF ORGANIZATION) have a board of directors, commission, or committee of citizens who review the recreation services which are provided?

[1] YES, BOARD OF DIRECTORS   [4] NO -- GO TO Q. 8

[2] YES, COMMISSION

[3] YES, COMMITTEE

7a. Does the (board's/commission's/committee's) authority include the power to determine....

Yes   No

[1]   [5]   The recreation budget?

[1]   [5]   Staff levels?

[1]   [5]   Recreation programs?

[1]   [5]   Recreation land acquisition?

[1]   [5]   Construction of recreation facilities?

7b. How many members serve on this body?

MEMBERS:_____

7c. How many members of the (board/commission/committee) are black or from other minority groups?

BLACK MEMBERS: _____

OTHER MINORITY GROUP MEMBERS: (SPECIFY GROUP)

GROUP: _____   MEMBERS: _____

GROUP: _____   MEMBERS: _____

7d. Are these persons appointed to this position or elected?

[1] APPOINTED   [5] ELECTED -- GO TO Q. 7f.

7e. Who appoints (board/commission/committee) members?

APPOINTED BY: _____

7f. How often do members of the (board/commission/committee) meet?

[1] WEEKLY OR MORE OFTEN   [3] MONTHLY

[2] 2-3 TIMES A MONTH   [4] LESS OFTEN THAN MONTHLY

7g. Are minutes of these meetings kept?

[1] YES   [5] NO

7h. When there is an important issue or business matter to be decided, how does the (board/commission/committee) determine the wishes of the citizenry?

_____

_____

_____

_____

8. What is your title (the title of the administrative officer responsible for recreation facilities and services)?

TITLE: _____

8a. Do you (does this person) work full-time or part-time on recreation matters?

[1] FULL-TIME   [5] PART-TIME

8b. Is this a paid or voluntary position?

[1] PAID   [5] VOLUNTARY

9. How many persons are employed by your organization, on a full-time and part-time or seasonal basis? (IF NONE, ENTER "0" BELOW AND GO TO Q. 10)

> 9a. How many of your employees (of each type) are white, black, or from other minority groups?

> | 9. | TOTAL | a. | WHITE | BLACK | OTHER |
> |---|---|---|---|---|---|
> | FULL-TIME: | _____ | | ____ | ____ | ____ |
> | PART-TIME OR SEASONAL: | _____ | | ____ | ____ | ____ |
> | TOTAL: | _____ | | ____ | ____ | ____ |

10. During the past year, about how many volunteer recreation workers were utilized by your organization in (NAME OF COMMUNITY)? ACCEPT RANGES

NUMBER OF VOLUNTEERS:_____   (IF NONE, GO TO Q. 11)

> 10a. What types of functions or activities do volunteers perform?
>
> _____
>
> _____
>
> _____

11. Have any citizen committees (other than the board of directors) been formed to help with the recreation programs and activities of your organization in (NAME OF COMMUNITY)?

[1] YES   [5] NO

> 11a. What types of committees have been formed?
>
> _____
>
> _____
>
> _____
>
> 11b. How are members of these committees recruited?
>
> _____
>
> _____
>
> 11c. Overall, would you say you are very satisfied, somewhat satisfied, somewhat dissatisfied, or very dissatisfied with the performance of these committees?
>
> [1] VERY SATISFIED   [3] SOMEWHAT DISSATISFIED
>
> [2] SOMEWHAT SATISFIED   [4] VERY DISSATISFIED

11d. Why do you say that?

_____

_____

_____

Finances

12. During 1972, what were the total annual operating expenditures of your organization for recreation areas, facilities, and services in (NAME OF COMMUNITY)?

RECREATION EXPENDITURES: $_____

    12a. What proportion of your organization's total expenditures did this represent? (ACCEPT ESTIMATES)

        PROPORTION OF TOTAL EXPENDITURES:_____%

13. What were your primary sources of revenue during 1972?

    [0] NONE -- GO TO Q. 14

Yes   No

[1]   [5]   COUNTY OR MUNICIPAL BUDGET ALLOCATIONS

[1]   [5]   SPECIAL RECREATION TAXES

[1]   [5]   USER CHARGES

[1]   [5]   MEMBERSHIP ASSESSMENTS

[1]   [5]   DONATIONS

[1]   [5]   OTHER (SPECIFY:_____)

14. During the past five years, have you had any financial difficulties or problems in providing recreation services in (NAME OF COMMUNITY)?

[1] YES   [5] NO

14a. What were these problems?

_____

_____

_____

15. INTERVIEWER: CHECK ONE

    1 PRIVATE OR SEMI-PUBLIC AGENCY -- GO TO Q. 17

    2 PUBLIC AGENCY -- ASK Q. 16

16. How many bond issue referendums for recreation areas, facilities, and/or services have been held during the past five years, including pending referendums?

    NUMBER OF REFERENDUMS: _____   (IF NONE, GO TO Q. 17)

    16a. In what year was this (the last) (will this) referendum (be) held?

         YEAR:_____

    16b. What was (is) the purpose of the bond issue?

         _____

         _____

    16c. What was (is) the amount of the bonds to be authorized?

         AMOUNT OF BONDS: $_____

    16d. Was the referendum approved?

         1 YES   3 PENDING   5 NO

17. INTERVIEWER: CHECK ONE

    1 CONTROL COMMUNITY -- GO TO Q. 20

    2 NEW OR RETIREMENT COMMUNITY -- ASK Q. 18

Developer Participation

18. In what ways, if any, has (NAME OF COMMUNITY DEVELOPER) contributed to the development and support of recreation in (NAME OF COMMUNITY)?

    0 NONE -- GO TO Q. 19

    _____

    _____

    _____

    _____

19. Do you feel (NAME OF COMMUNITY DEVELOPER) has given adequate attention to the recreation needs of people living in (NAME OF COMMUNITY)?

[5] NO   [1] YES

> 19a. Please explain.
>
> _____
>
> _____
>
> _____

Recreation Areas, Facilities, and Services

20. What is the total acreage owned by (NAME OF ORGANIZATION) in (NAME OF COMMUNITY)?

TOTAL ACRES OWNED: _____   (IF NONE, GO TO Q. 21)

21. Do you lease any recreation areas or facilities in (NAME OF COMMUNITY)?

[1] YES   [5] NO

> 21a. How many acres are leased at this time?
>
> ACRES LEASED:_____

22. Do you operate any recreation programs in (NAME OF COMMUNITY) on land or in facilities whose use, but not ownership, has been donated by another organization or individual?

[1] YES   [5] NO

> 22a. How many acres are involved in these programs?
>
> OTHER ACRES: _____

23. Have you developed any cooperative arrangements with local school boards for the recreational use of school facilities after school hours and/or during the summer?

[1] YES   [5] NO

> 23a. Please explain these arrangements, including financing of cooperative programs.
>
> _____
>
> _____
>
> _____

24. Can you tell me the name and location of each area or site in the community, including schools, where your organization owns recreation facilities or operates recreation programs?

	Name of Site or Facility	Location	
		Street	Cross Street
a.			
b.			
c.			
d.			
e.			
f.			
g.			
h.			
i.			
j.			
k.			
l.			
m.			
n.			
o.			
p.			
q.			
r.			
s.			
t.			
u.			
v.			
w.			
x.			

25. Now I have some questions about specific recreation facilities which are
     owned and/or operated by your organization in (NAME OF COMMUNITY).

---

a. Here is a list of the facilities in
   which we are interested. (HAND LIST
   A) Could you tell me which of these
   facilities are owned and/or operated   b. How many (facility)   c. Is there a
   by your organization in (NAME OF   does your organiza-   charge for the
   COMMUNITY)? Any others?   tion own or operate?   use of (facility)?

Facilities	No	Yes	Number	No	Yes	Amount
(1) Arts/crafts/hobby rooms	5	1 →	_____	5	1 →	
(2) Basketball courts	5	1 →	_____	5	1 →	
(3) Baseball diamonds	5	1 →	_____	5	1 →	
(4) Bathing beaches	5	1 →	_____	5	1 →	
(5) Bicycle trails	5	1 →	_____	5	1 → ___	
(6) Boating facilities	5	1 →	_____	5	1 → ___	
(7) Fields for soccer, foot-ball, etc.	5	1 →	_____	5	1 → ___	
(8) Fishing lakes	5	1 →	_____	5	1 → ___	
(9) Golf courses	5	1 →	_____	5	1 → ___	
(10) Gymnasiums	5	1 →	_____	5	1 → ___	
(11) Ice skating areas or rinks	5	1 →	_____	5	1 → ___	
(12) Parks with benches	5	1 →	_____	5	1 →	
(13) Playgrounds for children from 6-15 years old	5	1 →	_____	5	1 → ___	
(14) Picnic areas	5	1 →	_____	5	1 → ___	
(15) Recreation centers, club houses, or community centers	5	1 →	_____	5	1 → ___	
(16) Stables and/or bridle trails	5	1 →	_____	5	1 → ___	
(17) Swimming pools	5	1 →	_____	5	1 → ___	
(18) Teen centers	5	1 →	_____	5	1 → ___	
(19) Tennis courts	5	1 →	_____	5	1 → ___	

Facilities	No Yes	Number	No Yes	Amount
(20) Totlots or playlots for pre-school children	5 1 →	_____	5 1 →	_____
(21) Tracks for running	5 1 →	_____	5 1 →	_____
(22) Walking paths or trails	5 1 →	_____	5 1 →	_____
(23) Other (Specify:____ _____)	5 1 →	_____	5 1 →	_____
(24) Other (Specify:___ _____)	5 1 →	_____	5 1 →	_____

26. Does your organization conduct periodic evaluations of recreation needs and the performance of your recreation program?

    1 YES   5 NO

> 26a. What changes, if any, have occurred in recreation policies or plans as a result of these evaluations?
>
>   0 NONE -- GO TO Q. 27
>
> _____
>
> _____
>
> _____
>
> _____

27. What do you feel is the greatest need for recreation areas and/or facilities in (NAME OF COMMUNITY) at this time?

_____

_____

_____

Recreation Planning

28. Do you have a master plan for the development of additional recreation areas and facilities?

    1 YES (OBTAIN COPY)   5 NO -- GO TO Q. 30

28a. When was this plan prepared?

YEAR:_____

28b. Would you describe how the plan has been used in decision-making by your organization?

_____

_____

_____

29. What provisions, if any, have been made for citizen participation in the recreation planning process?

[0] NONE -- GO TO Q. 30

_____

_____

_____

30. Are developers and builders in (NAME OF COMMUNITY) required to dedicate land in new subdivisions or neighborhoods for open space and/or recreational use?

[1] YES   [5] NO

30a. Could you describe these regulations?

_____

_____

_____

31. What are your policies, if any, regarding the staging of recreational facility development in new residential areas?

[0] NONE -- GO TO Q. 32

_____

_____

_____

Recreation Program and Activities

32. Now I have some questions about recreation programs and activities provided for the people of (NAME OF COMMUNITY). Could you look at this list (HAND RESPONDENT LIST B) and check any organized activities and programs which were available for children, young adults and/or adults during 1972, excluding activities provided at the schools only during school hours.

33. From what you know of communities similar to (NAME OF COMMUNITY), would you say that participation in recreation activities in this community is very high, above average, average, or below average?

        1 VERY HIGH   3 AVERAGE

        2 ABOVE AVERAGE   4 BELOW AVERAGE

34. Have you developed any recreation or social programs or services aimed specifically at the needs of any of the following groups. First, what about...

    34a. ELDERLY PERSONS: _____

                _____

    34b. LOW INCOME PERSONS: _____

                _____

    34c. HANDICAPPED PERSONS: _____

                _____

35. Considering black families living in (NAME OF COMMUNITY), have the following types of problems occurred frequently, occasionally, or not at all in your recreation programs? What about...

    0 NO BLACK FAMILIES IN COMMUNITY -- GO TO Q. 38

		Frequently	Occasionally	Not at all
35a.	Whites and blacks segregating into separate groups at recreation facilities or centers...	1	3	5
35b.	Open conflicts or hostility between blacks and whites.......	1	3	5
35c.	Hostility between blacks and white recreation leaders........	1	3	5
35d.	Withdrawal of blacks or whites from participation in recreation programs...................	1	3	5

```
36. INTERVIEWER:  CHECK ONE

        1   NO PROBLEMS -- GO TO Q. 38

        5   SOME PROBLEMS -- ASK Q. 37
```

37. What steps, if any, have been taken to solve this (these) problem(s)?

    0   NONE -- GO TO Q. 38

    _____

    _____

    _____

38. Would you say that voluntary organizations are very active, somewhat active, somewhat inactive, or very inactive in providing recreation opportunities for the people of (NAME OF COMMUNITY)?

    1   VERY ACTIVE   3   SOMEWHAT INACTIVE

    2   SOMEWHAT ACTIVE   4   VERY INACTIVE

39. Considering everything we've discussed about recreation facilities and programs in (NAME OF COMMUNITY), how good would you say facilities and services are for people who live here (there) -- excellent, good, average, below average, or poor?

    1 EXCELLENT 2 GOOD 3 AVERAGE 4 BELOW AVERAGE 5 POOR

Finally, I have some general questions about your present position and background.

40. First, what is the exact title of your position with (NAME OF ORGANIZATION)?

    TITLE:_____

41. In what year did you assume this position?

    YEAR:_____

42. Have you held any other positions with (NAME OF ORGANIZATION)?

    1   YES   5   NO

    ```
    42a.  What were these?

          _____

    42b.  In all, how many years have you worked for (NAME OF ORGANIZATION)?

          YEARS:_____
    ```

43. What were the most important reasons you (first) came to work here (assumed this position)?

_____

_____

_____

44. Do you live in (NAME OF COMMUNITY)?

| 1 | YES | 5 | NO

44a. In what year did you move to (NAME OF COMMUNITY)?

YEAR:_____

45. How do you feel about (NAME OF COMMUNITY) as a place to live? From your own point of view, would you rate this area as an excellent place to live, good, average, below average, or poor?

| 1 | EXCELLENT | 2 | GOOD | 3 | AVERAGE | 4 | BELOW AVERAGE | 5 | POOR

45a. Why do you say that?

_____

_____

46. Before we conclude, could you help us to identify any other persons or organizations involved in providing recreation services for the people of (NAME OF COMMUNITY)? Who else would you recommend that we interview?

a. Organization:_____

Name:_____

Position:_____

Telephone Number:_____

b. Organization:_____

Name:_____

Position:_____

Telephone Number:_____

c. Organization:_____

　　　Name:_____

　　　Position:_____

　　　Telephone Number:_____

d. Organization:_____

　　　Name:_____

　　　Position:_____

　　　Telephone Number:_____

THANK YOU VERY MUCH. YOU'VE BEEN MOST HELPFUL.

47. Race of respondent

　　　　　1　WHITE　　　　　　　3　ORIENTAL

　　　　　2　BLACK　　　　　　　4　OTHER

48. Sex of respondent

　　　　　1　MALE

　　　　　5　FEMALE

<u>LIST A</u>

1. Arts/crafts/hobby rooms

2. Basketball courts

3. Baseball diamonds

4. Bathing beaches

5. Bicycle trails

6. Boating facilities

7. Fields for soccer, football, etc.

8. Fishing lakes

9. Golf courses

10. Gymnasiums

11. Ice skating areas or rinks

12. Parks with benches

13. Playgrounds for children from 6 - 15 years old

14. Picnic areas

15. Recreation centers, club houses, and/or community centers

16. Stables and/or bridle trails

17. Swimming pools

18. Teen centers

19. Tennis courts

20. Totlots or play lots for preschool children

21. Tracks for running

22. Walking paths or trails

ANY OTHERS?

Community:_____   Interview Number:_____

LIST B

Organized Recreation Activities

Please check those organized programs and activities you provided for children, young adults, and adults in the community during 1972.

Activities	For Children 13 Years Old and Under	For Young Adults 14-20 Years Old	For Adults 21 Years and Older
1. Arts and crafts.....................	☐	☐	☐
2. Baseball...........................	☐	☐	☐
3. Basketball.........................	☐	☐	☐
4. Boating............................	☐	☐	☐
5. Bowling - indoor...................	☐	☐	☐
6. Camping............................	☐	☐	☐
7. Dancing - Dances...................	☐	☐	☐
8. Drama..............................	☐	☐	☐
9. Field trips/outings................	☐	☐	☐
10. Football..........................	☐	☐	☐
11. Golf..............................	☐	☐	☐
12. Ice skating/ice hockey............	☐	☐	☐
13. Music instruction or programs.....	☐	☐	☐
14. Nature instruction................	☐	☐	☐
15. Soccer............................	☐	☐	☐
16. Softball..........................	☐	☐	☐
17. Supervised bicycling..............	☐	☐	☐
18. Swimming..........................	☐	☐	☐
19. Tennis............................	☐	☐	☐
20. Track and field..................	☐	☐	☐
21. Tumbling and gymnastics...........	☐	☐	☐
22. Volleyball........................	☐	☐	☐

Bibliography

Advisory Commission on Intergovernmental Relations. 1968. *Urban and Rural America: Policies for Future Growth.* A Commission Report (A–32). Washington, D.C.: U.S. Government Printing Office, April.

Alonso, William. 1970. "The Mirage of New Towns." *The Public Interest,* No. 19 (Spring), pp. 3–17.

American-Hawaiian Steamship Company. 1972. "Fact Sheet Number 1. General Facts About Westlake—A Planned Community." Westlake Village, Calif.: The Company, July 1.

American Institute of Planners, The AIP Task Force on New Communities. 1968. *New Communities: Challenge for Today.* American Institute of Planners Background Paper No. 2, Muriel I. Allen (ed.). Washington, D.C.: The Institute.

American Public Health Association. 1948. *Planning the Neighborhood.* Chicago: Public Administration Service.

Andrews, Frank M., and Withey, Stephen B. 1974. "Assessing the Quality of Life as People Perceive It." Paper Presented at the Annual Meeting of the American Sociological Association, Montreal, August.

Apgar, Mahlon, IV. 1971. *Managing Community Development: The Systems Approach in Columbia, Maryland.* New York: McKinsey & Company, Inc.

Barasch, Stephen B. 1974. *Recreational Planning for New Communities.* Jericho, N.Y.: Exposition Press, Inc.

Barker, Michael B. 1966. *California Retirement Communities.* Special Report No. 2. Berkeley, Calif.: Center for Real Estate and Urban Economics, Institute for Urban and Regional Development, University of California.

Bollens, John C., and Schmandt, Henry J. 1965. *The Metropolis, Its People, Politics, and Economic Life.* New York: Harper & Row, Publishers.

Breckenfeld, Gurney. 1971. *Columbia and the New Cities.* New York: Ives Washburn, Inc.

Brooks, Richard. 1971. "Social Planning in Columbia." *Journal of the American Institute of Planners,* Vol. 37 (November), pp. 373–379.

Bultena, Gordon L., and Wood, Vivian. 1969. "The American Retirement Community: Bane or Blessing?" *Journal of Gerontology*, Vol. 24 (April), pp. 209–217.

——. 1970. "Leisure Orientation and Recreational Activities of Retirement Community Residents." *Journal of Leisure Research*, Vol. 2 (Winter), pp. 3–15.

Burby, Raymond J., III. 1975. "Environmental Amenities and New Community Governance: Results of a Nationwide Study," in *Man-Environment Interactions: Evaluations and Applications* (EDRA 5 Community Development Series, Vol. 22), Daniel H. Carson (ed.). New York: Halstead Press, pp. 101–123.

Burby, Raymond J., III, and Donnelly, Thomas G. 1976. *Schools in New Communities*. Cambridge, Mass.: Ballinger Publishing Company.

Burby, Raymond J., III, and Weiss, Shirley F., with Donnelly, Thomas G., Kaiser, Edward J., Zehner, Robert B., and Lewis, David F., Loewenthal, Norman H., McCalla, Mary Ellen, Rodgers, Barbara G., and Smookler, Helene V. 1976. *New Communities U.S.A.* Lexington, Mass.: D.C. Heath and Company, Lexington Books.

Burby, Raymond J., III, and Weiss, Shirley F. 1974. "Planning for Population Target Groups in New Community Development." Paper Presented at Confer-In 74, Annual Conference of the American Institute of Planners, Denver, October 26–31.

Butler, George D. 1959. *Introduction to Community Recreation*. Prepared for the National Recreation and Park Association. New York: McGraw-Hill Book Company.

Cherry, Rona, and Cherry, Laurence. 1974. "Slowing the Clock of Age." *The New York Times Magazine*, May 11.

Christiansen, R. Paul. 1964. *Comprehensive Master Plan for Forest Park, Ohio*. Middletown, Oh.: R. Paul Christiansen, City Planner.

Cicchetti, Charles J. 1973. *Forecasting Recreation in the United States*. Lexington, Mass.: D.C. Heath and Company, Lexington Books.

Ciccheti, Charles J., Seneca, Joseph M., and Davidson, Paul. 1968. *The Demand and Supply of Outdoor Recreation*. Washington, D.C.: Bureau of Outdoor Recreation, U.S. Department of the Interior.

Clapp, James A. 1971. *New Towns and Urban Policy: Planning Metropolitan Growth*. New York: Dunellen Publishing Company.

Clawson, Marion, and Knetsch, Jack L. 1966. *Economics of Outdoor Recreation*. Baltimore, Md.: The Johns Hopkins Press.

The Columbia Commission. 1971. *Impact of New Town Zoning on Howard County, Maryland*. Report to the County Executive and County Council, Howard County, Maryland. Ellicott City, Md.: The Commission, May 19.

Columbia Park and Recreation Association. 1973. "Columbia Association Youth Survey." Columbia, Md.: The Association, June.

——. 1974. *The Briefing Book 1974*. Columbia, Md.: The Association.

Columbia Roles Study Committee. 1972. "Citizen Participation in Columbia: A Study of Roles, Relationships, and Processes in New Town Government." Columbia, Md.: Columbia Park and Recreation Association.

Department of Regional Planning, Metropolitan Washington Council of Governments. 1970. *New Communities in Metropolitan Areas: The Governmental Role*. Washington, D.C.: The Council.

Department of Resources Development, Michigan State University. 1962. *The Quality of Outdoor Recreation as Evidenced by User Satisfaction.* Outdoor Recreation Resources Review Commission Study Report 5. Washington, D.C.: U.S. Government Printing Office.

Duhl, Leonard J. 1966. "The Parameters of Urban Planning," in *Planning for Diversity and Choice*, Stanford Anderson (ed.). Cambridge, Mass.: The M.I.T. Press.

Eichler, Edward P., and Kaplan, Marshall. 1967. *The Community Builders.* Berkeley and Los Angeles: University of California Press.

Einsweiler, Robert C., and Smith, Julius. 1971. "New Town Locates in a Municipality: Jonathan Saves Money and Chaska Increases Tax Base." *Planners Notebook*, Vol. 1 (June-July), pp. 1–8.

Erskine, Hazel F. 1973. "The Polls: Hopes, Fears and Regrets." *The Public Opinion Quarterly*, Vol. 37 (Spring), pp. 132–145.

Foer, Albert A. 1969. "Democracy in the New Towns: The Limits of Private Governance." *University of Chicago Law Review*, Vol. 36 (Winter), pp. 379–412.

Foote, Nelson N., Abu-Lughod, Janet, Foley, Mary M., and Winnick, Louis. 1960. *Housing Choices and Housing Constraints.* New York: McGraw-Hill Book Company.

Ford, Russell C. 1974. *New Towns: Toward an Innovative Leisure System.* Research Report Prepared for the New Towns Research Seminar. Chapel Hill, N.C.: Center for Urban and Regional Studies, The University of North Carolina, Spring.

Fucick, William C. 1975. "The Challenge of Implementing Federally Assisted New Communities." *Public Administration Review*, Vol. 35 (May/June), pp. 249–256.

Gans, Herbert J. 1967. *The Levittowners: Ways of Life and Politics in a New Suburban Community.* New York: Pantheon Books, A Division of Random House, Inc.

Godschalk, David R. 1972. *Participation, Planning, and Exchange in Old and New Communities: A Collaborative Paradigm.* Chapel Hill, N.C.: Center for Urban and Regional Studies, The University of North Carolina, November.

———. 1973a. "New Communities or Company Towns? An Analysis of Resident Participation," in *New Towns: Why—And for Whom?* Harvey S. Perloff and Neil C. Sandberg (eds.). New York: Praeger Publishers, pp. 198–220.

———. 1973b. "Reforming New Community Planning." *Journal of the American Institute of Planners*, Vol. 39 (September), pp. 306–315.

Griffin, Nathaniel M. 1974. *Irvine: The Genesis of a New Community.* ULI Special Report. Washington, D.C.: ULI–the Urban Land Institute.

Guggenheimer, Elinor C. 1969. *Planning for Parks and Recreation in Urban Areas.* New York: Twayne Publishers, Inc.

Hanson, Royce. 1971. "Background Paper," in *New Towns: Laboratories for Democracy.* Report of the Twentieth Century Fund Task Force on Governance of New Towns. New York: The Twentieth Century Fund, pp. 25–73.

———. 1972. *Managing Services for New Communities.* A Report of the Symposium on the Management of New Communities, Held at Columbia, Maryland, and Reston, Virginia, October 25–28, 1970. Washington, D.C.: The Washington Center for Metropolitan Studies and The New Communities Study Center, Virginia Polytechnic Institute and State University.

Hatry, Harry P., and Dunn, Diana R. 1971. *Measuring the Effectiveness of Local Government Services: Recreation.* Washington, D.C.: The Urban Institute.

Haworth and Anderson. n.d. "Interim Open Space, Parks and Recreation Elements of the City of Irvine." Irvine, Calif.: Haworth and Anderson.

Hertel, Michael M. 1971. *Irvine Community Associations.* A Research Report of the Claremont Urban Research Center. Claremont, Calif.: Claremont Urban Research Center, Claremont Graduate School.

Hjelte, George, and Shivers, Jay S. 1972. *Public Administration of Recreational Services.* Philadelphia: Lea & Febiger.

Houston, Lawrence. 1974. "Of Land, Leisure & Energy." *HUD Challenge,* Vol. 5 (October), pp. 26–30.

Institute of Government, The University of North Carolina. 1971. *How Govern Soul City?* Report of Organizational Studies for Region K/New Communities Program (NCP–192). Chapel Hill, N.C.: Institute of Government, The University of North Carolina, September.

Jackson, Mercer L., Jr. 1972. "Housing for Older Americans." *HUD Challenge,* Vol. 3 (July), pp. 4–7.

Jackson, Samuel C. 1972. "New Communities." *HUD Challenge,* Vol. 3 (August), pp. 4–7.

Jensen, Clayne R. 1970. *Outdoor Recreation in America.* Minneapolis, Minn.: Burgess Publishing Company.

Jonathan Development Corporation. 1971. *Jonathan New Town: Design and Development.* Chaska, Minn.: The Corporation, February.

Kaiser, Edward J. 1976. *Residential Mobility in New Communities: An Analysis of Recent In-movers and Prospective Out-movers.* Cambridge, Mass.: Ballinger Publishing Company.

Kelly, Burnham. 1974. *Social Facilities for Large-Scale Housing Developments.* Ithaca, N.Y.: Center for Urban Development Research, Cornell University, October.

Kraus, Richard. 1968. *Public Recreation and the Negro.* New York: Center for Urban Education, March.

Lackawanna County Planning Commission. 1963. *Recreation and Open Space Plan.* Prepared by Candeub, Cabot and Associates. Scranton, Pa.: The Commission.

Lansing, John B., and Hendricks, Gary. 1967. *Living Patterns and Attitudes in the Detroit Region.* Detroit, Mich.: Detroit Regional Transportation and Land Use Study.

Lansing, John B., Marans, Robert W., and Zehner, Robert B. 1970. *Planned Residential Environments.* Ann Arbor, Mich.: Institute for Social Research, The University of Michigan.

Lawton, M. Powell, and Byerts, Thomas O., eds. 1973. *Community Planning for the Elderly.* Report Prepared for the U.S. Department of Housing and Urban Development by the Gerontological Society. Washington, D.C.: U.S. Department of Housing and Urban Development, September.

Mandell, Lewis, and Marans, Robert W. 1972. *Participation in Outdoor Recreation: A National Perspective.* Ann Arbor, Mich.: Institute for Social Research, The University of Michigan, June.

Manilow, Lewis. 1971. "New Communities in the Seventies, Part III: Park Forest South, Illinois," in *New Community Development: Planning Process, Implementation, and Emerging Social Concerns,* Vol. 2, Shirley F. Weiss, Edward J. Kaiser, and Raymond J. Burby, III (eds.). Chapel Hill, N.C.: New Towns Research Seminar, Center for Urban and Regional Studies, The University of North Carolina, October, pp. 217–241.

Marans, Robert W. 1971. *Determinants of Outdoor Recreation Behavior in Planned Residential Environments.* Ph.D. Dissertation. Ann Arbor, Mich.: University Microfilms.

Marans, Robert W., and Rodgers, Willard. 1972. "Toward an Understanding of Community Satisfaction." Ann Arbor, Mich.: Institute for Social Research, The University of Michigan, December.

———. 1973. "Evaluation of Resident Satisfaction in Established New Communities," in *Frontiers of Planned Unit Development: A Synthesis of Expert Opinion,* Robert W. Burchell (ed.). New Brunswick, N.J.: Center for Urban Policy Research, Rutgers University, pp. 197–227.

"Measuring the Quality of Life in America." 1974. *ISR Newsletter,* Vol. 2 (Summer), pp. 3–8.

Meltzer, Jack. 1953. "Administrative Problems of New Towns," in *Planning 1952.* Chicago: American Society of Planning Officials, pp. 77–78.

Meyer, Harold D., and Brightbill, Charles K. 1956. *Recreation Administration: A Guide to Its Practice.* Englewood Cliffs, N.J.: Prentice-Hall, Inc.

———. 1964. *Community Recreation: A Guide to Its Organization.* 3rd Edition. Englewood Cliffs, N.J.: Prentice-Hall, Inc.

Mields, Hugh, Jr. 1973. *Federally Assisted New Communities: New Dimensions in Urban Development.* A ULI Landmark Report. Washington, D.C.: ULI–the Urban Land Institute.

Mueller, Eva, and Gurin, Gerald. 1962. *Participation in Outdoor Recreation: Factors Affecting Demand among American Adults.* Outdoor Recreation Resources Review Commission Study Report 20. Washington, D.C.: U.S. Government Printing Office.

National Academy of Sciences. 1969. *A Program for Outdoor Recreation Research.* Washington, D.C.: The Academy.

National Association of Counties. 1964. *County Parks and Recreation: A Basis for Action.* Washington, D.C.: The Association.

National Recreation Association. 1962. *Standards for Municipal Recreation Areas.* Revised Edition. New York: The Association.

———. 1965a. *Outdoor Recreation Space Standards.* New York: The Association.

———. 1965b. *Standards: Playgrounds, Recreation Buildings, Indoor Facilities.* New York: The Association.

"The Nebulous Art of New Community Management." 1971. *Columbia Today,* Vol. 4 (March), pp. 8–15.

"New Communities." 1972. *HUD Challenge*, Vol. 3 (August), pp. 4–23.

"New Communities Checklist Update." 1974. *Systems Building News*, Vol. 5 (August), pp. 30–32.

New Communities Division, Community Resources Development Administration, U.S. Department of Housing and Urban Development. 1969. "Survey and Analysis of Large Developments and New Communities Completed or Under Construction in the United States Since 1947." Washington, D.C.: The Department, February.

New Community Services, Inc. 1972. *Jonathan General Development Plan 1972*. Chaska, Minn.: Jonathan Development Corporation, September.

Norcross, Carl. 1966. *Open Space Communities in the Market Place*. Technical Bulletin 57. Washington, D.C.: Urban Land Institute, December.

––––––. 1973. *Townhouses & Condominiums: Residents' Likes and Dislikes*. A Special Report. Washington, D.C.: ULI–the Urban Land Institute.

Park Forest Properties. 1968. *Village of Park Forest South*. Park Forest, Ill.: Park Forest Properties.

Park Forest South Developers, Inc. n.d. *Park Forest South: New Town of the Seventies*. Park Forest, Ill.: Park Forest South Developers, Inc.

Perry, Clarence A. 1929. *Regional Survey of New York and Its Environs*. Vol. VII. New York: Russell Sage Foundation.

––––––. 1939. *Housing for the Machine Age*. New York: Russell Sage Foundation.

Phillips, Proctor, Bowers & Associates. 1960. *A Master Plan for Elk Grove Village*. Prepared for Centex Construction Company. Dallas, Tex.: Phillips, Proctor, Bowers & Associates.

Prestridge, J.A. 1973. *Case Studies of Six Planned New Towns in the United States*. Lexington, Ky.: Institute for Environmental Studies, University of Kentucky Research Foundation, March.

"Project Agreement Between United States of America and Jonathan Development Corporation." 1970. October 8.

"Project Agreement Between United States of America and Park Forest South Development Company." 1971. March 17.

Rabinovitz, Francine F., and Lamare, James. 1970. *After Suburbia, What? The New Communities Movement in Los Angeles*. Los Angeles: Institute of Government and Public Affairs, University of California, Los Angeles.

The Reston Home Owners Association. 1973. *Reston Residents' Handbook*. Reston, Va.: The Association, January.

Rossi, Peter H. 1955. *Why Families Move*. Glencoe, Ill.: The Free Press.

Scott, Stanley, 1965. "Local Government and the Large New Communities." *Public Affairs Report*, Vol. 6, (June), pp. 1–5.

––––––. 1967. "The Homes Association: Will 'Private Government' Serve the Public Interest?" *Public Affairs Report*, Vol. 8 (February), pp. 1–4.

Slidell, John B. 1972. *The Shape of Things to Come? An Evaluation of the Neighborhood Unit as an Organizing Scheme for American New Towns*. Chapel Hill, N.C.: Center for Urban and Regional Studies, The University of North Carolina, January.

Smookler, Helene V. 1976. *Economic Integration in New Communities: An Evaluation of Factors Affecting Policies and Implementation.* Cambridge, Mass.: Ballinger Publishing Company.

So, Frank S., Mosena, David R., and Bangs, Frank S., Jr. 1973. *Planned Unit Development Ordinances.* Planning Advisory Service Report No. 291. Chicago: American Society of Planning Officials, May.

The Study Team on RHOA Role & Structure. 1972. "Toward New Town Governance." Reston, Va.: The Study Team, January.

Twentieth Century Fund Task Force on Governance of New Towns. 1971. *New Towns: Laboratories for Democracy.* Report of the Twentieth Century Fund Task Force on Governance of New Towns. New York: The Twentieth Century Fund.

ULI–the Urban Land Institute and CAI–the Community Association Institute. 1974. *Managing a Successful Community Association.* Washington, D.C.: The Institutes.

The Urban Land Institute. 1964. *The Homes Association Handbook.* Technical Bulletin 50. Washington, D.C.: The Institute.

U.S. Congress, House of Representatives, Committee on Banking and Currency. 1973. *Oversight Hearings on HUD New Communities Program.* Hearings Before the Subcommittee on Housing of the Committee on Banking and Currency, House of Representatives, Ninety-third Congress, First Session, May 30 and 31, 1973. Washington, D.C.: U.S. Government Printing Office.

U.S. Department of Health, Education, and Welfare, Office of Human Development, Administration on Aging. 1973. *New Facts about Older Americans.* DHEW Publication No. (SRS)73–20006. Washington, D.C.: U.S. Government Printing Office, June.

U.S. Department of the Interior, Bureau of Outdoor Recreation. 1967a. *Outdoor Recreation Space Standards.* Washington, D.C.: U.S. Government Printing Office, April.

––––. 1967b. "The 1965 Survey of Outdoor Recreation Activities." Washington, D.C.: U.S. Department of the Interior, Bureau of Outdoor Recreation, October.

Van Beckum, William G., Jr. 1971. "Developer vs. Residents in a California New Town: A Study of the Evolution of Democracy in Foster City." Master of Urban Planning Thesis, University of Oregon, August.

Village of Park Forest, Illinois. 1972. *Concept: A Plan for the Future.* Park Forest, Ill.: The Village.

Vivrett, Walter K., and Wilkinson, George R. 1972. *Development of Jonathan.* Report to the Ford Foundation, Grant #69–0525. Minneapolis, Minn.: School of Architecture and Landscape Architecture, University of Minnesota, September 30.

Watson, Raymond L. 1973. "Phasing Growth: How Fast? Where Next?" in *New Towns in America: The Design and Development Process*, James Bailey (ed.). New York: Published for the American Institute of Architects by John Wiley & Sons, pp. 87–89.

Weiss, Shirley F. 1973 *New Town Development in the United States: Experiment in Private Entrepreneurship.* Chapel Hill, N.C.: Center for Urban and Regional Studies, The University of North Carolina.

Werthman, Carl, Mandel, Jerry S., and Dienstfrey, Ted. 1965. *Planning and the Purchase Decision: Why People Buy in Planned Communities.* A Prepublication of the Community Development Project. Berkeley, Calif.: Institute for Urban and Regional Development, Center for Planning and Development Research, University of California, July.

Whyte, William. 1968. *The Last Landscape,* Garden City, N.J.: Doubleday & Company, Inc.

Zehner, Robert B. 1976. *Indicators of the Quality of Life in New Communities.* Cambridge, Mass.: Ballinger Publishing Company.

Index

About the Author

Raymond J. Burby, III is assistant director for research at the Center for Urban and Regional Studies of The University of North Carolina at Chapel Hill. He was co-principal investigator and deputy project director of the NSF/RANN New Communities Project. He received the M.R.P. and Ph.D. in planning from The University of North Carolina at Chapel Hill. Dr. Burby is the author of *Planning and Politics: Toward a Model of Planning Related Policy Outputs in American Local Government*, co-author of *New Communities U.S.A.*, and co-editor of *New Community Development: Planning Process, Implementation, and Emerging Social Concerns*. In addition to his research on new community development, Dr. Burby has been the author of many monographs and articles on planning, urban growth, and the land conversion process.